Motivating Others

Motivating Others

Nurturing Inner Motivational Resources

Johnmarshall Reeve
University of Wisconsin-Milwaukee

Allyn and Bacon
Boston · London · Toronto · Sydney · Tokyo · Singapore

Dedication

Once in a while, we all read an article or book that changes our way of thinking, that informs and enlightens us in a way that extends us beyond our expectations. Such an opportunity came my way back in 1991 when I read "Inner Resources for School Achievement: Motivational Mediators of Children's Perceptions of Their Parents." It was the first time I had heard the term *inner motivational resource,* and the authors demonstrated convincingly that such resources, when supported by those around us, energize and direct our behaviors in ways that are healthy, adaptive, and productive. So I wish to dedicate the book to the authors of that article—Wendy Grolnick, Richard Ryan, and Ed Deci.

Copyright © 1996 by Allyn & Bacon
A Simon & Schuster Company
Needham Heights, Massachusetts 02194

Library of Congress Cataloging-in-Publication Data
Reeve, Johnmarshall.
    Motivating others : nurturing inner motivational resources / Johnmarshall Reeve.
        p.   cm.
    Includes bibliographical references (p.   ) and index.
    ISBN 0-205-16969-4
    1. Motivation in education.   2. Motivation (Psychology)
    3. Teacher–student relationships.   I. Title.
    LB1065.R395   199695-20280
    370.15′4—dc20CIP

Printed in the United States of America

10 9 8 7 6 5 4 3 2 1   99 98 97 96 95

Contents

Preface

Educators know a motivated student when they see one—a student who is active, excited, persistent, optimistic, quick to begin tasks; one who seeks challenges, concentrates deeply, and shows high effort. Such a student learns a great deal; indeed, learning seems to come naturally.

Educators also know motivational problems when they see them. With ever-increasing frequency, teachers and parents see apathy, listlessness, helplessness, defensiveness, avoidance of challenge, immature coping responses, anxiety about achievement, absenteeism, truancy, underachievement—even woeful, jaw-dropping levels of underachievement. We see students ask for easy successes rather than for optimal challenges. We see them give up in the face of difficulty and failure rather than persist. We listen as they complain about academic challenges, and we see defensive emotions like fear and anxiety guide their educations, rather than approach-oriented emotions like interest and enthusiasm. We watch as students display low or even nonexistent levels of effort and submit work that fulfills only minimal standards. We see too many students who are motivationally empty: They lack the ability to generate motivation for themselves.

Motivation addresses more than just the problems of students' low effort, disaffection, and disengagement. Motivation is also about fostering psychological growth and healthy development. Every motivation theorist I know is optimistic about students and about their potentialities. Like teachers, they see in students a natural motivation to learn, grow, and develop in a healthy way. With this optimistic view, most people who study motivation spend their lives searching for and researching in depth those aspects of classrooms that support and nurture students' natural motivational tendencies. Theories of motivation, then, speak not only to our worst students but also to our best—to those students who are motivationally rich and routinely generate their own motivation.

Audience

This book concerns all those interpersonal relationships in which one person tries to motivate another. Primarily, however, I write to classroom teachers interested in acquiring knowledge and developing skills to motivate their students. In each theoretical statement and in each example, the relationship foremost in my mind is the one between teacher and student. But the book has a larger purpose as well. The intended audience also includes parents motivating children, tutors motivating pupils, coaches motivating athletes, principals motivating teachers, employers motivating employees, doctors motivating patients, therapists motivating clients, directors motivating volunteers—all relationships in which one person seeks to motivate another. The intended audience is anyone interested in motivating others—anyone who wants to enhance others' efforts, improve their performances, foster their growth, or optimize their development.

Orientation

In speaking about relationships in which one person tries to motivate another, I take a theoretical orientation that is humanistic and constructivistic. A humanistic approach to motivation values human freedom and self-determination, and it argues that one person best motivates another by supporting the development of his or her inner motivational resources. A constructivistic approach to learning views students as engaged learners who actively construct meaning and personal understandings from the information available to them. Both approaches value a student-centered approach to instruction and to education in general. Many approaches to education exist, but von Glaserfeld and Steffe (1991) argue there are two general approaches to the practice of education—mechanistic and organismic. A humanistic, constructivistic orientation embraces the organismic approach that stresses the importance of the motivational processes that exist as an inherent part of human nature. Motivating others, therefore, becomes the task of tapping into and nurturing those natural, organismic motivational processes. But I also understand that sometimes the best way to teach students information is just to tell them the information outright. Mathematical knowledge and procedures, for instance, seem amenable to direct instruction. This approach, however, solves the problem of motivation by ignoring it. In contrast, I see motivation as the central issue around which the whole educational experience revolves. Before instructing others, I always ask myself, "Does this student want this information? Is this student enthusiastic about what I have to say?" If not, I see the role of the teacher as that of the facilitator, not the instructor.

Observational Activities

This book communicates the relevance of motivation in two ways. The first is the traditional, theoretically based review of the experimental findings and empirically validated theories that combine to give the field its body of knowledge. That is, the content of each chapter revolves around presenting the theories and findings related to one particular domain of knowledge about motivation theory and reviewing the findings and theories related to that particular area of study (e.g., there is a chapter on "competence," another on "curiosity," and so on). Another way of understanding motivational phenomena is a nontraditional, hands-on approach that relies on learning through personal experience—through face-to-face interviews with teachers and through careful observations of teachers and their students in school. To help you in this latter way of understanding motivational phenomena, each chapter offers two "observational activities." One relies on interviewing either teachers or students, the other on observing them in action.

Whether asking you to interview or to observe, each activity brings the phenomena discussed in the chapter to life in a personally meaningful way. In most cases, the individuals you will observe or interview will not be too hard to find: teachers in the local school district, students you encounter in schools, friends' children, children in campus child care centers, work colleagues, neighbors, and so on. For some activities, you will not need to interact with your subjects, but you should—out of courtesy and professional obligation—inform the student's caretaker (parent, teacher, or other individuals involved in that student's well-being) that you are engaged in an observational exercise as part of a college course. For other activities, it might be necessary first to have your project reviewed and cleared by the college's or university's Human Subjects Review Board. Your professor can help you if this becomes necessary, but I have tried to design each activity to be so unobtrusive as to remove the need for a formal review by an ethics committee.

The observational activities appear at the end of each chapter. To begin each activity, work through the following steps. First, provide the requested background information on items 1–6. Items 7 and 8 constitute the heart of your report. These two items require you to answer the questions asked on the observational activity.

1. *Purpose* of your observation: Each Observational Activity begins with an explicit statement of its purpose, although the reader can add to or refine that purpose.
2. *Place* or location of your observation
3. *Date* of your observation
4. Subject(s)' *age, sex, and any special characteristics* you need to note
5. *Length* of your observation in minutes

6. Whether *permission* was granted for the observation, and if so, by whom
7. A careful *record of your observation,* with notes describing the incident and setting in enough detail so that you can later answer questions about what happened. Stick to the facts—what actually was done and said by the subject. Use the record of your observation to answer the questions posed to you in the observational activity.
8. A brief paragraph of *conclusions or findings* developed from your observation.

In presenting these observational activities to the reader, I want to pay a special tribute of gratitude to Anne Gormly and David Brodzinsky (Gormly & Brodzinsky, 1993) for coming up with the idea of the observational activity.

Acknowledgments

I want to acknowledge my threefold gratitude to all those who contributed to the book. First, I thank those educators who dedicated so much of their time and energy to reviewing early drafts of the book: Helene Anthony of Moorhead State University, Kay S. Bull of Oklahoma State University, Myron H. Dembo of the University of Southern California, Theresa Garcia of the University of Texas—Austin, Dale Schunk of Purdue University, and Anita Woolfolk of Ohio State University. Second, I thank my friends and colleagues who helped me prepare and revise various parts of the book: John Surber, Sally Lynch Reeve, Judy Robinson, Dick Schrader, and especially Dawn Robinson. Third, I express my gratitude toward the professionals at Allyn and Bacon who contributed so much enthusiasm, assistance, patience, and expertise toward the project: Greg Bell, Kate Wagstaffe, and Nancy Forsyth.

Finally, I want to acknowledge a special debt of gratitude toward editor Forsyth; thanks.

1

Introduction

Motivating others is challenging. Even motivating ourselves is challenge enough. For instance, have you ever procrastinated in writing a term paper? Have you ever exerted only lackluster effort toward a goal that you wanted for yourself, such as exercise? We all have our hands full just trying to generate our own motivation.

Fortunately, in motivating others we have two advantages on our side. First, personal experience in feeling both motivated and unmotivated gives us the empathy we need to understand what others are going through as they face the motivational problems in their lives. We also know what it feels like when others try to motivate us. Second, motivating others is an attainable skill. If you begin this book with only a vague sense of how a teacher might go about motivating students, then I can promise you that the skill of motivating others will improve as you gain knowledge, practice, and experience. I'll leave the experience up to you, but the twofold purpose of this book is to supply you with the knowledge (via the contents of each chapter) and practice (via the chapter-ending observational activities) to motivate others.

Introductory Questions

To begin the journey, let me ask you to generate your own answers to a set of questions that are basic to motivating others:

- What is motivation?
- Why motivate others?

I hope you will pause to produce your own answer to each question. My experience with classroom teachers leads me to anticipate hearing great vari-

1

ation in teachers' answers. Given the diversity of teachers' perspectives on these questions, I invite you to consider the merits of what people who study motivation have learned and can bring to bear on the attempt to define motivation and to understand why one person would want to increase the motivation of another.

What Is Motivation?

Trying to define *motivation* is like trying to define *personality*. As with personality, everyone feels sure he or she knows what motivation is—until asked to define it! Defining motivation is deceptively difficult, so let me spare you the "Oh, you know . . . It's sort of like . . ." struggle, and offer the definition that people in the field of motivation use.

Motivation involves the internal processes that give behavior its energy and direction. Energy means that behavior is relatively strong, intense, and persistent; *direction* means that behavior aims itself toward achieving a particular purpose or goal. The phrase *internal processes* is necessary because environmental events such as rewards and requests by other people can give our behavior energy and direction, too. In a motivational analysis, however, we examine not how environmental events energize and direct behavior but, rather, how these environmental events affect the individual's internal processes, which, in turn, energize and direct behavior. These internal processes include needs, emotions, and cognitions (*cognition,* incidentally, is a general term that includes mental events such as thoughts, beliefs, and expectations). These internal processes—needs, cognitions, and emotions—constitute the subject matter for the study of motivation in schools.

It is only part of the story to say that motives energize and direct behavior, because motives influence behavior in multiple ways. That is, motives start behavior, sustain it over time, heighten its intensity, direct it toward some goals but away from others, and stop it (e.g., Jones, 1955). So the short answer to the question "What is motivation?" is that motivation is the study of the internal processes that give behavior its energy and direction. A more involved answer would add that motivation originates from a variety of sources (needs, cognitions, and emotions), and that these internal processes energize and direct behavior in multiple ways such as starting, sustaining, intensifying, focusing, and stopping it.

Why Motivate Others? (Observational Activity 1.1)

Does this question strike you as a silly one that only an educational psychologist could ask? If it does, I suspect that is because many teachers take it for granted that motivation is the stuff that produces greater academic achievement in students. Motivation is the trick, the secret, to achieving academic excellence. Stated differently, the problem in the classroom is to foster student achievement, and the means to do this is to arouse and sustain high motivation. Thus, the obvious reason that a teacher would want to motivate students would be to promote achievement and academic excellence.

Few educators would argue with the goal of motivating for achievement and excellence. The tricky part emerges only when it becomes clear that there are at least two markedly different approaches to motivate achievement and excellence (Ryan, Connell, & Grolnick, 1992). One approach (popular with educational conservatives and back-to-basics advocates) calls for more discipline, longer hours, fixed curricula, and higher educational standards. This view assumes that motivation is something that can be produced by providing more direction for students. An authority figure or an expert (e.g., a teacher or a parent) directs students by disseminating important information and by the effective use of incentives to guide and shape students toward desirable (and away from undesirable) behaviors. There is something appealing about this traditional view because children *can* be externally regulated, and they will indeed work harder when they desire approval or seek rewards. An alternative approach, however, is to support students' motivation from within. According to this humanistically oriented approach, increasing motivation is not only an achievement issue, but also a developmental issue. The attempt is to encourage students to move away from a dependence on teachers and parents to create motivation for the student and to move toward an increased capacity for self-regulation in which the student accepts a personal responsibility for learning, generates motivation from within, and discovers the satisfactions that exist within the learning process itself.

In practice, most of the attempts of one person to motivate another take place within a relationship that involves an interpersonal power differential (Deci & Ryan, 1987). For example, consider the following interpersonal relationships in which the first person has some sense of responsibility or accountability for motivating the second person:

- teacher–student
- principal–teacher
- parent–child
- employer–employee
- doctor–patient
- therapist–client
- coach–athlete
- clergy–parishioner

In each case, the first person has some basis of power and influence over the second person, whether the basis of that power and means of influence manifests itself in the form of expertise, rewards, status, or position. Consequently, the person who is one-down in the power relationship is vulnerable to being controlled by the person who is one-up in power. This vulnerability is the impetus to my question as to why one person would want to motivate another.

When such a vulnerability exists, powerful people sometimes desire to motivate others in a way that simply produces compliance (i.e., the desired behavior). Suppose that Ms. Smith "motivates" her class of fifth-graders to pay attention in class, and she does so because she wants the noise level to lessen so she can finish the lesson. Suppose Mr. Jones "motivates" his child to hone those piano skills, and he does so because he wants to boast to his friends and feel good about himself as a parent. Suppose Ms. Lawrence "motivates" her employees to increase their productivity, and she does so because she wants to look good to the company president and maybe even get a fat bonus. I use quotation marks around "motivates" to communicate that each of these cases involves interpersonal coercion more than it does motivation per se. Let me be explicit and say directly that the issue that separates these two approaches to motivating others is one of control versus motivation. In this book, I will actively resist the idea that the reason to motivate others is to manipulate them into doing what it is you think they should or ought to be doing. Motivating others does *not* mean controlling others. In contrast, I will promote the idea that the fundamental rationale for motivating others is to cultivate inner motivational resources that allow them the greatest opportunity possible to develop, grow, and regulate their own behavior.

Inner Motivational Resources

This book is about cultivating in students rich inner motivational resources. Inner motivational resources refer to growth-promoting needs, cognitions, and emotions. Consider the analogies of intelligence as an inner cognitive resource and interpersonal support as an outer social resource. Intelligence functions as a valuable resource to fall back on whenever a person faces a difficult problem to solve. Having rich intelligence to draw on as an inner resource allows the student to understand and solve problems that would otherwise be too difficult an undertaking. A social support network of family and friends functions as a valuable resource to fall back on whenever a student faces a potent environmental stressor, such as a lack of money or a breakup in a relationship. Having a reliable network of friends to fall back on as an outer resource allows the student to cope successfully with stress that would otherwise be overwhelming.

As intelligence and social support networks function as valuable resources, so needs, cognitions, and emotions function as motivational resources that people can fall back on when they face problems that are motivational in nature.

When people encounter failure, when they set high goals for themselves, or when they need to marshal great effort to face academic challenges, it helps them tremendously if they have inner motivational resources to tap into to initiate their behavior, to direct their behavior, and to maintain it over time. In this book, I detail the significance of eleven inner motivational resources and discuss carefully how teachers can structure their classrooms in ways that nurture the development of these inner motivational resources toward strength and resiliency. The eleven inner motivational resources include three psychological needs (self-determination, competence, and relatedness), five cognitive domains (self-efficacy, personal control beliefs, achievement strivings, goal setting, and the self), and three emotional states (curiosity, interest, and enjoyment/positive affect).

People do not always rely on inner motivational resources to motivate their behavior. Often, people rely on outer motivational resources to decide when it is time to initiate or to continue action. That is, students rely on tomorrow's test to prompt their studying, on deadlines to begin their papers, on teachers to choose which book to read, on a scholarship to work for a high grade point average, and on the advice of their parents to take challenging honors courses. Instead of generating motivation from within, people frequently wait for the environment to supply motivation for them. The world of work provides many clear examples of how outer motivational resources can motivate behavior—paychecks to come to work, time clocks to encourage punctuality, approvals from the boss to work hard, and so on. Sometimes, the same mentality that operates in the world of work carries over to the world of education as students learn to become dependent on others for their motivation.

This issue of who motivates the student—the student or some outside force—is particularly important in education because learning is an active process and occurs optimally when there is an intrinsic motivation on the part of the learner to engage and assimilate information (e.g., Thomas, 1980). The same can be said, I think, for development: It too is an active process and occurs optimally when there is an intrinsic motivation to grow and to improve on oneself. As we shall see throughout this book, learning and development do indeed progress optimally when there is an active participation from the student to take personal responsibility for his or her own learning and developing.

Intrinsic and Extrinsic Motivations

In many people's minds, motivation is a unitary concept. In other words, the only feature of motivation that varies is its amount or its intensity, and the only concern about motivation is "How much?" In contrast, several motivation theorists suggest that types of motivations exist and can be distinguished (Ames

& Archer, 1988; Condry & Stokker, 1992; Deci, 1992a). For instance, we can distinguish "motivation to learn" from "motivation to perform" (discussed in Chapters 8 and 11), the "tendency to approach success" from the "tendency to avoid failure" (also in Chapter 8), as well as "intrinsic" from "extrinsic" motivation (discussed below). In each of these cases, the behavior itself can look precisely the same, as in, say, reading a book or going to the library; but the person's reasons for reading the book or going to the library can be very different. These differences in types of motivation produce significant differences in students' classroom experiences and in the qualities of their academic work. In this section, I introduce the distinction between intrinsic and extrinsic motivation.

Intrinsic motivation is the innate propensity to engage one's interests and exercise one's capacities, and, in doing so, to seek out and master optimal challenges (Deci & Ryan, 1985). It emerges spontaneously from the student's needs, personal curiosities, and innate strivings for growth. Intrinsic motivation provides a natural force that fosters learning and development, and it therefore can motivate behavior without the assistance of extrinsic rewards and pressures. For instance, even in the absence of rewards and pressures, curiosity can spark a child's desire to read a book, and competence strivings can involve a student in a challenge for hours. Functionally, intrinsic motivation provides the student with an innate motivational force to exert the effort necessary to exercise and develop skills and capabilities.

Extrinsic motivation, on the other hand, is motivation that arises from external contingencies. When a student acts in order to gain a high grade, win a trophy, or comply with a deadline, that student's behavior is extrinsically motivated. In essence, extrinsic motivation is an environmentally created reason to carry out an action. Extrinsic motivation is a means-to-an-end type of motivation in which the means is the behavior and the end is some attractive consequence (or the prevention of an unattractive consequence). For instance, when a student reads a book, she may do so out of a strong desire to please her parents. The desire to please her parents provides an environmentally produced reason to exert the effort necessary to read the book. The desired end is parental approval, and reading just happens to be the means to obtain it.

Often, intrinsically and extrinsically motivated behaviors look precisely the same—the student reads a book, paints a picture, or volunteers to answer a question in class. The essential difference between the two types of motivation lies in the source that energizes and directs the behavior. With intrinsically motivated behavior, the source of the student's activity emanates from personal curiosities, needs, and strivings—that is, from inner motivational resources; with extrinsically motivated behavior, the source of the student's activity emanates from events taking place in the environment—that is, from outer motivational resources.

Motivation researchers became intrigued by the distinction between behavior that is intrinsically versus extrinsically motivated when they asked the following question: "If a person is involved in an intrinsically interesting activity and begins to receive an extrinsic reward for doing it, what will happen to his or her intrinsic motivation for the activity?" (Deci & Ryan, 1985, p. 43). For example, if a child engages in an enjoyable puzzle under the surveillance of an adult and is rewarded by the adult with an attractive prize for doing so, what happens to that child's intrinsic motivation for puzzle-playing? Clearly, the surveillance and attractive reward increase the child's extrinsic motivation for puzzle-solving, but does intrinsic motivation increase, decrease, or remain unaffected by these environmental events?

Generally speaking, extrinsic rewards and constraints decrease intrinsic motivation (Condry, 1977; Deci & Ryan, 1985; Lepper & Greene, 1978). The previous paragraph describes Lepper and Greene's (1975) experiment with children who solved puzzles either with or without rewards and with or without an adult's surveillance at one time and who were then observed two weeks later to see how much time they spent playing with the same puzzle during a free-choice opportunity. The study's behavioral measure of intrinsic motivation was whether or not the child played with the puzzle two weeks later (because

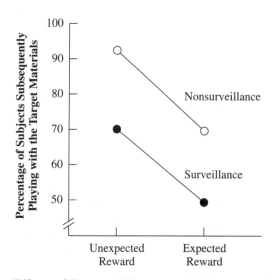

FIGURE 1-1   Effects of Expected Reward and Adult Surveillance on Children's Intrinsic Motivation

Source: Lepper, M. R., & Greene, D. (1975). Turning play into work: Effects of adult surveillance and extrinsic rewards on children's intrinsic motivation. *Journal of Personality and Social Psychology, 31,* 479–486. Copyright 1975 by the American Psychological Association. Reprinted with permission.

such free-choice play shows the child's willingness to engage the puzzle in the absence of external contingencies to do so). Figure 1-1 shows the effect that surveillance and reward had on intrinsic motivation. Children who solved puzzles under surveillance and for a reward played with the puzzle the least (50%), whereas children who puzzle-solved without surveillance and without reward played with the puzzle the most (92%). People who study motivation refer to this adverse effect on intrinsic motivation as "the hidden cost of rewards" (Lepper & Greene, 1978), because our culture typically regards events like rewards and surveillance to be positive contributors to motivation.

Can You Foresee the Hidden Costs of Rewards?

Foreseeing the hidden costs of rewards is difficult. Our culture values rewards, and most of us see external events like receiving a good player award as a positive source of motivation. So foreseeing hidden costs in rewards is counter-intuitive. I do not expect teachers to think of rewards as motivational antago-nists, and I am not surprised by classroom observations that show teachers use extrinsic motivators liberally and for the explicit purpose of motivating students (Marshall, 1987; Newby, 1991).

To see the extent to which people do foresee the hidden costs of rewards, one researcher invited people to participate in the following exercise and make predictions about students' intrinsic motivation (Hom, 1994). First, the class discussed whether preschool children like to draw and receive recognition for doing so in the form of "good player" awards. The researcher asked his listeners to imagine that they were conducting an experiment in their own local preschool center and to make predictions of what the results would look like (before learning the actual outcome of the experiment). To introduce the experimental scenario, the experimenter read the following synopsis of a second Lepper and Greene study (Lepper, Greene, & Nisbett, 1973):

> *Only preschoolers showing high interest in drawing during free play-time were selected for the research. The children were tested individu-ally and assigned randomly to one of three conditions. In the* expected reward *condition, children were shown a good player badge and told that if they did a good job of drawing, they could earn a good player badge and have their names put on the school honor roll board. All children in this condition got the expected awards. In the* unexpected reward *condition, children were asked to draw without any mention of the rewards. Unexpectedly, at the end of the drawing, all of these chil-dren were given the awards. Finally, in the* control *condition, children were asked simply to draw without the promise or presentation of the awards. After this task, children were observed back in the classroom*

during free playtime, and the amount of time spent drawing was re-corded. (Hom, 1994, p. 36, italics added).

After hearing the synopsis, each listener predicted how much time children in each of the three conditions would spend drawing during their subsequent free playtime. Which group of children would play the most? Which group would play the least? Would all the children play about the same? The Lepper, Greene, and Nisbett (1973) study found that children in the expected reward condition drew less than children from either the unexpected reward condition or the control condition. No significant difference emerged between the amount of drawing time for children in the unexpected reward and control conditions. Hom (1994) reported that fewer than 1% of students accurately predicted these findings (including educational psychology students!).

These "hidden costs of reward" findings highlight three phenomena. First, types of motivation exist—intrinsic and extrinsic. The children's natural curiosity supported their intrinsic motivation to draw, whereas the teacher's artificial good player awards supported their extrinsic motivation to draw. Second, well-intentioned teacher practices such as rewarding children and monitoring their task engagements can have detrimental effects on (intrinsic) motivation. Third, it is not the reward per se that undermines intrinsic motivation but, rather, its anticipation. Notice that the children in the unexpected reward condition received an award for their drawing, but the fact that the reward was an unexpected surprise effectively inoculated them from approaching it with a means-to-an-end orientation. In contrast, when the children expected the awards, they developed an "in order to" way of approaching the drawing, such as "I draw *in order to* get the award." Under such an approach, when the awards ended, so did the instrumental behavior (i.e., during the free playtime).

Developmental Decline in Academic Intrinsic Motivation

Just as Lepper and Greene used "good player" badges to encourage children to draw, teachers often rely on external contingencies to encourage students to want to work on science projects, familiarize themselves with computers, and read books. Stickers, candy, grades, prizes, deadlines, surveillance, and other incentives are ubiquitous in the classroom. As teachers and parents subject students to a constant barrage of external contingencies, students naturally adapt to the demands of the school culture. In their adaptation, however, students take on a greater extrinsic motivational orientation by focusing increasingly less on the process of learning and increasingly more on its products—grades, evaluations, jobs, scholarships, approval, and the like. Gradually, students experience an ever-growing increase in their academic extrinsic motivation and, therefore, an ever-diminishing developmental decline in their academic intrinsic motivation (Harter, 1981, 1992). From the third through the ninth (but especially between the sixth and seventh) grades, children move from a predominantly intrinsic motivational orientation to a predominantly extrinsic motivational orientation (Bacon, 1993; Harter, 1981). With each advancing grade, students perceive that school becomes more impersonal, more formal, more evaluative, more competitive, and basically less intrinsically motivating (Eccles, 1993; Eccles & Midgley, 1989; Eccles, Midgley, & Adler, 1984).

Once intrinsic motivation diminishes, educators find themselves in quite a mess. Students who have little or no intrinsic motivation have only extrinsic motivation to fall back on. To motivate such a student, an educator is put into the difficult position of having to use extrinsic rewards and controls to get any motivation out of the students at all. The cycle can be a vicious one—students have little intrinsic motivation, so teachers use powerful and salient extrinsic inducements that work in the short term but that further erode intrinsic motivation in the long term.

Rewards, prizes, and the like do not always undermine intrinsic motivation (Cameron & Pierce, 1994). To undermine intrinsic motivation, task interest must be relatively high to begin with. When tasks are interesting and enjoyable in their own right, extrinsic rewards and controls are superfluous sources of motivation. In contrast, with tasks that are inherently dull, extrinsic incentives do not undermine intrinsic motivation because there is so little intrinsic motivation there to undermine in the first place. In other words, extrinsic rewards and controls are problematic on relatively interesting tasks. In addition, rewards must be expected and made contingent on task engagement to undermine intrinsic motivation (e.g., "If you do your homework, then I'll give you a prize when you are finished."). It is this "if–then" contingency that establishes the "in order to," or means-to-an-end, approach to a task that is the telltale sign of an extrinsic motivational orientation. Thus, intrinsic motivation is put most at risk during interesting tasks when the external events are expected and made contingent on task engagement. Unfortunately, the temporal coexistence of these conditions is not uncommon in the practice of education.

Extrinsic supports for learning are sometimes necessary. Very few children that I have met show themselves to be intrinsically interested in sitting still for long periods of time, in voluntarily waiting their turn in the lunch line, or in doing their math homework when it is full of routine problems. Children are not intrinsically motivated to do these sorts of behaviors, but as a society we value them and wish our children to internalize them as important ways of behaving. Of course, such a plight says more about educational practice than it does student motivation. Thus, the challenge educators face is not to remove extrinsic contingencies from the classroom but, rather, to learn to use them judiciously so to avoid their detrimental effects on children's intrinsic motivation. Intrinsic motivation and inner motivational resources more generally are simply too precious to undermine inadvertently. To meet this challenge of using extrinsic supports while also maintaining intrinsic motivation, teachers can develop a complementary pair of skills:

1. Discover and utilize teaching strategies that support students' intrinsic motivation by enriching their sense of autonomy and self-determination (i.e., the topic of Chapter 2).
2. Discover and utilize teaching strategies that effectively use extrinsic supports for learning in a way that contributes to rather than interferes with students' intrinsic motivation to learn (i.e., the topic of Chapter 3).

Two Precautions in the Attempt to Motivate Others

Chapters 2 and 3 address the issue of students' intrinsic and extrinsic motivation more fully, but at this stage in the discussion two preliminary points need to be made explicit about how teachers might best structure their classrooms to motivate students. The first is an appeal to consider the merits of what researchers have learned about effective and ineffective motivational strategies—namely, that motivation theory is not necessarily consistent with common sense. The second concerns the effort to translate motivation theory into practice—namely, it is a good idea to keep in mind the medical credo-Do no harm in the fervor to heal).

Motivation Theory Is Not Necessarily Consistent with Common Sense

Classroom teachers face a myriad of problems that are motivational in nature. Student apathy, achievement anxiety, helplessness, immature coping strategies, challenge avoidance, and absenteeism are only a sampling of these problems. When faced with motivational problems, teachers fall back on the understandings they possess in regard to generating possible courses of action to alleviate the problems before them, sometimes on an hourly basis. Years of experience in the classroom supply teachers with trial-and-error learning and common sense to fall back on. One precaution in motivating others, however, is to recognize that motivation theory is not necessarily commonsensical (although sometimes it is). I hope that the previous discussion on the hidden costs of rewards successfully communicates that, sometimes, common sense and motivation theory make predictions that stand at odds with each other. I do not wish to argue that theories of motivation should replace common sense! Rather,

I simply invite the reader to consider the opportunity that motivation theories offer to complement personal experience and common sense. As an exercise, glance through the following two questions and, as you do so, actively monitor your thoughts as you generate possible solutions.

1. For a student with strong potential but a poor track record and low motivation in a particular course, what could you do to encourage his or her motivation and achievement during that course?
2. When you read books or listen to lectures, what is it about some of them that grabs your attention and fills your imagination with interest and intrigue, while other books and lectures leave you uninspired and listless?

As you think about possible solutions to each problem, monitor your own thought processes as you generate possible solutions and courses of action. Perhaps you begin with common sense. Alternatively, you might recall a similar problem from your personal experience, or you might pick up the telephone or walk over to the bookshelf to get some advice from another person. Perhaps the words of a mentor or role model leap to mind. These are all fine resources for a teacher to fall back on, but this book offers yet another resource—a set of motivation theories. A *theory* is simply a set of variables (e.g., teaching style, student interest, academic achievement) and the relationships that are assumed to exist among those variables (e.g., teaching style affects interest, which, in turn, affects achievement). Theories provide frameworks for interpreting observations and serve as bridges that link research with the practice of teaching (Gerrity, 1994). With a motivation theory in mind, the teacher might frame a solution to a problem along the lines of, "Well, according to goal-setting theory, . . ." or "According to self-determination theory, . . ." or "Brophy's research findings of the effect of teachers' praise on student performance suggests that . . ." As you read this book, I invite you to become familiar with these and several other motivation theories and bodies of research findings. Each theory represents extensive scientific analysis on which you can capitalize to gain an increased understanding of the dynamics involved in student motivation.

Keep in Mind the Medical Credo

A second precaution in motivating others is to keep in mind the medical credo: Do no harm. The medical practitioner must resist initiating any intervention effort that might very well put the patient into a worse condition than before he or she walked through the door. To respect the spirit of the medical credo, a teacher needs to be cognizant of the possible *multidimensional consequences* of his or her attempts to address a motivational problem. Consider again Lepper and Greene's studies using the good player awards, which increased extrinsic motivation but also decreased intrinsic motivation. Before a teacher initiates a classroom intervention, the teacher should have a comfortable grasp of the expected results, or outcomes, of such an effort. To this end, each chapter covers the empirical studies that spell out the advantages as well as the disadvantages of applying particular theories of motivation. When an educator understands how and why a motivation theory produces the particular sought-after outcomes, and when an educator can anticipate specific advantages and disadvantages of putting a theory into practice, then that teacher is well positioned to act every bit as responsibly as the medical doctor.

What Is the Purpose of Education? (Observational Activity 1.2)

There remains one final subject to cover in introducing the book: What is the purpose of education? Education is about fostering high student achievement, but it is also about much more. Education is about developing in students the personal resources they need to meet the requirements they will face in their personal lives and in the society at large. In the spirit of inviting discussion, Table 1-1 lists four major goals for education. Certainly, one major goal is to foster

TABLE 11-1 Four Major Goals of Education

A. Academic achievement
   1. Grade point average
   2. Standardized test scores
   3. Awards and scholarships (e.g., National Merit finalists)
   4. Academic skills, abilities, and talents (e.g., computers, public speaking)
   5. Life skills (e.g., driver's training, shop, home economics)
   6. Career preparation
   7. Mastery of content-based knowlede (e.g., history)
B. Continuing motivation to learn—becoming a lifelong learner
C. Development
   1. Toward autonomy or self-regulation
   2. Positive interpersonal relationships
   3. Healthy sense of self and identity
   4. Mastery (vs. helpless) orientation
   5. Subjective well-being (i.e., happiness)
   6. Positive emotional tone
D. Adjustment to society
   1. Socialization
   2. Internalization of cultural values
   3. Balance between independence and conformity
   4. Cooperativeness
   5. Personal contribution to society

student achievement, and educators can evaluate their success in this regard by paying attention to students' grade point averages, test scores, awards, acquired skills and abilities (in both academic and life-skill domains), career preparation, and content-based knowledge. In addition, education aspires to cultivate in students a love for learning itself. A second major goal of education, then, is to foster in students a continuing motivation to learn that manifests itself in students becoming lifelong learners. Third, education aspires to optimize students' development. Some of the major aspects of educationally relevant development include progress towards autonomy or self-regulation, the capacity for positive interpersonal relationships, a healthy sense of self and identity, a sense of personal mastery or competence, subjective well-being, and an optimistic emotional tone. Education also strives for a fourth goal—namely, to support the individual's successful adjustment into the society. Educators can evaluate their success in this regard by paying attention to the quality of students' socialization, internalization of cultural values, balance between independence and conformity, cooperativeness, and willingness and readiness to offer a personal contribution to the welfare of the society.

This list of goals is a tall order for any school system. Often, students have different goals for education and schooling than do educators. For instance, teachers generally see the purpose of education as the promotion of understanding of the world, social responsibility, and a commitment to learning, whereas students often see the purpose of education as securing a job and gaining wealth and status (e.g., Nicholls, Patashnick, & Nolen 1985). Despite the difficulty of the undertaking, the premise of this book is that when students acquire inner motivational resources such as self-determination, self-efficacy, and personal control beliefs, then the educational goals summarized in Table 1-1 are significantly more likely to occur. By asking you to pause and consider that the goals of education extend beyond maximizing student achievement outcomes, I am also asking you to consider that the goals of motivating others extend beyond maximizing achievement outcomes.

Conclusion

Motivation involves the internal processes that give behavior its energy and direction. In practice, people motivate others in one of two general ways—through a reliance on external motivational resources such as attractive rewards and incentives or through the nurturing of internal motivational resources such as needs, cognitions, and emotions. Most of us find the task of motivating others challenging, so we often seek strategies that work and that work in a hurry. On first glance, outer motivational resources seem to work just fine—students read, come to class, turn in assignments, and do all sorts of academic accomplishments that we like to see them do. On second glance, however, outer motivational resources produce a number of side effects that are simply too damaging to ignore—they sometimes undermine intrinsic motivation and risk leaving students motivationally empty after their removal (as students become increasingly dependent on outer resources to regulate their future motivation). The problem with nurturing inner motivational resources, on the other hand, is an obvious one—namely, that it is not readily apparent just how to do so. How does one nurture students' sense of self-determination or their interest in mathematics? Nor is it clear just how long the process will take before the teacher sees any sign of progress. Answering these concerns is the focus of the chapters to come.

Am I taking too hard a position against the use of extrinsic motivators? After all, is it not commonplace for students to come to like activities that teachers once had to coerce them into trying? Perhaps you can recall an instance in which a teacher made you do some activity you did not want to do but which, over time, you came to like. Perhaps you came to enjoy playing the piano only after Mom made you take lessons, or perhaps you now love reading Shakespeare or writing poetry after first doing so only to pass an exam. My own experience was with cheesecake. As a kid, I thought "cheesecake" sounded perfectly revolting, and I came to like it only after being forced to eat it during Thanksgiving dinners. But, having gone through these examples, I want to argue that, no, I do not think this is a commonplace occurrence. For task interest to increase when others use extrinsic motivators requires a special skill in the effective use of such motivators. Extrinsic motivators *can* be used effectively, and they can even be used in a way that increases intrinsic motivation. For instance, verbal praise is an extrinsic motivator that consistently increases intrinsic motivation (Anderson, Manoogian, & Reznick, 1976). I take a hard position against the use of extrinsic motivators only when one person is using them to control or pressure another person.

Instead of dangling rewards in front of students to coerce them into participation, what else can a teacher do? This question, more than any other, introduces the chapters to come. Instead of using extrinsic motivators, teachers can carefully explain the rationale, importance, and value inherent in engaging the activity (Chapter 3). They can point out the challenges it offers and provide competence-related feedback (Chapter 4). Or they can build in students the skills and confidence necessary to perform the task well enough so as not to be overwhelmed by fear and anxiety (Chapter 5). They can ask questions to pique curiosity or find ways to make the task more interesting than it now is (Chapter 9), and so on. Teachers who nurture students' inner motivational resources have more than just behavioral compliance to look forward to; in addition, inner motivational resources cultivate in students a continuing motivation to learn, positive developmental trajectories, and the inner guides to a successful and harmonious adjustment into society.

Recommended Readings

Condry, J. (1977). Enemies of exploration: Self-initiated versus other-initiated learning. *Journal of Personality and Social Psychology, 35,* 459–475.

Deci, E. L., & Ryan, R. M. (1987). The support of autonomy and the control of behavior. *Journal of Personality and Social Psychology, 53,* 1024–1037.

Harter, S. (1981). A model of intrinsic mastery motivation in children: Individual differences and developmental change. In A. Collins (Ed.), *A social developmental perspective* (Vol. 14). Hillsdale, NJ: Lawrence Erlbaum.

Hom, Jr., H. L. (1994). Can you predict the overjustification effect? *Teaching of Psychology, 21,* 36–37.

Lepper, M. R., & Greene, D. (1975). Turning play into work: Effects of adult surveillance and extrinsic rewards on children's intrinsic motivation. *Journal of Personality and Social Psychology, 31,* 479–486.

Marshall, H. (1987). Motivational strategies of three fifth-grade teachers. *Elementary School Journal, 88,* 135–150.

Rogers, C. R. (1969). The interpersonal relationship in the facilitation of learning. In *Freedom to learn* (pp. 103–127). Columbus, OH: Merrill.

Ryan, R. M. (1993). Agency and organization: Intrinsic motivation, autonomy, and the self in psychological development. In J. E. Jacobs (Ed.), *Nebraska symposium on motivation: Developmental perspectives on motivation* (Vol. 40, pp. 1–56). Lincoln: University of Nebraska Press.

Ryan, R. M., Connell, J. P., & Grolnick, W. S. (1992). When achievement is not intrinsically motivated: A theory of internalization and self-regulation in school. In A. K. Boggiano & T. S. Pittman (Eds.), *Achievement and motivation: A social-developmental perspective* (pp. 167–188). New York: Cambridge University Press.

Weiner, B. (1990). History of motivational research in education. *Journal of Educational Psychology, 82,* 616–622.

Observational Activities

Observational Activity 1.1: Strategies People Use to Motivate Others

The purpose of this observation is to attend to, observe, and classify the strategies and techniques people use to motivate others in their daily interactions. To begin, consider the interpersonal relationships listed in the section "Why Motivate Others?" (e.g., teacher and student, coach and athlete, doctor and patient). Observe three of these interpersonal exchanges as they occur naturally. Each exchange will probably be quite brief, lasting only five minutes or so. Identify who in the relationship is one-up in power and who is one-down, and then identify the strategy or technique that the first person uses to motivate the second person. Name and classify each strategy you see used by the person in power. Some possible strategies might be "used authority—just told them to do it," "used persuasion—convinced them that it was a fun thing to do," or "used bribery—promised them something in return." Also, note the emotional reaction of the person who is one-down as he or she is asked or told to do the task in question. How would you describe the person's emotional reaction—interested? upset and angry? compliant? tense or stressed? glad?

Following your observations, briefly describe the strategies you observed and the emotional reactions they caused. Then answer the following questions: What strategies did powerful people use to motivate others? Did any of these strategies occur more than once? Was there any pattern between the type of strategy used by one person and the type of emotional reaction from the second person? How active versus passive did the person being motivated seem, and did their activity or passivity depend on the type of strategy used? How voluntary was the second person's performance on the task—would you call their task participation compliance, or was it more voluntary and willful? Did you think one strategy in particular was significantly better than or worse than the others? If so, what led you to this impression?

Observational Activity 1.2: Perspectives on the Purposes of Education

The purpose of this interview is to discover the varieties as well as the commonalities in people's perspectives about the purposes of education. You will need to interview one person from at least three of the following categories: (1) students, (2) parents, (3) teachers, (4) school administrators, (5) property tax payers (i.e., home owners), and (6) employers or business managers. For instance, interview a student, a parent, and a teacher. Each interview will be brief, lasting 5 to 10 minutes. To conduct your interviews, you can use open-ended questions such as, "What do you think are the purposes of education?" or you can use the items listed in Table 1-1 to construct a questionnaire in which each entry in Table 1.1 lists a separate goal for education. Use a five-point scale (as shown below) to structure people's responses to each question. Feel free to improvise on the questionnaire and alter the phrasing of each question to fit your own interests and needs. You can delete some of the items or add some of your own. Eventually, your questionnaire will look something like this:

The purpose of education is to . . .

	Strongly Disagree				*Strongly Agree*
1. Increase students' academic achievement.	1	2	3	4	5
2. Increase students' standardized test scores.	1	2	3	4	5
3. Win attractive awards and scholarships.	1	2	3	4	5

	Strongly Disagree				*Strongly Agree*
17. Enable students to make a personal contribution to society.	1	2	3	4	5

Finish your interview with the following open-ended question: "What advice or recommendations could you give to school teachers to motivate their students?" Write down the advice the person gives.

Once you are done with the interviews, answer the following questions: Did any pattern emerge in what people see as the purposes of education? Did everyone agree that some goals were clearly the purposes of education, or did people's answers vary widely? Did the category of the person predict what he or she emphasized as the purposes of education, or did some other factor, such as age or gender, predict people's views better? Did you see any link emerge between what people said the purposes of education were and the advice they offered to teachers? Did you see any relationship between people's category and the type of advice they gave to teachers?

2

Self-Determination

Imagine being a university student preparing to become a teacher in the local school district. In one of your courses this semester, you have the opportunity to visit a local elementary school and observe teachers and students in action. Today's schedule includes visits to two fifth-grade classrooms for one hour each. During the first class, one characteristic of the teacher captures your attention. This teacher is clearly in charge. She cares about maintaining discipline, and she is masterful at doing so. Clearly, she is the center of attention and functions as a leader: She teaches from the lesson plan, assigns projects to complete, pushes everyone to keep on task, praises students when they do what she tells them to do, and evaluates the quality of their work. Confidently, she directs her students: "Listen carefully." "Read the instructions." In her class, students do not goof off. You admire her air of authority.

The hour ends, and off you go to the second class. Here, you notice that this teacher acts nothing like the first. She is not the center of attention. Rather, she invites questions and listens to the opinions of her students. She values spontaneity and promotes self-reliance in her students. Her students participate more actively and spend more time working independently or in groups. This teacher does not come across as a leader in charge, and you never see her trying to push her students to learn. Instead, she puts her effort into involving students in the lesson plan, offering them feedback, and supporting their autonomous behaviors.

With your observations completed, you ask yourself which of the two teachers you would rather emulate. Both were active, and both did what they thought was best for the students. Yet their teaching styles differed markedly. Though reported in a somewhat stereotypical manner, these two teaching styles correspond to what educators refer to as *controlling* versus *autonomy-supportive* (Deci & Ryan, 1987). Research shows that students say they like and prefer to have teachers who tell them what to do and then show them how to do it over teachers who give them choices and ask them to discover how to solve problems for themselves (Boggiano, Flink, Shields, Seelbach, & Barrett, 1993; Flink, Boggiano, & Barrett, 1990). Further, parents say they want their children to have teachers who are in charge (Boggiano, Barrett, Weiher, McClelland, & Lusk, 1987). That is, students and teachers alike prefer controlling teachers. The same research, however, shows that the students of autonomy-supportive teachers actually show more positive educational outcomes. Students of supportive teachers perceive themselves to be more competent, perform better on tests of academic achievement, and show a greater motivation to learn (Boggiano et al., 1993; Deci, Schwartz, Scheinman, & Ryan, 1981; Flink et al., 1990).

The discussion in Chapter 1 laid out the argument as to why controlling techniques are not a panacea for motivating students to learn. In this chapter, I continue that line of reasoning by arguing that a teaching strategy that facilitates students' autonomy, or self-determination, produces positive educational and developmental outcomes for students. In this chapter, the inner motivational resource under discussion is *self-determination*. The teaching strategy that facilitates self-determination is supporting students' autonomous behavior, or *autonomy support*. In addition, I will be explicit about how to teach in an autonomy-supportive manner.

The Nature of Self-Determination

We all have a need to experience choice in the initiation and regulation of our behavior. We desire to have our own choices, rather than environmental rewards and pressures, determine our actions (Deci & Ryan, 1985). We prefer to choose behaviors based on inner needs and desires. In other words, we have a need for *self-determination*. Behavior is self-determined when aspects of the self (e.g., needs, beliefs, feelings) guide the decision whether or not to spend time engaged in a particular activity. We are not self-determining (i.e., our behaviors are other-determined) when some outside force pressures us to think, feel, or behave in particular ways (Deci, 1980).

Perceived Locus of Causality

A concept that is fundamental to our understanding of self-determination is *perceived locus of causality* (Heider, 1958). Perceived locus of causality, an individual's perception of why he or she initiated a behavior, exists on a continuum that ranges from internal to external. When students believe that their behavior originates from their own needs, thoughts, feelings, and desires, then the locus for their behavior is an internal one. When students believe that their behavior originates from environmental influences, then the locus for their behavior is an external one. Typical environmental influences include another person (teacher, parent), rewards (gold star, paycheck), pressures (deadline), threats (loss of a privilege), constraints (rule), or behavioral contingencies (grade). In terms of self-determination, an internal perceived locus of causality is synonymous with self-determination, whereas an external perceived locus of causality is synonymous with other-determination (i.e., environment-determination).

Origins and Pawns

Some educators use *origins* and *pawns* as metaphorical shorthand terms to communicate the distinction between students whose behavior is free, self-determined, and emanates from an internal perceived locus of causality versus students whose behavior is forced, other-determined, and emanates from an external perceived locus of causality (deCharms, 1976, 1984; Ryan & Grolnick, 1986). To be an origin is to be the originator of one's behavior. To be a pawn is to be a "mere pawn" in the game that powerful other people play as they push their subordinates around like puppets—"like pawns." To be an origin is to be active, instrumental, and personally responsible, with a willingness to set goals for oneself in the classroom; to be a pawn is to be passive, reactive, and possessing little personal responsibility for school-related activities (Ryan & Grolnick, 1986).

When deCharms (1976) went into the public school system in St. Louis, his impression was that children were too frequently treated as pawns to the dictates of classroom teachers. Knowing the detrimental effects of being treated like a pawn, he decided to initiate a four-year origin-training program for fifth-graders from lower-middle-class families and the teachers those students would encounter in their coming grades. deCharms believed that the classroom climate established by the teacher determined whether a student felt like a pawn. Before he could empower students as origins, deCharms's strategy was first to give teachers an empathic dose of what it felt like to be treated like a pawn to the whims of an authority figure. As part of an extensive teacher-training program, the St. Louis teachers participated in a series of two dozen different activities to give them firsthand experiences of being treated as pawns and being treated as origins. For instance, in the Block-Stacking Game, teachers were paired in such a way that one teacher performed a block-stacking task with his or her non-preferred hand and wearing a blindfold, while the second teacher assumed the role of teacher to help the block-stacker, who was to try to build 18 stacks in a five-minute period. Some teachers took control and dominated the blindfolded block-stacker; other teachers were less directive, more supportive, and "warmer." The point of the exercise was to enliven discussion on the role of the teacher as a helping agent (deCharms, 1976, p. 49).

A second task was the Blindfold Game, in which one teacher was blind-folded while a second, sighted teacher served as the first teacher's guide during a walk across the school grounds. The activity was an exercise in the variety of leadership styles, and its purpose was to raise awareness about issues of guidance and control.

A third activity was the Origin–Pawn Game. During this activity, a staff member organized the teachers to sit together around a number of conference tables and introduced a (sort of) tinker-toy task with the following instructions (deCharms, 1976, pp. 57–58):

> *"Arrange the boxes in the center of the table. . . . Don't prop the boxes up, I want them flat. . . . Remove everything else but the boxes from your table. . . . Sit up straight; put your hands in your lap. . . . You may not talk, smoke, or chew gum. . . . Listen carefully to me; don't leave the room; if you need something, raise your hand. . . . Listen to these instructions. . . . This is a yellow rod; this is a blue rod; this is a red rod; this is a cylinder. . . . Follow these directions carefully. . . . Get six spools with narrow holes and place them in a straight line in front of you. . . . I said a* horizontal *straight line, not a* vertical *line; follow directions." And, then, later: "Take a spool, connect it to a red rod on the round side of the spool. . . . I did* not *say to put the assembly down. . . . Put the assembly down now. . . . Pick up the assembly. . . . Connect another round spool to the other side of the red rod. . . . Connect it to the* round *side; don't you know how to follow* directions?"*

As you can see, the staff member began to give contradictory directions as the instructions continued, and he began to state rules without explanation. Near the end of the session, he refused to listen to the teachers' attempts to correct him or to open a dialogue at all. That is, over time the staff member became less and less supportive of the teachers' autonomy and more and more controlling and demanding in his instructions and tone. At first, the teachers responded with passive acceptance and conformity. Near the end, however, many teachers rejected the instructions and some even rebelled against the control imposed on them.

After their experiences in the training program, the teachers went into the St. Louis public school system aware of the origin–pawn distinction. deCharms found that when teachers became more supportive of students' autonomy, their students' attitudes and behaviors changed from relatively pawnlike to relatively originlike. Specifically, the students showed greater tendencies toward active goal setting in which they translated their personal motives into behavioral actions, greater commitment to academic tasks, acceptance of personal respon-sibility for learning (e.g., volunteering for extra tasks, offering aid to less skilled students), greater academic confidence, less anxiety and pretentiousness, increased sense of personal responsibility for their own educational outcomes, and reported relatively internal perceived loci of causality (deCharms, 1976).

Individual Differences in Autonomy
(Observational Activity 2.1)

Two factors determine how much (or how little) a student feels like an origin. On the one hand, whether a student feels like an origin depends on the orientation of the teacher and of the classroom in general (Deci et al., 1981); on the other hand, whether a student feels like an origin depends on personality characteristics (Ryan & Grolnick, 1986). Just as deCharms noticed the effect that teachers had on students' origin–pawn perceptions, Ryan and Grolnick noticed that wide variability existed among students in the same classroom in terms of origin–pawn perceptions. Ryan and Grolnick argued that before students enter any particular classroom, they bring with them a host of prior experiences that influence how they interpret a teacher's support and control as well as how much they "pull" (i.e., ask) for either supportiveness or controllingness from the teacher. Variability in students' origin–pawn perceptions comes from experiences with previously encountered teachers, experiences within the home environment (parents, too, have orientations toward support or control; Grolnick & Ryan, 1989), and from experiences in other settings such as sports and music. To test their ideas, the researchers measured 600 elementary-grade children on both individual differences in perceptions of autonomy and perceptions of classroom climates. They found that individual differences exerted an even greater influence on students' origin–pawn perceptions than did classroom and teacher influences. In addition, both factors—individual differences and classroom climates—predicted all their measures of student motivation: self-worth, perceived competence, and mastery motivation (Ryan & Grolnick, 1986).

Positive Outcomes from Supporting Students' Autonomous Behavior

Educational researchers find that positive educational and developmental outcomes occur when teachers support students' autonomous classroom behaviors and when students posses originlike personalities. To investigate the effects of self-determination, educators adopt one of two research strategies. In the first, researchers categorized teachers in terms of how supportive versus controlling they are, and researchers then measure the educational and developmental outcomes of the students of those teachers. In the second, students report their own origin–pawn perceptions, and then the students complete measures of their educational and developmental outcomes. The first strategy looks for the effect of teacher and classroom differences; the second strategy looks for the effect of individual differences. Compared to students of controlling teachers and to pawnlike students, students of autonomy-supportive teachers and originlike students show the following positive educational and developmental outcomes:

1. Higher academic achievement
2. Greater perceived competence
3. Higher sense of self-worth and self-esteem
4. Enhanced conceptual learning
5. Greater creativity
6. Preference for challenge
7. More positive emotional tone
8. Increased school attendance and retention

Higher Academic Achievement

Perhaps the most important of all educational outcomes is academic achievement. Therefore, before educators can take a teaching strategy such as autonomy support seriously, evidence needs to exist that it does indeed promote academic achievement. Such evidence does exist, as autonomy-supportive teachers have students who show higher academic achievement than do the students of controlling teachers. Further, this is true whether researchers measure academic achievement via national test scores (Boggiano, Barrett, Silvern, & Gallo, 1991; Deci et al., 1981; Flink, Boggiano, Main, Barrett, & Katz, 1992) or via classroom grades (deCharms, 1976).

Greater Perceived Competence and Higher Self-Worth

Perhaps the most important developmental outcomes during the school years are perceived competence and a sense of positive self-worth. Sense of self-worth is particularly important because many educators view it as an index for a student's overall adjustment and well-being (Harter, 1982). Educators find that self-determination, like academic achievement, promotes perceptions of both competence and positive self-worth. When teachers support students' autonomy, rather than controlling their behavior, perceived academic competence increases (Deci, Schwartz, Sheinman, & Ryan, 1981; Ryan & Grolnick, 1986). Further, originlike students have higher perceived competence than do pawnlike students, in both the academic and social domains (Ryan & Grolnick, 1986). The logic of the link between self-determination and high perceived competence is that when teachers ask students to take personal responsibility for their own learning and for solving their own academic problems, then when those students face academic challenges, they tend to rely on their own inner motivational resources rather than on outer resources (i.e., the teacher). Deci, Nezlek, and Sheinman (1981), for instance, argue that teachers' support for students' self-reliance affirms students' sense of competence.

As is the case for perceived competence, originlike students hold relatively high self-worth, compared to pawnlike students (Harter, 1981, 1982; Ryan & Grolnick, 1986). Similarly, students of autonomy-supportive teachers report higher self-esteem than do students of controlling teachers (Deci, Schwartz, Sheinman, & Ryan, 1981). The link between self-determination and a positive self-worth occurs because self-worth increases when students (1) feel personally responsible for their own actions and academic accomplishments and (2) perceive that significant others support and respect their autonomous functioning.

Enhanced Conceptual (but Not Factual) Learning

Learning and conceptual understanding are additional key educational outcomes. When teachers are supportive, students show a greater flexibility in their way of thinking (McGraw & McCullers, 1979), show a more active mode of information processing (Grolnick & Ryan, 1987), and learn in a way that is conceptual rather than rote (Benware & Deci, 1984; Boggiano et al., 1993; Flink, Boggiano, & Barrett, 1990; Grolnick & Ryan, 1987). A self-determined approach to academic material allows the student to think about and integrate information in a flexible, less rigid, and less pressured way. A controlled, test-determined approach to learning produces a relatively rigid way of thinking as students' attention narrows to focus specifically on information that best answers questions on a test. In virtually every study showing that supportiveness enhances conceptual learning, the learning of factual information, however, does not differ between the two groups. Thus, a self-determined approach to learning does not increase learning in general; rather, it enhances only learning that is conceptual or thematic.

Greater Creativity

When teachers control students, student creativity diminishes. Specifically, creativity decreases when students expect their work to be evaluated (Amabile, 1979), when others closely watch their performances (i.e., surveillance; Amabile, 1983), when students perform under pressuring limits (Koestner, Ryan, Bernieri, & Holt, 1984), and when there are extrinsic rewards at stake for expert performance (Amabile, Hennessey & Grossman, 1986). In one study, for instance, students composed a short poem either under an extrinsic set ("think about impressing the teacher with your talent") or an intrinsic set ("think about playing with words"). Results showed that the writers with an intrinsic set wrote the more creative poems (as judged by experts) (Amabile, 1985). The findings linking self-determination to creativity are so consistent and so robust that

Amabile and Hennessey (1992) offer the following *intrinsic motivation principle of creativity*: "People will be most creative when they feel motivated primarily by the interest, enjoyment, satisfaction, and challenge of the work itself—rather than by external pressures."

Preference for Challenge

Preference for challenge refers to students' willingness to undertake tasks that are difficult or moderately difficult; avoidance of challenge refers to students' desires to minimize effort or undertake only the easiest tasks. When extrinsic rewards are at stake and students have a choice of activities that vary in their difficulty, students prefer the task's least challenging version (Harter, 1974, 1978b; Pittman, Emery, & Boggiano, 1982; Shapira, 1976). The rationale behind choosing the easiest version of a task is that by doing so the student positions herself best to gain the reward. In contrast, self-determined students prefer to choose the optimally challenging version of a task (Shapira, 1976) and prefer to engage in more difficult rather than less difficult follow-up tasks (Boggiano, Main, & Katz, 1988; Boggiano, Pittman, & Ruble, 1982; Boggiano & Ruble, 1986). Self-determined (rather than reward-determined) persons choose optimal challenges because their reason to engage the task in the first place is to strive for mastery and improvement, rather than to strive for external gain. Incidentally, when I think about these studies, I cannot help but speculate about their implications as undergraduates make their curricular choices for the upcoming semester (e.g., "Should I pick that easy course to help boost my GPA, or should I pick that more difficult course to help boost my teaching skills?").

More Positive Emotional Tone

When classrooms are relatively autonomy-supportive, students' moment-to-moment emotional state centers around interest and enjoyment rather than tension and anxiety (Csikszentmihalyi, 1985; Csikszentmihalyi & Rathunde, 1993; Ryan & Connell, 1989). In contrast, controlling classrooms create in students a negative emotional tone because these classrooms force students to think, feel, or behave in a way with which they are not necessarily comfortable (Ryan, 1982; Ryan & Connell, 1989). Instead of cultivating a positive emotional tone, controlling classrooms lead students to feel alienated, distressed, and even angry (Patrick, Skinner, & Connell, 1993).

Increased School Attendance and Retention

The final educational and developmental outcome affected by supportive versus controlling classrooms is attendance and retention. The more originlike students are, the more likely they are to come to class on time, attend their classes, and remain in school from one year to the next (deCharms, 1976; Vallerand & Bissonnette, 1992). As one point of illustration, Vallerand and Bissonnette (1992) asked each of one thousand first-year students at a Canadian college to complete a questionnaire that assessed their reasons for attending school. After scoring each student for how originlike versus pawnlike were their reasons, the researchers checked back a year later to see which students had dropped out of school by their sophomore years. The attrition rate of the pawnlike students was substantially greater than that of the originlike students.

How Does Autonomy Support Facilitate Positive Outcomes?

Clearly, autonomy-supportive classrooms promote positive educational and developmental outcomes for students. That leaves us with the question: *How* do supportive classrooms produce such positive outcomes? What is the process (or processes) though which support produces outcomes such as creativity and academic achievement?

To answer these questions, one group of researchers sought to study the most controlled students they could find—medical students (Williams, Weiner, Markakis, Reeve, & Deci, 1994). Traditionally, medical students learn in a dehumanizing learning climate that is rich in controlling sources of pressure such as unusual stress, interpersonal humiliation, and public verbal abuse (Smith & Kleinman, 1991). Williams and colleagues focused on internal medicine (i.e., general practice) interns because they noticed the national trend that many interns in this field were changing careers to pursue specialized practice. The researchers suspected that if the training climate were more autonomy-supportive, then the interns would experience greater interest and value in the practice of internal medicine and therefore would become more likely to choose to pursue the career. If controlling, on the other hand, then the interns' decisions to pursue internal medicine would not be guided by internal concerns (i.e., competence or interest) but by extrinsic concerns (i.e, pay and status). Because the extrinsic payoffs for specialized practice are universally greater than those for general practice, the researchers predicted that the interns would, when controlled, opt out of the internal medicine career path.

Table 2-1 lists ways in which interns might feel supported. When instructors supported the interns' self-determination, they did so by conveying confidence in the interns (item 1), by listening to how the interns would approach a problem (items 5 and 7), and by providing the interns with choices and options for how to treat their patients' problems (item 8). Figure 2-1 illustrates how the instructors' support enhanced the interns' motivational processes—perceived competence increased, interest grew, and tension and pressure decreased. When equipped with increased competence, increased interest, and an atmosphere of positive emotion, the interns did indeed become more likely to make a career choice for internal medicine. (The variable *prior likelihood* is important because

TABLE 2-1 Autonomy Supportiveness Questionnaire

1. The instructors conveyed confidence in my abilities to contribute to the care of my patients.
2. I felt accepted by the instructors.
3. The instructors encouraged me to ask questions.
4. The instructors were clear and informative.
5. The instructors would listen to how I would do things before giving their opinion.
6. I felt able to share my feelings with the instructors.
7. The instructors tried to understand how I saw things before suggesting how they would handle the situation.
8. The instructors provided me with choices and options for how to treat my patients' problems.

Source: Adapted with permission from Williams, G. C. (1993). *Internalization of biopsychosocial values by medical students.* Unpublished doctoral dissertation, University of Rochester, NY.
Note: In the questionnaire used by Williams, the phrase "attendings and residents" appeared in place of "instructors."

it mathematically controls for factors such as salary and occupational status that are obviously important variables when considering one's career choice.) Figure 2-1 therefore shows that supportive learning climates fostered students' inner motivational resources (competence, interest), and these inner resources, in turn, facilitated positive career outcomes. I want to argue that the results depicted in Figure 2-1 would also hold true in other settings (e.g., teacher-training programs) and would hold true for other outcomes such as academic achievement or retention in school.

Creating Autonomy-Supportive Classrooms

Given the merits of autonomy-supportive learning climates, a practical question arises: "How does a teacher establish an autonomy-supportive classroom, one that will facilitate students' self-determination?" Several investigators addressed precisely this question (e.g., Deci, Connell, & Ryan, 1989; Deci, Eghrari, Patrick, & Leone, 1994; Koestner et al., 1984). Foremost, researchers affirm the need to rethink rationales for using rewards and controls in the classroom that might threaten self-determination. The first step in supporting students' autonomy is to minimize the use of superfluous social controls. Once superfluous controls are eliminated, five specific teaching behaviors promote autonomy and self-determination in students. Table 2-2 lists these behaviors.

Acknowledging the Students' Points of View

The fundamental step for a teacher to take in creating an autonomy-supportive climate is to strive to understand and appreciate the students' points of view. To do so, the teacher needs to put the proverbial shoe on the other foot to best

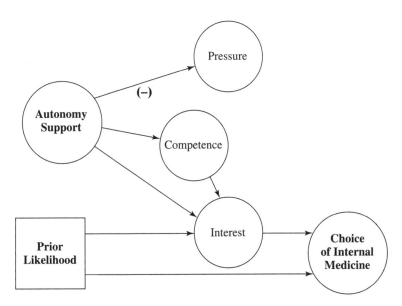

FIGURE 2-1   Autonomy-Supportive Model: Instructor Facilitates Student's Interest

Source: Williams, G. C., Weiner, M. W., Markakis, K. M., Reeve, J., & Deci, E. L. (1994). Medical students' motivation for internal medicine," *Journal of General Internal Medicine, 9,* , pp. 327–333.

identify the needs, interests, and feelings of the students. One way for a university professor to gain a sense of how students experience his or her course is to sit through or even audit another professor's course. The professor will soon learn what it feels like to sit still for an hour listening to a lecture, taking notes, writing papers, participating in discussions, taking examinations, and the like. After taking the role of the student, the teacher is then in an improved position to identify the needs and feelings of his or her students. When teachers identify students' concerns in an emotionally meaningful way, they can work to create a learning environment that encourages students' strivings and enables learning to take place in an atmosphere of interest and enthusiasm. When teachers structure the learning climate in a student-centered way, they make

TABLE 2-2   Five Teaching Behaviors That Support Students' Autonomous Behavior

1. Teacher acknowledges the students' points of view.
2. Teacher encourages students' choices and initiatives.
3. Teacher communicates rationale for any behavioral limits or constraints placed on students.
4. Teacher acknowledges that negative emotion is a valid reaction to teacher control.
5. Teacher's communication style relies on noncontrolling, positive feedback.

decisions with a primary concern for the needs and interests of the students (rather than for the needs and interests of the teacher) (Rogers, 1969).

Encouraging Students' Choices and Initiatives

As a teacher identifies students' needs, desires, and feelings, he or she is better positioned to create for students opportunities for choice, initiative, and self-reliance (McCombs & Pope, 1994). Greater opportunities for choice occur when there is a variety of learning centers or stations in the classroom, when there are options of which tasks to do, or even when students can choose which book to read for an assignment. Greater opportunities for initiative revolve around students making decisions whether or not to participate in educational tasks, when to do them, and especially how to solve problems as they arise. Greater opportunities for self-reliance occur as teachers give students more time for (directed) independent work and greater personal responsibility for their own learning and outcomes. Overall, to create an autonomy-supportive classroom climate, the teacher works to provide students with choices, options, and personal responsibility rather than relying on pressuring students to behave in a particular way.

Communicating the Rationale for Behavioral Limits or Constraints

Rules, constraints, and limits are a necessary and important part of the classroom structure. The important point is not whether rules, constraints, and limits are necessary (they are) but, rather, how these elements of classroom structure should be used—in a way that is informational or in a way that is controlling (Deci & Ryan, 1985; Koestner et al., 1984). When informational, the teacher communicates the rationale with which these limits ("no talking," "keep the table clean") are imposed by explaining the importance and necessity of the constraints and by clearly and unambiguously spelling out what the good reason for the "no talking" and "keep the table clean" constraints are. The logic in communicating the rationale for the teacher's display of social control is that students will internalize and accept as their own the teacher's rules, constraints, and limits (a process of internalization, discussed in Chapter 3).

Acknowledging That Negative Emotion Is a Valid Reaction to Teacher Control

Students naturally experience negative emotion when teachers impose limits, rules, and constraints and when teachers ask them to engage tasks that offer little appeal. Students feel frustrated when constrained to wait their turn in line and anxious when asked to read a difficult book. The strategy behind acknowledging and accepting the validity of students' negative emotional reactions to rules, limits, constraints, and unappealing tasks is this: Avoid pitting a student's negative, task-withdrawing emotionality (this is so boring! so frustrating!) against the teacher's request for the student to engage and persevere. In those cases in which the task itself is unable to generate the positive emotion that would otherwise facilitate on-task behaviors, then the teacher's rationale for doing the task—why the task is important, valuable, and meaningful—needs to be able to sustain the on-task activity. If the student learns to accept that part of learning and engaging in educational activities includes feeling bored, frustrated, and confused, then the student will be better equipped to initiate and persist in educational activities when the teacher is absent (as during homework).

Communication Style Relies on Noncontrolling, Positive Feedback

At times students perform poorly, and at other times they behave inappropriately. To create an autonomy-supportive climate, the teacher treats poor performance and behavioral problems as problems to be solved rather than as targets for criticism. The art of using noncontrolling feedback involves learning to resist using coercive language such as saying that the student "should," "must," "ought to," or "has to" do such-and-such (e.g., "Johnny, you should try harder to improve your spelling"). Instead, a teacher with a noncontrolling, supportive communication style would ask, "Johnny, I've noticed your spelling has not been improving lately; do you have any idea why this might be?" The art of using positive feedback is to resist using critically negative feedback (e.g., "Your handwriting is sloppy") and, instead, make a special effort to identify points of improvement and progress (e.g., "I noticed that your *t*'s are clearer than before; can you make your *l*'s as straight as your *t*'s?").

Teacher Orientation (Observational Activity 2.2)

Teacher orientation refers to the extent to which a teacher solves the problems that arise in the classroom in a supportive or a controlling way. An autonomy-supportive teacher orientation centers around a problem-solving approach in which students diagnose and solve their own problems with the support of the teacher. To measure type of teacher orientation, Deci and his colleagues (1981) developed a questionnaire that lists hypothetical problems that occur in school settings and asks teachers to make a recommendation in how to solve each problem. Table 2-3 shows one of Deci et al.'s "problems in school" and lists four possible ways of responding to the problem. Take a moment to read the problem and decide for yourself how appropriate versus inappropriate each of the four ways of dealing with the problem seems to you.

TABLE 2-3   One Vignette from the Problems in School Questionnaire

Instructions

Here is a vignette that describes an incident and lists four conceivable ways of responding to it. Think about each story and then consider each response in turn. Consider how appropite you believe each response to be for dealing with the problem described. You may find the option to be perfect—in other words, "extremely appropriate"—in which case you would want to circle a number around 7. You may find the option to be highly inappropriate, in which case you would want to circle a number around 1. If you find the option reasonable, then you would want to circle a number somewhere between 1 and 7. There are no right or wrong answers. People's styles differ, and this questionnaire simply asks for what you consider to be appropriate for this particular problem, according to your own style.

Vignette

Jim is an average student who has been working at grade level. During the past two weeks he has appeared listless and has not been participating during reading group. The work he does is accurate, but he has not been completing assignments. A phone conversation with his mother revealed no useful information. The most appropriate thing for Jim's teacher to do is:

(a) Make him stay after school until that day's assignments are done.

1	2	3	4	5	6	7
Highly Inappropriate					Highly Appropriate	

(b) She should impress upon him the importance of finishing his assignments since he needs to learn this material for his own good.

1	2	3	4	5	6	7
Highly Inappropriate					Highly Appropriate	

(c) Let him see how he compares with the other children in terms of his assignments and encourage him to catch up with the others.

1	2	3	4	5	6	7
Highly Inappropriate					Highly Appropriate	

(d) Let him know that he doesn't have to finish all of his work now and see if she can help him work out the cause of his listlessness.

1	2	3	4	5	6	7
Highly Inappropriate					Highly Appropriate	

Source: Deci, E. L., Schwartz, A., Sheinman, L., & Ryan, R. M. (1981). An instrument to assess adults' orientations toward control versus autonomy in children. Reflections on intrinsic motivation and perceived competence. *Journal of Educational Psychology, 73,* 642–650. Copyright 1981 by the American Psychological Association. Adapted with permission.

According to Deci, Schwartz, Scheinman, and Ryan (1981), the first strategy is a highly controlling one, because the teacher literally controls the student to behave in a particular teacher-defined way. The second strategy is moderately controlling because the teacher's control is less explicit, although it clearly pressures the student to act and believe in a way that the teacher thinks is appropriate. The third strategy is only slightly controlling and is, in fact, slightly autonomy-supportive, because the teacher suggests nonevaluative information the student can use to decide whether or not to follow the example. The final strategy is highly autonomy-supportive because the student, not the teacher, possesses the responsibility for diagnosing and solving the problem in his or her own way.

Specific Autonomy-Supportive Instructional Strategies.

Autonomy-supportive classroom climates satisfy students' needs for self-determination and foster a high intrinsic motivation to learn throughout the school year. Teachers' day-to-day concerns, however, typically are more concrete and often revolve around the problem of fostering student motivation to learn particular tasks at particular times. Any specific attempt to motivate students' learning on a particular task can be classified in terms of (1) how controlling and (2) how directed that strategy is.

Controlling (versus noncontrolling) motivational strategies differ with respect to how much the teacher relies on grades, tangible rewards, rules, or a pressuring style of praise to initiate students' learning behavior. Directed (versus nondirected) motivational strategies differ in respect to how much the teacher gives the student an instruction to learn specific information. According to Grolnick and Ryan (1987), the most effective and the most autonomy-supportive instructional strategy to use is a noncontrolling, directed one.

In an experimental demonstration of the effectiveness of a noncontrolling, directed teaching strategy, Grolnick and Ryan (1987) asked fifth-grade students to read two passages from a grade-level social studies textbook. On the first (warm-up) passage, all students read it at their leisure and completed a brief questionnaire about how interesting it was, how much pressure they felt while reading it, and how difficult the passage was to read. Before reading the second passage, the researchers divided students into one of three experimental conditions based on the type of instructions the student heard: (1) controlling and directed, (2) noncontrolling and directed, or (3) noncontrolling and nondirected. Controlling, nondirected instructional strategies are rare (if they exist at all), so the researchers included only the three experimental conditions. After reading the second passage, then all students completed a second questionnaire to assess their interest, pressure, recall of factual information, and conceptual understanding of the passage.

Controlling, directed instructions: "After you are finished, I'm going to test you on it. I want to see how much you can remember. You should work as hard as you can because I'll be grading you on the test to see if you're learning well enough."

Noncontrolling, directed instructions: "After you are finished, I'm going to ask you some questions about the passage. It won't really be a test, and you won't be graded on it. I'm just interested in what children can remember from reading passages. Read it in whatever way is best for you."

Noncontrolling, Nondirected Instructions: "After you are finished, I'll be asking you some questions similar to the ones I asked about the other passage."

The researchers wanted to know what effect each teaching strategy would have on students' learning. They measured two types of learning: factual and conceptual. Factual learning was greatest following the two directed instructions and least following the nondirected instruction. With directed instruction, the teachers told the students to focus their attention on learning the factual information, and indeed they did. Conceptual learning was greatest following the two noncontrolling instructions and least following the controlling instruction. Conceptual learning is highest with noncontrolling instruction because what is read is more likely to be processed actively, with greater interest, and with greater perceived relevance (as opposed to being merely a means to get a good grade). Conceptual learning is highest with nondirected instruction because attentional span is wider and freer to process and integrate information actively. Further, the researchers found that pressure was highest following the controlling, directed instruction relative to the two noncontrolling conditions, while interest was highest in the two noncontrolling conditions and lowest in the controlling, directed instructions.

Taken as a whole, the results confirm the efficacy of a noncontrolling, directed approach to instruction. With this approach, interest was high, pressure was low, factual learning was high, and conceptual learning was high. In other words, all aspects of learning were optimal. The second best strategy (in this study) was the noncontrolling, nondirected instruction, as interest was high, pressure was low, and conceptual understanding was high; the problem with nondirected instruction was that the learning of specific, factual information was relatively low. As for controlling, directed instruction, its benefit was that factual learning was relatively high (but no higher than for controlling, directed instruction); its problems, however, were many, as interest was low, pressure was high, and conceptual learning was low.

Freedom within Limits

Another way of conceptualizing a noncontrolling, directed style of instruction is "freedom within limits" (Rogers, 1969). A noncontrolling approach to instruction allows students to learn in their own way (i.e., freedom), while a directed approach to instruction establishes a climate with a firm, consistent structure (i.e., within limits). Koestner and colleagues (1984) demonstrated how classroom teachers can translate "freedom within limits" into clear, usable classroom instruction. The researchers invited elementary-grade children to engage in an enjoyable painting activity under one of three instructional sets (shown below). The noncontrolling (informational) limits condition corresponds to freedom within limits. Unlike the earlier Grolnick and Ryan study, which asked students to *do* something (read), the Koestner et al. study used instructions to ask students *not* to do something—not to make a mess during their painting.

Controlling limits: "Before you begin, I want to tell you some things that you will have to do. They are rules that we have about painting. You have to keep the paints clean. You can paint only on this small sheet of paper, so don't spill any paint on the big sheet. And you must wash out your brush and wipe it with a paper towel before you switch to a new color of paint, so that you don't get the colors all mixed up. In general, I want you to be a good boy (girl) and don't make a mess with the paints."

Noncontrolling (i.e., informational) limits: "Before you begin, I want to tell you some things about the way painting is done here. I know that sometimes it's really fun to just slop the paint around, but here the materials and room need to be kept nice for other children who will use them. The smaller sheet is for you to paint on, the larger sheet is a border to be kept clean. Also, the paints need to be kept clean, so the brush is to be washed and wiped in the paper towel before switching colors. I know that some kids don't like to be neat all the time, but now is a time for being neat."

The "no limits" children received no such pretask, limit-setting instructions. After ten minutes of painting, the researchers measured each child on his or her painting enjoyment, quality of painting (as measured by raters), creativity (also measured by raters), and intrinsic motivation (measured during a free-choice playtime). The children followed the limits equally well in the two limit-setting conditions; but with the noncontrolling limits, students enjoyed the task more, performed better, showed high creativity, and showed high intrinsic motivation. The children without limits also showed all these same effects—high enjoyment, quality performance, high creativity, and high intrinsic motivation (though they did make a mess of things). In fact, statistical tests showed no difference on these measures between the children with the noncontrolling limits and children with no limits. Children who painted with the controlling limits, however, showed significantly lower enjoyment, poorer performance, less creativity, and less intrinsic motivation.

Criticisms of Supporting Students' Autonomy

When teachers first learn of research on intrinsic and extrinsic motivations, origins and pawns, and support and control, their reactions are full of enthusiasm and interest. At the same time, however, teachers quickly counterargue that to lose control over a classroom is the quickest way they know to open the door to chaos. Behavior management does have its virtues. But autonomy support is *not* permissiveness run amuck. Teacher support does not preclude classroom rules, constraints, and limits. Teacher students need structure; and rules, constraints, and limits provide some of that structure. The question is not whether classrooms should have rules and limits; rather, the question is how these external events will be put into practice. The study by Koestner and his colleagues (1984) contrasting "controlling" versus "informational" limits, for instance, showed that only the controlling limits produced an adverse effect on students' performances, creativity, and intrinsic motivation. In other words, external events such as limits *can* be administered in a relatively autonomy-supportive manner (Ryan, 1982).

A second criticism is that if a teacher spends all of his or her time on supporting students' self-determination, then the teacher loses critical time and opportunity to teach arithmetic, reading, science, or whatever the specific content of the course may be. After all, first and foremost teaching involves instruction. There is merit to the basic idea that "if you want somebody to know something, you teach it to them" (Detterman, 1993, p. 15). Such a "direct instruction" approach stands at odds with the more supportive, "constructivistic" approach taken in the present chapter (von Glaserfeld & Steffe, 1991). This criticism makes it sound as if the selection of a teaching strategy boils down to an either–or choice. The dilemma resolves itself, I think, because empirical research confirms that students of supportive teachers demonstrate higher academic achievement on tests of traditional subject matter than do students of controlling teachers. Through supporting students' autonomy, a teacher gets the best of both worlds: healthy student development *and* higher academic achievement.

A final criticism I hear from teachers goes something like this: "If support is so great, then why are most teachers controlling? And why do most teachers prefer to be that way?" I think there are three reasons teachers are so frequently controlling in their interactions with students:

1. Many teachers (and parents) endorse the philosophy that controlling techniques, such as rewards, deadlines, and surveillance, are more effective for promoting learning, motivation, and achievement than are autonomy-supportive techniques (Barrett & Boggiano, 1988; Boggiano et al., 1987).
2. Teachers who use controlling strategies are rated by both students and parents as more competent than those teachers who use autonomy-supportive strategies (Flink et al., 1990). Thus, students and parents frequently "pull" for classroom teachers to conduct themselves in a controlling way.
3. Teachers themselves are pressured to meet performance standards by the people who employ them (i.e., principals, the general public). Teachers who are told "Your role is to ensure that students learn, and it is your responsi-

bility to make sure they perform up to standards" teach in a more controlling manner than do teachers told "Your role is to facilitate students' learning, and there are no specific performance requirements" (Deci, Spiegel, Ryan, Koestner, & Kauffman, 1982).

We must be willing to balance the pressures placed on us as teachers with the knowledge that students benefit most from autonomy-supportive classrooms.

Conclusion

Most teachers would agree that learning is an active process that occurs most readily when students bring their own motivation to the assimilation and accommodation of academic material (e.g., Thomas, 1980). This chapter focused on the need that underlies energizing and directing students' intrinsic motivation, self-determination. From the empirical research on this topic, we can draw three conclusions:

1. A teacher's orientation toward support (versus control) influences the self-determination of students in that classroom (e.g., Deci, Schwartz, Scheinman, & Ryan, 1981)
2. Teacher-training programs can enhance students' senses of self-determination in the classroom (e.g., deCharms, 1976).
3. Substantial individual differences exist among students in the same classroom on the origin–pawn experience (Ryan & Grolnick, 1986).

Thus, teachers express orientations toward support or control; teacher support is an acquirable skill and, when acquired, facilitates a host of positive educational and developmental outcomes in students.

The discussion of teachers' support of students' autonomous behavior is important because it strongly challenges one of the most traditional assumptions in the teaching profession—namely, that the best way to ensure that students learn is to control and pressure them until they do so. Often, that pressure comes in seductive ways (e.g., praise, gold stars, scholarships), but it is control and pressure nonetheless. The literature on autonomy support, however, communicates that the most effective way to encourage students to learn is to facilitate their autonomy and interest. If this sounds intuitive, I invite you to watch and listen with the ear of the clinician as coaches talk to athletes, managers talk to employees, and doctors talk to patients (as in Observational Activity 1.1). Also, read the editorials on public education that appear in the local newspaper. As often as not, the language and interaction style of the person who is one-up in interpersonal power is much closer to a controlling, dictatorial, hard-line approach than it is to an autonomy-supportive one. No one wants to argue that teachers should not direct their students' behavior and teach them the information that the culture values. In the same spirit, however, no one can deny the aversive, negative emotions one experiences while being treated as a pawn (as in deCharms' Origin–Pawn game).

Recommended Readings

Amabile, T. M. (1985). Motivation and creativity: Effect of motivational orientation on creative writers. *Journal of Personality and Social Psychology, 48,* 393–399.

Benware, C., & Deci, E. L. (1984). The quality of learning with an active versus passive motivational set. *American Educational Research Journal, 21,* 755–765.

deCharms, R. (1984). Motivation enhancement in educational settings. In R. E. Ames & C. Ames (Eds.), *Research on motivation in education: Student motivation* (Vol. 1, pp. 275–310). New York: Academic Press.

Deci, E. L., Driver, R. E., Hotchkiss, L., Robbins, R. J., & Wilson, I. M. (1993). The relation of mothers' controlling vocalizations to children's intrinsic motivation. *Journal of Experimental Child Psychology, 55,* 151–162.

Deci, E. L., Schwartz, A. J., Sheinman, L., & Ryan, R. M. (1981). An instrument to assess adults' orientations toward control versus autonomy with children. *Journal of Educational Psychology, 73,* 642–650.

Deci, E. L., Spiegel, N. H., Ryan, R. M., Koestner, R., & Kauffman, M. (1982). The effects of performance standards on teaching styles: The behavior of controlling teachers. *Journal of Educational Psychology, 74,* 852–859.

Flink, C., Boggiano, A. K., & Barrett, M. (1990). Controlling teaching strategies: Undermining children's self-determination and performance. *Journal of Personality and Social Psychology, 59,* 916–924.

Grolnick, W. S., & Ryan, R. M. (1987). Autonomy in children's learning: An experimental and individual difference investigation. *Journal of Personality and Social Psychology, 52,* 890–898.

Koestner, R., Ryan, R. M., Bernieri, F., & Holt, K. (1984). Setting limits on children's behavior: The differential effects of controlling versus informational styles on intrinsic motivation. *Journal of Personality, 52,* 233–248.

Ryan, R. M., & Grolnick, W. S. (1986). Origins and pawns in the classroom: Self-report and projective assessments of individual differences in children's perceptions. *Journal of Personality and Social Psychology, 50,* 550–558.

Observational Activities

Observational Activity 2.1: Projective Assessment of Students' Autonomy

The purpose of this interview is to assess students' autonomy from both an individual difference perspective as well as from a classroom perspective. You will need to enlist the participation of three students. You can test more than one student at a time, and, if possible, you can test everyone simultaneously as one group.

For these interviews, you will use a projective test. In projective testing, a test administrator (e.g., a school psychologist) typically shows an ambiguous scene depicted in a drawing and asks the examine to look at the drawing and create a story that makes sense of the scene. The picture used in this activity (from the original version of the Michigan Pictures Test) is copyrighted material, so you will use the narrative depicted under the section "The Scene" (instead of using the actual picture). To begin, hand out on a single piece of paper that has the sections "The Scene" and "Instructions" typed on the top third of the page. Leave the bottom two-thirds of the page blank, because that is where students are to write their stories.

The Scene
The classroom is a typical one with 25 students sitting in rowed seats in the schoolroom. A female teacher stands at the head of the schoolroom near her desk. While the other 24 students sit in their desks, a single boy (girl) stands next to his (her) desk. At this moment, every one of the other students and the teacher have their attention focused on the boy (girl).

Instructions
Write a story about what is going on. It can be any kind of story you like. Tell something about what is happening now, what happened in the past, what is going to happen in the future, and include something about what the people are thinking and what they are feeling.

After ten minutes, call time and collect the stories. To score and interpret the stories, score each narrative on these two dimensions:

1. *Student autonomy, or self-determination:* Score on a 1–7 scale your impression of how autonomy-oriented versus controlled the protagonist's behavior and thoughts are. At one end of the scale put "self-determined" and at the other end of the scale put "controlled by others."
2. *Teacher support:* Score on a 1–7 scale your impression of how autonomy-supportive versus controlling the teacher seemed to be. At one end of the scale put "highly supportive," and on the other end of the scale put "highly controlling."

You might find the original scoring procedure in Ryan and Grolnick (1986) to be helpful.

Once you have scored the stories for both student autonomy and teacher support, answer the following questions:

- How easy or difficult was it to identity themes of autonomy and control in the stories?
- How much variance (difference) appeared among the three students in your two measures?
- Did the two variables—student autonomy and teacher support—correlate with one another?
- If so, why do you think these variables related to one another?
- Did the examiners focus mostly on the student, mostly on the teacher, or equally on the student and the teacher? Do you consider this important; why or why not?

Observational Activity 2.2:
Controlling versus Supportive Teaching Styles

The purpose of this interview is to become sensitive to interpreting a teacher's classroom style for its support versus control. Teachers vary along many dimensions—how experienced they are, what their personalities are like, and a host of other variables. The dimension emphasized here is how controlling versus autonomy-supportive teachers are in their interactions with students. To understand controlling versus autonomy-supportive teaching styles more fully, interview two teachers. Each interview will last 30 to 40 minutes. If possible, select teachers who work with the same grade level of students that you plan to teach. Include in your list of questions the following:

1. How would you describe your students in terms of their motivation?
2. What do you usually do when your students are listless and apathetic—that is, when they fail to show a motivation to learn? What do you do when they fail to behave in a way that you would like?
3. Do you make most of the classroom decisions, or do you create opportunities for your students to make decisions? Can you give me an example of the sort of decisions you tend to make and an example of the sort of decisions the students tend to make?
4. Can you recall a recent interaction you had in which you consciously tried to motivate a student to learn? What did you do? How did the student react?
5. Do you use extrinsic incentives, such as stickers or privileges, to motivate your students. Why or why not?
6. Do people outside the classroom—parents, principals, and so on—pressure you to motivate your students more, or in a particular way, or for a particular purpose?

With your list of questions in hand, interview each teacher separately. Begin by introducing yourself (if the teacher is a stranger) and your purpose in asking the questions. After your interviews, compile a description of each teacher's orientation toward motivating students. Compare the different styles. What similarities and differences do you notice? Which teaching style would you prefer if you were a student in a class taught be these teachers? Did one or both of the teachers appear to be *both* autonomy-supportive and controlling? What did you learn in terms of controlling versus supportive styles by conducting these interviews?

3

Internalization and Self-Regulation

Imagine that you have a nine-year-old daughter who attends the local public school. Today she came home in tears, saying that the teacher had sent her to the time-out room because she was late for class. You telephone the teacher for an explanation, and her teacher tells you that the punishment teaches your daughter that punctuality is desirable while tardiness is not. You sense that punishment is not the way to encourage your daughter to learn the value of punctuality. After all, she continues to insist that punctuality is "no big deal." Like her teacher, you wish for your daughter to value punctuality; yet, at the same time, you understand your daughter's point of view that there is no fun in arriving early only to sit and wait for class to begin as everyone else lingers in the hallway having fun, talking, and laughing. Your daughter knows what punctuality is, and she is fully able to be punctual if she so desires; she just does not see the same personal value in punctuality that her teacher does. You wonder if there is a better way to approach this problem.

Dozens of other examples exist in which a student's desires stand in conflict with adult prescriptions and proscriptions. Adults often attempt to overcome students' lack of desire by *prescribing* specific behaviors: Do homework, pay attention, take advanced classes, wait your turn in line, and—my personal favorite from childhood—stand up straight! In the next breath, parents and teachers restrain students' desires by *proscribing* a variety of behaviors: talking in class, fighting, cheating, chewing gum, and so on.

Internalization is not just a one-way street in which adults prescribe and proscribe directives to children. Children, too, desire self-regulation for themselves. This socialization process to encourage internalization and self-regulation is largely an adult-regulated relationship in the early grades, mostly a negotiated and cooperative relationship in the middle grades, and largely a student-regulated undertaking in the later grades (Borman, 1978).

At whatever age, teachers encourage students to become increasingly active participants in their own learning—to become willing and able to take a personal responsibility for regulating their own academic achievement (Corno, 1992). It is a cornerstone belief of educators in this area of research (e.g., Schunk & Zimmerman, 1994) that students' abilities to monitor and regulate their own learning and studying are at least as important to academic achievement (if not more so) than are their cognitive abilities (see Pintrich & DeGroot, 1990). Such a belief arises from data like those from a 1990 report of the National Assessment of Educational Progress group showing that 25 percent of twelfth-graders *never* study, whereas 71 percent study *no more than one hour a day*. When students are unwilling to invest time and effort in their schoolwork, expectations for academic achievement must be low and the possibilities for academic excellence remote. These data, like teachers' daily observations in the classroom, support the contention that academic achievement is not only an ability issue; it is also a motivational issue—perhaps even *mostly* a motivational issue.

Internalization

Much in early development occurs spontaneously and naturally. Children naturally exercise their skills and pursue their curiosities and, through such spontaneity, develop talents and acquire knowledge. As children develop, however, other people (e.g., parents and teachers) place increasing limits on the exercise of these capacities and interests. By kindergarten, more than half of all adult communications to children come in the form of directives ("Tie your shoes"; "Quit running"; Borman, 1978). Adults require children to engage in behavior that they would not do naturally (e.g., completing routinized homework assignments) and to disengage from behavior they do spontaneously (e.g., screaming with excitement). In the classroom, teachers ask children for voluntary participation in uninteresting but culturally valued activity (e.g., homework) and for voluntary restraint from interesting but culturally proscribed activity (e.g., daydreaming).

Internalization refers to the process through which an individual transforms a formerly externally prescribed regulation or value into an internal one (Ryan, Rigby, & King, 1993). During internalization, one adopts the value or regulation of others as one's own. Figure 3-1 illustrates the internalization process whereby a competent adult helps a child develop the capacity for self-regulation (from Henderson & Cunningham, 1994).

Central to the contents of Figure 3-1 is Vygotsky's (1978) "zone of proximal development," which refers to some aspects of development (e.g., reading, penmanship) that lie outside the child's current independent capacities yet within

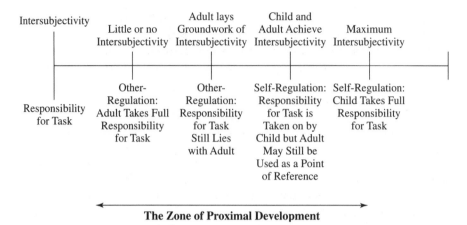

The Zone of Proximal Development

FIGURE 3-1 Advancing from Other-Regulation to Self-Regulation in the Zone of Proximal Development

Source: Henderson, R. W., & Cunningham, L. (1994). Creating interactive sociocultural environments for self-regulated learning. In D. H. Schunk & B. J. Zimmerman (Eds.), *Self-regulation of learning and performance: Issues and educational applications* (pp. 255–281). (Hillsdale, NJ: Lawrence Erlbaum).

the child's current capacities given the assistance of a competent adult. That is, the zone of proximal development communicates the full bandwidth of self-regulation in which heteronomy (dependence on others) appears on the left-hand side while autonomy (dependence on the self) appears on the right-hand side.

At first, the adult assumes the responsibility for externally regulating the child's behavior. At this point (far left-hand side), the child has little or no understanding of the meaning of the adult's regulations (little or no *intersubjectivity*). In time, the adult communicates the meaning of the activity in terms the child can understand. When the child understands some of the meaning for the regulated activity, he or she gains some intersubjectivity and assumes some of the responsibility for the task or behavior. Adult–child (or teacher–student) interactions become increasingly reciprocal and decreasingly directive. As the child understands more of the meaning and rationale for the task, he or she gains an increasing sense of responsibility for his or her own self-regulation. As the capacity for self-regulation increases, the child frequently uses the adult as a reference point as to the appropriate course of action. During these interactions, the child often mimics aloud the adult's speech concerning what to do. Through an increasing number of reciprocal interactions, the child internalizes the adult's task-related instructions as his own self-instructions—first in the form of repeating aloud the adult's instructions verbatim and then in the form of internalized, inaudible, and private self-talk. With self-administered instructions (self-talk), the child takes full responsibility for the task and the adult need no longer be present during the child's performance. After internalization has occurred— that is, after intersubjectivity is high, private self-talk regulates action, personal responsibility for the task is high, and the adult serves only in an advisory capacity (far right-hand side of the figure)—the adult no longer needs to externally regulate the child, as she "can do it herself."

Internalization and the passing along of cultural knowledge from adult to child is a joint problem-solving venture (Rogoff, 1990; Vygotsky, 1978). The teamwork that takes place within the zone of proximal development between child and adult enables the child to participate in activities beyond those he or she currently can handle independently. Internalization and self-regulation advance when the child can independently perform tasks that originally oc- curred only between the two partners. The whole process is a developmental apprenticeship (Rogoff, 1990).

Three Developmental Issues

Three issues underscore the importance of the internalization process for educators:

1. There are two different processes through which internalization occurs.
2. Students engage in internalization actively and intentionally.
3. Relatedness to others provides the social context to support internalization.

The process of internalization. There are two different processes through which internalization outcomes occur (Deci, Eghrari, Patrick, & Leone, 1994). At one extreme, children internalize beliefs and regulatory styles in a rigid, unreflective fashion; at the other extreme, children internalize beliefs and regulatory styles in a flexible, open-minded fashion (Fromm, 1941). In the first case, the impetus that drives the internalization process is social pressure or a sense of fear and guilt. The social context sometimes uses pressure (e.g., threats, punishments), fear (e.g., loss of approval or love), and guilt (e.g., activity condemned as "sin") to force a person into thinking, feeling, or behaving in particular ways. Though internalized, such a set of beliefs carries with it little in terms of personal volition and much in the sense of anxiety, internal pressure (to do what one "should"), and intrapsychic conflict (to do "X," although one would rather do "Y"; Ryan, 1982). The result is adherence to an internally controlling style in which the person self-administers affective and self-esteem contingencies to force the self into particular ways of thinking, feeling, or behaving (Ryan, 1991, 1993).

In the second case, an individual adopts beliefs and regulations through an acceptance of their meanings, rationales, and utilities. For beliefs and regulations to be internalized in this manner, the social context must explain the significance, purpose, and utility of thinking or acting in a particular way. Beliefs internalized in this fashion carry with them a strong sense of choice, volition, and personality integration and little in the way of coercive pressures and anxieties (Ryan & Connell, 1989). So the first issue to keep in mind is that not all internalizations are equal in that some internalizations are qualitatively more healthy and adaptive than are others.

Internalization is an active, intentional process. Children strongly desire to interact *effectively* with their social environment. To do so, children actively and intentionally learn those societal regulations that allow them to interact as effectively with others as possible (Deci & Ryan, 1985), although age-related differences exist in determining how active the child is in his or her own socialization (Higgins & Parsons, 1983). A child might learn, for instance, that when she is punctual, polite, and cooperative, then her interactions with the social context are most effective and rewarding. Such learning is not necessarily of a passive, observational nature; rather, in the course of interacting with others the child actively seeks those ways of interacting that enhance social interaction. Of course, another child might learn that a selfish and aggressive style pays off best, but even in this case the child is attempting to interact effectively with the social context. So the second issue to keep in mind is that internalization has a strong, active component such that the child will initiate efforts to learn the beliefs and behaviors she perceives to be instrumental in attaining effectiveness in the social world.

Relatedness to others provides the social context that supports internalization. Students do not internalize the prescriptions and proscriptions of every adult who comes along. Rather, students select the prescriptions and proscriptions of some adults but ignore those offered by others. Relatedness to others provides the social context that supports internalization (Goodenow, 1993; Ryan & Powelson, 1991). *Relatedness* refers to the quality of the interpersonal relationship that exist between the teacher and the student, and it captures the student's sense of belongingness and support—of being liked, respected, and valued by another person. When the student feels emotionally connected to and interpersonally involved with the teacher, relatedness is high and internalization occurs willingly. When the student feels emotionally distant from and interpersonally neglected, relatedness is low and internalization does not occur willingly. When parents and teachers are responsive and receptive to students and when they provide a relationship characterized by interpersonal security, autonomy support, and involvement, internalization flourishes (Ryan & Powelson, 1991). Relatedness, however, does not make internalization an automatic process. For internalization to occur, students must also see the value, meaning, and utility in the adults' prescriptions and proscriptions. So relatedness is a necessary but not sufficient condition for cultural transmission to occur.

Self-Determination Theory

According to self-determination theory (Deci & Ryan, 1985, 1991), the distinction between intrinsically and extrinsically motivated behavior (discussed in Chapter 1) is fundamental to understanding internalization. To understand internalization, researchers translate the intrinsic-versus-extrinsic dichotomy into the more sophisticated continuum of self-determination, a continuum that extends from "fully self-determined" to "not at all self-determined" (i.e., fully other-determined) behavior (Rigby, Deci, Patrick, & Ryan, 1992). Self-determination theory recognizes that types of extrinsic motivation exist, types that vary in how self-determined people experience them. These three types of extrinsic motivation are *identified regulation* (self-determined extrinsic motivation), *introjected regulation* (somewhat self-determined extrinsic motivation), and *extrinsic regulation* (not at all self-determined extrinsic motivation). Table 3-1 shows the full continuum of motivation, according to self-determination theory.

External Regulation
External regulation is the prototype of non-self-determined extrinsic motivation. For the person who is externally regulated, motivation arises from environmental events such as rewards, pressures, and constraints. For instance, a student who is externally regulated may have a very difficult time beginning her homework unless there is some external prompt (e.g., an upcoming examination, the wrath of a parent).

Introjected Regulation
Introjected regulation involves taking in—but not truly accepting—other people's rules or demands to think, feel, or behave in a particular manner. In essence, the person, *acting as a proxy for the environment,* emotionally rewards himself for any performance of other-defined good behavior and emotionally punishes himself for any performance of other-defined bad behavior. For instance, a student might come to class on time or may resist cheating during an examination, not because he or she chooses to be punctual or honest but because being late or dishonest produces feelings of guilt and shame (i.e., self-adminis-

TABLE 3-1 The Self-Determination Continuum of Motivation

Three Types of Extrinsic Motivation			Intrinsic Motivation
External Regulation	Introjected Regulation	Identified Regulation	
Complete Absence of Self-Determination		Full Endorsement of Self-Determination	

tered punishments), while being on time or honest produces feelings of pride and approval (i.e., self-administered rewards). Under introjected regulation, the person regulates their motivation as if she were carrying the rules and commands of a teacher or parent around inside his or her head to such an extent that the internalized voice, not the student, regulates the student's motivation. Notice, however, that introjected regulation does indicate some degree of self-control, as the person's behavior does not require explicit external contingencies the way it does with extrinsic regulation.

Identified Regulation
Identified regulation occurs when a student comes to accept the logical merits of a belief or behavior because she sees it as important and personally useful. Thus, if a student comes to believe that extra work in mathematics is important (e.g., for a career in science) or that learning the muscles of the human body is important (e.g., to become a physician), then the motivation to study is extrinsic but it is freely chosen. Extra work in mathematics or anatomy is extrinsic because these behaviors are instrumental to other aims (a career as a scientist or physician), yet they are freely chosen because they are perceived to be useful and valuable for one's life. For instance, many people exercise religiously, not because they enjoy jogging and lifting weights but because they value what such behaviors can do for them. So with identified regulation the person weighs the merits and utility of being extrinsically motivated and freely chooses to be so.

Intrinsic Motivation
Intrinsic motivation is the prototype of self-determined motivation. As discussed in Chapter 1, when intrinsically motivated, the person engages in an activity for the need-satisfying interest and pleasure that participation in the activity brings. For instance, a student works on a shop project because she enjoys its challenge and the way it allows her to feel competent and self-determining. At first glance, intrinsic motivation and identified extrinsic motivation seem similar, but the distinction is this: The regulatory process underlying intrinsic motivation is "Is the activity enjoyable?" whereas the regulatory process underlying identified regulation is "Is the activity important?" (Deci, 1992a).

Researchers have developed questionnaires to assess students' regulatory styles in school settings (Harter, 1981; Gottfried, 1985; Ryan & Connell, 1989; Vallerand, Pelletier, Blais, Briere, Senecal, & Vallieres, 1992). Table 3-2 lists some sample items from one of those questionnaires, Ryan and Connell's (1989) Academic Self-Regulation Questionnaire (ASRQ) for children. This questionnaire asks the respondent to agree or disagree with various reasons that he or she participates in four domains of school-related activity: (1) Why do I do my homework? (2) Why do I work on my classwork? (3) Why do I try to answer hard questions in class? (4) Why do I try to do well in school? The reasons reflect

TABLE 3-2 Sample Items from the Academic Self-Regulation Questionnaire (ASRQ)

Question 1

When I participate actively in class, I do so . . .
    because I'll get in trouble if I don't. (external regulation)
    because, if I didn't, I would feel guilty. (introjected regulation)
    because doing so helps me improve important skills. (identified regulation)
    because it is fun to do so. (intrinsic motivation)

Question 2

When I study, I do so . . .
    because I should, because that is what is expected of me. (introjected regulation)
    because I enjoy it. (intrinsic motivation)
    because, to me, studying is both meaningful and important. (identified regulation)
    because I have to; it's the rule. (external regulation)

Source: Ryan, R.M., & Connell, J. P. (1989). Perceived locus of causality and internalization: Examining reasons for acting in two domains. *Journal of Psychology and Social Psychology, 57,* 749–761. Copyright 1989 by the American Psychological Association. Adapted with permission. *Note.* I adapted these sample items for use by college students.

various styles of extrinsic regulation, introjected regulation, identified regulation, and intrinsic motivation.

After looking at the ASRQ sample items, you might wonder why the self-determination continuum is important to the practice of education. A graduated understanding of extrinsic motivation carries implications for teachers' attempts to engage students academically. Chapters 1 and 2 emphasized only three motivational states—intrinsic motivation, extrinsic motivation, and amotivation (i.e., without motivation). Because internalization pertains most specifically to the motivation to engage in uninteresting activities, teachers generally cannot expect students to be intrinsically motivated. Thus, the teacher's options for motivational strategies boil down to either extrinsic motivation or no motivation. Indeed, when asking students to engage in routinized work, teachers (especially beginning teachers) routinely rely on a steady administration of extrinsic incentives to push students to learn (Newby, 1991). In addition to extrinsic regulation, however, identified regulation represents a form of extrinsic motivation that relies relatively little on a teacher-generated source of motivation and much on a student-generated source.

To test the benefits of identified regulation, one group of researchers asked participants to engage in a terribly boring computer task (Deci et al., 1994). As they stared at a dot on the computer screen, some participants experienced a social context that (1) provided them with a convincing rationale for why do this tedious task, (2) acknowledged and accepted as legitimate the participants' inevitable conflict between feeling bored and wanting to quit versus wanting to persist because the task was important, and (3) offered a communication style between experimenter and participant that minimized pressure. Other participants, however, experienced a social context that offered no such rationale for doing the task, failed to acknowledge the conflict between boredom and persistence, and used a communication style characterized by a coercive, pressuring language. Internalization—as measured by time spent voluntarily doing the task—was greater in the first case.

This study and others like it (e.g., Koestner et al., 1984) confirm that there is an art to inviting students to participate in tasks that are not necessarily fun. *Having fun is not the only reason students voluntarily engage in tasks; students also voluntarily engage in tasks that are important to them.* Understanding the perceived importance of a task—its value, meaningfulness, and utility to the person—is at the heart of facilitating identified regulation in others. To recognize the truth of this assertion, we need only think of the endless hours of deliberate practice musicians, athletes, authors, scientists, dancers, and others put into practicing routinized work that they perceive to be important (Ericsson, Krampe, & Tesch-Romer, 1993). Anyone who has voluntarily tried to diet or exercise also understands the essence of identified regulation. In this spirit, stop for a moment and pause to reflect on the subject matter(s) you teach (or plan to teach) and see if you can answer with clear, convincing, honest, and persuasive rationale the student's question: "Why do I have to learn this?" Whether you plan to teach English literature, American history, algebra, or whatever, see what sort of list of reasons you generate for yourself as to why students should engage themselves and care about this subject matter. What is it that makes it important, useful, or meaningful? A teacher's answer to the "Why do I have to learn this?" question, more than anything else, is critical to the internalization process (see Observational Activity 3.2).

Academic Self-Regulation

Academic self-regulation refers to the thoughts, plans, and actions students generate for themselves as they strive to attain their academic goals (Schunk & Zimmerman, 1994; Zimmerman, 1989). More often than not, the thoughts, plans, and actions that are necessary to the attainment of academic goals and to the successful negotiation of the demands of school do *not* come naturally and spontaneously to students. Rather, students learn and eventually internalize such patterns of thinking, planning, and behaving from teachers, other adults, and peers. To illustrate the self-regulatory strategies students use to help them learn and succeed in school, Table 3-3 shows the most common learning strategies high school students reported using, given questions such as the following (from Zimmerman & Martinez-Pons, 1986, p. 53):

> *Assume your teacher is discussing with your class the history of the civil rights movement. Your teacher says that you will be tested on the topic the next day. Do you have a method that you would use to help you learn and remember the information being discussed?"*

Assume your teacher asks students in your class to write a short paper on a topic such as the history of your community or neighborhood. Your score on this paper will affect your report card grade. In such cases, do you have any particular method to help you plan and write your paper?

For each self-regulating learning strategy, Table 3-3 provides a definition and an example (in italics), from Zimmerman (1989). Notice that the strategies include mostly self-initiated plans (e.g., organizing and transforming, goal-setting) and self-initiated behaviors (e.g., seeking information, self-consequating).

To illustrate how students put these self-regulatory strategies into practice, consider a hypothetical student trying to learn the essentials of economics for a test at the end of the week. This student might begin the effort by taking notes in class, organizing them into a student-designed outline or knowledge map, and reviewing the outline or map daily (strategies 5, 2, and 10 in Table 3-3). Once familiar with the demands of the test, the student might plan a study timeline for the week (strategy 3). To carry out the plan, the student might arrange a favorable learning environment (strategy 6) and proceed to use that setting to write down, rehearse, and memorize answers about how the economy works (i.e., "supply and demand relate inversely to each other and together they determine the price of a good . . .") (strategy 8). As she tests herself, the student might evaluate the quality of her learning as poor, acceptable, or excellent (strategy 1). If her learning shows itself to be less than excellent, she might conclude that she needs assistance and either seek an opportunity for cooperative learning with a classmate (strategy 9) or pull a book on economics off the shelf (strategy 4). As she studies, the student might promise to treat herself to a weekend of fun if she performs well (strategy 7).

How do students learn such self-regulating strategies in the first place? One answer is that students learn these strategies through necessary trial-and-error efforts and by attending to which ones improve and which ones do not improve understanding and performance outcomes. Successful strategies will be retained, and unsuccessful strategies will be abandoned (Schunk, 1989a). But students also learn these strategies through interactive learning with teachers (Corno, 1992; Schunk, 1989b). Graham and Harris (1994) use the writing process to illustrate how teacher-student interactions proceed in such a way that students acquire the learning strategies that promote academic self-regulation. The authors provide the following seven step framework:

1. Teacher begins by helping the student develop writing preskills. Such preskills involve self-regulation strategies (e.g., planning, organizing, goal-setting).
2. Teacher and student discuss prior writing performances. Teacher asks the student to express and then explain the strategies used to accomplish a writing assignment.

3. Teacher introduces one proven strategy (e.g., one listed in Table 3-3 that seems appropriate for that particular student). Teacher explains its purpose as well as how and when to use it.
4. Teacher models the strategy and vocalizes self-instructions (e.g., error detection, planning). After the modeling, teacher and student collaborate to refine the strategy so it will be more efficient or effective for that particular student.

TABLE 3-3 Learning Strategies Underlying High School Students' Academic Self-Regulation

Strategy	Definition (with an Example in Italics)
1. Self-evaluating	Student-initiated evaluations of the quality or progress of their work: *I check over my work to make sure I did it right.*
2. Organizing and transforming	Student-initiated overt or covert rearrangement of instructional materials to improve learning: *I make an outline before I write my paper.*
3. Goal-setting and planning	Students' setting of educational goals or subgoals and planning for sequencing, timing, and completing activities related to these goals: *First, I start studying two weeks before exams, and I pace myself.*
4. Seeking information	Student-initiated efforts to secure further task information from nonsocial sources when undertaking an assignment: *Before beginning to write the paper, I go to the library to get as much information s possible concerning the topic.*
5. Keeping records and monitoring	Student-initiated efforts to record events or results: *I took notes of the class discussions. I kept a list of the words I got wrong.*
6. Environmental structuring	Student-initited efforts to select or arrange the physical setting to make learning easier: *I turned off the radio so I can concentrate on what I am doing.*
7. Self-consequating	Student arrangement or imagination of rewards or punishments for success or failure: *If I do well on a test, I treat myself to a movie.*
8. Rehearsing and memorizing	Student-initiated efforts to memorize material by overt or covert practice: *In preparing for a math test, I keep writing the formula down until I remember it.*
9. Seeking social assistance	Student-initiated efforts to solicit help from peers, teachers, and adults: *If I have problems with math assignments, I ask a friend to help.*
10. Reviewing records	Student-initiated efforts to re-read notes, tests, or textbooks to prepare for class or further testing: *When preparing for a test, I review my notesl*

Source: Zimmerman, B. J. (1989). A social cognitive view of self-regulated academic learning. *Journal of Educational Psychology, 81,* 329–339. Copyright 1989 by the America Psychological Association.

5. Student memorizes the strategy.
6. Student and teacher practice the strategy and the self-instructions collaboratively.
7. Student uses the strategy and self-instructions independently.

Teaching students self-regulatory strategies is both possible and productive (Graham & Harris, 1994; Graham & MacArthur, 1988; Graham, MacArthur, Schwartz, & Voth, 1992; MacArthur, Schwartz, & Graham, 1991). So it is interesting that classroom observations find little evidence that teachers model or even talk with their students about self-regulation strategies (Anthony & Anderson, 1987; Pokay & Blumenfeld, 1990). By modeling and supporting students' efforts to learn self-regulation strategies, teachers empower students with metacognitive, motivational, and behavioral resources that enable them to become active participants in their own learning (Zimmerman, 1986, 1989).

An Example of Academic Self-Regulation: Writing

Self-regulation is important to virtually all aspects of academics and schooling, but writing offers a special illustration of the importance of academic self-regulatory skills. Compared to other academic endeavors, writing is an especially self-scheduled and self-paced undertaking. Writing is often done alone; it is carried out for unusually long periods of time without extrinsic reinforcement; and it necessitates editing, revision, and reengagement that take place mostly to satisfy personal standards of competence (Zimmerman & Bandura, 1994). In other words, the writing process is largely a self-disciplined, self-regulated undertaking (Zimmerman, Bandura, & Martinez-Pons, 1992).

Students differ in their abilities to regulate their own writing behavior, and they differ in their internalized standards of what constitutes an adequate or self-satisfying performance. One group of researchers separated these two aspects of the writing process by asking students (1) how confident they were that they could construct a good opening sentence quickly, rewrite wordy or confusing sentences clearly, and revise a first draft of a paper so as to shorten or better organize it (to measure self-regulatory capacity), and (2) how satisfied they would be if they made each possible grade (i.e., A, A–, B+, . . . F) in the writing course (to measure personal standards of writing excellence). The researchers found that both self-regulatory capacities and personal standards of excellence explained which students received both the highest and the lowest grades. In addition, self-regulatory capacities and personal standards of excellence predicted grades better than did a measure of students' verbal ability (SAT verbal aptitude score). These findings reinforce the claim that it is one thing to possess the ability and skills to do well in school and yet another thing to be able to translate those skills into competent performance through self-regulation.

Without self-regulatory skills, writers—even highly able ones—are prone to procrastination, distraction, and lackluster effort; without internalized personal standards of excellence, writers are too willing to accept minimal performances and see little reason to edit, revise, and voluntarily improve their work.

How to Facilitate Students' Internalization and Self-Regulation

It is hard to imagine much internalization occurring in children without adult intervention. This section outlines three teaching strategies to encourage internalization and self-regulation in students: scaffolding; autonomy support; and noncontrolling, positive feedback.

Teacher Assistance, or Scaffolding

Teachers assist students' internalization and self-regulatory processes in a number of ways, such as by communicating the rationale for a requested behavior, modeling self-regulation strategies, providing feedback on the student's effectiveness in interacting with the social context, and generally doing that class of behaviors referred to as "tutoring" (Wood, Bruner, & Ross, 1976). Much of this tutoring occurs as a negotiated effort between student and teacher. Part of what gets negotiated is just how much responsibility students have for their own learning and academic achievement. Before internalization, the teacher assumes the responsibility for regulating the student's behavior and learning; after internalization, the student assumes the responsibility. During the transition process, the teacher acts as and when needed by the student in a socially negotiated process referred to as *scaffolding* (Wood et al., 1976; Vygotsky, 1978).

Scaffolding requires providing support during the student's task engagements through clues, reminders, encouragement, assistance, problem-solving strategies, illustrative examples, or anything else that allows the student to grow in independence as a learner (Woolfolk, 1995). Peers also can scaffold their fellow students. Schunk, Hanson, and Cox (1987), for instance, showed that underperforming math elementary-grade students learn strategies from peers such as eliminating errors, high concentration, persistence, and increased (rather than decreased) effort. Similarly, in their work on "cooperative learning," O'Donnell and her colleagues showed that peers can co-regulate academic tasks through shared participation in planning, prompting, and monitoring (O'Donnell et al., 1986; O'Donnell et al., 1988). The picture that emerges is that scaffolding enables internalization to take place as a collaborative effort between teacher and student (or student and peer) in which the more competent individual guides, encourages, and otherwise supports the less competent individual's strivings toward internalized self-regulation.

Autonomy Support

Internalization is an active, intentional, developmental process, which occurs most adaptively in the absence of undue pressure and control. To achieve internalization, a child must be free to try out the self-regulation, to succeed and to fail, and to learn about the consequences of his or her actions (both to the self and to others). Unfortunately, however, teachers sometimes want students to perform inherently boring and dull tasks. In such cases, the teacher might be willing to settle for the student's momentary compliance (rather than internalization). Seeking compliance, however, raises the issue of social control.

In practice, social control can take three different forms (Lepper, 1983). Explicit social control, with its reliance on rewards, coercion, and punishment, produces compliance and external regulation. Subtle social control, with its reliance on others' approval and regard, produces a mixture of compliance and internalization in the form of introjected regulation. Autonomy support, with its reliance on minimal social pressures and clear rationale, produces internalization in the form of identified regulation. Autonomy support promotes identified regulation when socializing agents provide such clear, sufficient, justifiable, and honest rationale for the social control that the child voluntarily says, "Oh, O.K., that makes sense; I see why that is important to you; I can see why it could be important to me, too." In the delicate process of negotiation and compromise that takes place between socializing agent and object, the agent's use of power-assertive techniques generally promotes external and introjected regulation in the object, whereas the agent's use of autonomy-supportive techniques generally promotes internalized, identified regulation.

The Role of Noncontrolling, Positive Feedback

Autonomy support, with its emphasis on providing rationale and resistance to controlling pressures, sets the stage for internalization to occur, but students also need follow-up information from the social context as to when they are and are not interacting in an effective and competent fashion. Noncontrolling, positive feedback from the social context communicates to the student a message of competence, of a job well done. It also communicates a message of support and public recognition from the person giving the positive feedback to the person receiving it. Students internalize external regulations in order to promote more competent and effective interactions with the social world.

Consequently, positive feedback from a teacher serves as a marker of which particular behaviors produce the most effective interactions.

Conclusion

Why would a student ever internalize an adult prescription or proscription in the first place? Students internalize the regulations of others because they desire to interact effectively in the social world. But students do not internalize the regulations of all adults, and they do not internalize all the regulations from any one particular adult. Rather, students internalize regulations communicated by adult with whom they share an emotional relatedness, and they internalize only those regulations for which the adult provides a rationale in term of its value, meaning, or utility. Adults emotionally involved in the student's life communicate those regulations and skills students need to be effective, through the apprenticeship process referred to as scaffolding. Adult scaffolding allows students to master skills that otherwise lie outside the limits of their current capacities (to perform individually). In the schools, teachers scaffold students to master self-regulating learning strategies such as organizing, environmental restructuring, and goal setting. Students, in turn, employ these learning strategies on their own to master academic challenges such as writing and studying.

There are essentially three reasons for a student to do any task—because it is fun, because it brings forth some external contingency, or because it is seen as an important and useful thing to do. These three reasons correspond to intrinsic motivation, extrinsic motivation, and identified regulation. When a teacher faces unmotivated students, he or she has three routes to motivate them:

1. *Intrinsic motivation:* Find a way to make the task more interesting and enjoyable.
2. *Extrinsic motivation:* Associate an extrinsic reward or constraint with task participation.
3. *Identified regulation:* Explain carefully to students precisely why this particular task is important, meaningful, relevant, and valuable to them.

Introducing an academic task with a "relevance" strategy promotes greater on-task participation by students than does introducing an academic task with an extrinsic incentive (Newby, 1991). Adding teaching strategies to promote identified regulation to the previously discussed intrinsic and extrinsic approaches to motivating others is particularly important because it makes the point that not all extrinsic motivation is the same (and that some types of extrinsic motivation—identified regulation—are better than other types—introjected and extrinsic regulation). Identified regulation gives teachers a viable alternative to extrinsic regulation on those tasks that are not intrinsically motivating to students.

Recommended Readings

Borman, K. (1978). Social control and schooling: Power and process in two kindergarten settings. *Anthropology and Education Quarterly, 9,* 138–153.

Corno, L. (1992). Encouraging students to take responsibility for learning and performance. *Elementary School Journal, 93,* 69–83.

Deci, E. L., Eghrari, H., Patrick, B. C., & Leone, D. R. (1994). Facilitating internalization: The self-determination theory perspective. *Journal of Personality, 62,* 119–142.

Graham, S., & MacArthur, C. (1988). Improving learning disabled students' skills at revising essays produced on a word processor: Self-instructional strategy training. *Journal of Special Education, 22,* 133–152.

Newby, T. J. (1991). Classroom motivation: Strategies of first-year teachers. *Journal of Educational Psychology, 83,* 195–200.

Rigby, C. S., Deci, E. L., Patrick, B.P., & Ryan, R. M. (1992). Beyond the intrinsic–extrinsic dichotomy: Self-determination in motivation and learning. *Motivation and Emotion, 16,* 165–185.

Ryan, R. M., & Connell, J. P. (1989). Perceived locus of causality and internalization: Examining reasons for acting in two domains. *Journal of Personality and Social Psychology, 57,* 749–761.

Schunk, D. H. (1989). Social cognitive theory and self-regulated learning. In B. J. Zimmerman & D. H. Schunk (Eds.), *Self-regulated learning and academic achievement: Theory, research, and practice* (pp. 83–110). New York: Springer-Verlag.

Wood, D., Bruner, J. S., & Ross, G. (1976). The role of tutoring in problem solving. *Journal of Child Psychology and Psychiatry, 17,* 89–100.

Zimmerman, B. J. (1989). A social cognitive view of self-regulated academic learning. *Journal of Educational Psychology, 81,* 329–339.

Observational Activities

Observational Activity 3.1: Assessing Students' Self-Regulatory Styles

The purpose of this interview is to gain an understanding of the variability in students' self-regulatory styles in terms of the type of motivation they rely on to engage in school-related activities. Before you begin this activity, you might wish to read Experiment 1 from Ryan and Connell (1989).

In this activity, assess the self-regulatory styles of three students. The interviews will be brief, lasting about ten minutes each. Try to solicit the assistance of a variety of students—males and females, overachievers and underachievers, those who enjoy school and those who don't. Before you begin, you will first need to construct a Learning Motivation Questionnaire by taking the eight items listed in Table 3-2 and using the following instructions and five-point response scale:

Instructions
The following questions ask about your reasons for participating in school. Different people have different reasons for participating in class and for studying, and I simply would like to know how true versus untrue each of the reasons listed below is for you. Please use the following scale:

1	2	3	4	5
Very untrue	Mostly untrue	Somewhat true	Mostly true	Very true

Feel free to adjust the Learning Motivation Questionnaire to fit you own needs (i.e., ask a different question, such as "The reason that I will continue my education is . . ." or include different reasons, such as "because I want to get a well-paying job").

After each student completes the questionnaire, ask him or her a few questions to assess the emotional and scholastic quality of his or her educational experience. Some questions to ask might include: "How much or how little do you enjoy school?" "How much do you desire to continue your education and go to college?" "How much is your desire to get out of school as fast as you can?" "Would you say that you feel mostly bored and stressed in school or mostly interested and happy?" You can ask these questions either in an interview setting or on a questionnaire format with a 1–5 scale for each question.

After you collect your data, look for any patterns that seem to occur. Do your students seem mostly externally regulated, introjected regulated, identified regulated, or intrinsically motivated? Or did you find that most students show a constellation of two or more of these styles? Did any of these four self-regulatory styles seem to correlate with the students' answers to your questions about the emotional and scholastic quality of their educational experience? Did any student characteristics—grade level, gender, grades/GPA, and the like—predict self-regulatory style?

Observational Activity 3.2: Clarifying the Rationale for "Why Do I Have to Learn This?"

The twofold purpose of this observational activity is (1) to understand experienced teachers' rationales for why students should be actively engaged in school, and (2) to let you clarify and improve upon the rationales you hear. This activity has three parts.

Part 1

Interview three teachers who have at least three years of experience. Each interview will be brief and should take only about ten minutes. To start, ask teachers what subject matter they teach, what grade level they teach, and if their students ever complain to them, "Why do I have to learn this?" Then, ask each teacher to pause for a moment and answer this question as if you were the student asking it. Give the teacher time to think about the answer or answers and allow him or her enough time to give as full an answer as he or she would like to give. Try not to bias the teachers' responses. Write down each reason each teacher gives.

Part 2

Following the interviews, rate the rationale statements for (1) what type of motivation it appeals to in terms of external regulation, introjected regulation, identified regulation, or intrinsic motivation (e.g., "because it will be on the test" would be extrinsic regulation) and (2) how clear, convincing, honest, persuasive, and satisfying the rationale seems to you.

Part 3

Finally, take each rationale statement and see if you can reword it and improve on it so that the reason will be clearer, more convincing, more honest, more persuasive, or more satisfying. Keep editing each rationale until you feel you can truly say, "Oh, O.K., that makes sense to me; I can understand why this subject/activity is important, valuable, meaningful, and/or relevant for my life."

4

Competence

Imagine being a tenth-grade math teacher with a classroom full of capable but underachieving students. After extensive effort to make the lessons clear and meaningful, you find yourself moving toward the pessimistic conclusion that these students are just not going to apply themselves. After yet another lackluster day, you walk by the gym and wander inside for a moment to escape the winter's cold. Sounds from bouncing basketballs and people enjoying themselves dominate the interior of the gym and capture your attention. You see a group of students practicing and quickly notice that many of them are in your math class. With a basketball in their hands, they act nothing like they act when their hands hold a book or pencil. These students are exerting great effort, experimenting with and refining their techniques, running up and down the court with excitement, and grinning and pumping their fists with each success. You wonder what is going on—why don't they act like this in math class? You take a seat and watch carefully to see if you can discover what in the world it is about playing basketball that makes these students enjoy it so much. You wonder what it would take to help these athletes become "math-letes."

The Elements of Enjoyment

Specific, identifiable elements within the structure of an activity set the stage for people to experience enjoyment. Emotion researchers agree that enjoyment arises chiefly from an experience of either need satisfaction or personal accomplishment (Izard, 1977). From a motivational point of view, the question then becomes "What are the specific and identifiable elements with an activity that produce a sense of satisfaction and personal accomplishment?" Csikszentmihalyi (1975, 1990) finds there are at least four core elements within all enjoyable tasks:

- They can be completed, or finished.
- They offer clear goals to pursue.
- They provide immediate feedback in how well or poorly one is doing.
- They challenge and stretch the performer's skills and capacities.

Looking over Csikszentmihalyi's list of the elements of enjoyment, one can deduce why students enjoy basketball more than mathematics. In basketball, participants play for a specific length of time or to a number of points (task completion), focus and continually refocus on the objective of outscoring their opponents (clear goal), see and hear the ball swish through the net within a second after trying to do so (immediate performance feedback), and find a ten-foot-high, 27-inch-wide hoop to be a moderately difficult test of their shooting skills (optimal challenge). In contrast, math classes go on day after day (no completion), seem sometimes pointless (no clear goals), offer delayed, ambiguous performance feedback (an examination returned a day later with answers marked only right or wrong), and offer problems that alternate between being simplistic and being overwhelming in difficulty. But no rule declares that math lessons have to be void of the elements of enjoyment. A class that focused on, say, statistics, could begin, "We are going to learn how to calculate and apply the concepts of *mean* and *standard deviation,* and we will spend the week on these two concepts (for task completion). I want you be able to apply each formula to a problem such as computing means and standard deviations of the classes' ages, heights, or test scores (for goal). For practice, I'll give you a worksheet so you can check whether you can understand formulas, solve problems correctly, solve problems more quickly than before, and make fewer errors than before (for immediate feedback). If you feel ready for it, on Friday we will solve for the means and standard deviations of whatever variables interest you—scoring totals from last week's football games, the daily temperatures this month, or whatever anyone suggests (for challenge)."

Maximal Enjoyment: Flow

As he observed hundreds of people engaged in all sorts of activities (e.g., surgery, rock climbing, socializing, watching television, preparing for an examination), Csikszentmihalyi (1975, 1982, 1990) noticed that maximal enjoyment (or "flow") came at a very specific point in almost everyone's activity—whenever the person perceived that the challenges offered by the task equaled, or matched, his or her task-relevant skills. That is, optimal challenge gave birth to flow, or maximal enjoyment. Students experience flow as a state of concentration that amounts to an absolute absorption in an activity (Csikszentmihalyi, 1990), one that closely resembles that of intrinsic motivation (Csikszentmihalyi & Nakamura, 1989).

Figure 4-1 illustrates the relationship between task challenge on the one hand and personal skill on the other, and the figure shows the emotional consequences arising from the different pairings of challenge and skill. When challenge outweighs skill (challenge is high, skill is low), people worry about being overwhelmed as they experience a threatened sense of competence. Under conditions of challenge overwhelming skill, students feel anxious or intensely worried. When challenge matches skill (challenge and skill are both high), people feel enjoyment, show focused concentration, and achieve a relatively intense task involvement. When skill outweighs challenge (skill is high, challenge is low), people feel bored, show a dispersion of concentration, and achieve only minimal task involvement.

Being overchallenged or overskilled produces emotional problems and suboptimal experience, but the worst profile of experience actually emanates from the co-occurrence of low challenge and low skill (the lower left corner). With both challenge and skill at relatively low levels, literally all measures of emotion, motivation, and cognition are at their lowest levels—the person simply could not care less (Csikszentmihalyi, Rathunde, & Whalen, 1993). Hence, flow is a bit more complicated that just the balance of challenge and skill. Balancing low skill and low challenge produces only apathy, not flow. Flow emerges only in those situations in which challenges and skills both exceed the student's average (Csikszentmihalyi & Csikszentmihalyi, 1988). Thus, another way to

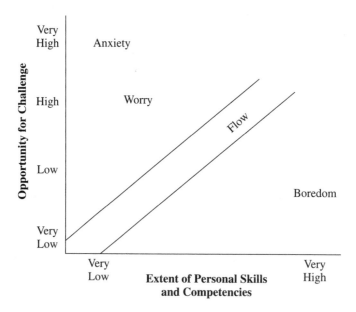

FIGURE 4-1   Csikszentmihalyi's Model of Flow

Source: Csikszentmihalyi, M. *Beyond Boredom and Anxiety: The Experience of Play in Work and Games.* Figure 1, p. 49, adapted as submitted. Copyright 1975 Jossey-Bass Inc., Publishers. Code 7514. (San Francisco: Jossey-Bass, 1975)

look at Figure 4-1 is to divide the figure into four quadrants, with the upper left quarter representing conditions for anxiety, the lower left quarter representing conditions for apathy, the lower right quarter representing conditions for boredom, and the upper right quarter representing conditions for flow.

Perhaps the most important implication of flow theory is this: Given the appropriate balance of skill and challenge, *any* activity can be enjoyed. Csikszentmihalyi (1982) confirmed this assumption by finding that people actually experience flow most often in work situations, not in leisure settings. Doing electrical work, writing papers, debating contemporary issues, sewing, analyzing a play, mowing the lawn, and other such activities do not necessarily make the top of anyone's list of must-do Saturday afternoon joys, but the balance of high skill with high challenge adds the spice of optimal experience. In another study, Csikszentmihalyi and his colleagues (1993) found that students enjoyed doing homework and working on part-time jobs more than they enjoyed viewing (challengeless) television programs.

To enjoy an educational task, then, must a student find the means to balance relatively high skill with relatively high challenge? Well, this is not necessarily true. Under some conditions, people find enjoyment when challenge overwhelms skill (Stein, Kimiecik, Daniels, & Jackson, 1995). People enjoy relatively high challenge in learning situations in which they perceive the dominance of challenge over skill as high challenge but low threat. With high challenge, a student sees a potential for gain, growth, and personal improvement; with high threat, a student sees a potential for loss, harm, and self-depreciation (Lazarus & Folkman, 1984). Thus, when challenge outweighs skill—a common situation in the schools as teachers ask students to learn new tasks—the classroom climate must orient the students toward perceptions of challenge (and gain) rather than toward perceptions of threat (and loss). The easiest way to do this is to focus students on *learning goals* (which emphasize improvement, progress, effort, and a tolerance for and acceptance of errors as part of the learning process) rather than on *performance goals* (which emphasize doing better than others and publicly proving one's high ability) (e.g., Ames & Archer, 1988).

The opposite situation of challenge overwhelming skill is the situation of skill overwhelming challenge. Under some circumstances, students can enjoy these circumstances too (Stein et al., 1995). When students perform, rather than learn, they enjoy having a level of skill that is above and beyond the challenge of the task. That is, if the student's goal is to prove to others that she has high ability and competence, then she will welcome and enjoy opportunites to show others just how smart she is—whether that situation involves solving problems on the blackboard or running faster than everyone else on the playground. However, I take it as a telltale sign that when students enjoy situations in which skill overwhelms challenge, then they engage in those situations with performance, rather than learning, goals. A performer will enjoy such a situation; a learner will be bored by it.

Flow and Challenge in School Settings

To link his theoretical model to the experiences of students and teachers, Csikszentmihalyi asked students to wear personal pagers day after day, and he beeped them at random times daily to ask them to report the following: the task they were doing, how challenged they felt, how skilled they were at that task, how well versus poorly they were concentrating, and their current emotional state. Csikszentmihalyi found that students spent all too much time in nonchallenging, low-skilled activities (reading simple texts, listening to slow-paced lectures—from the students' point of view, mind you) and all too little time in challenging, skill-advancing activities (e.g., art projects, debating issues in small groups, performing musically in front of an audience). Csikszentmihalyi et al. (1993) reasoned that if students are to enjoy school, then teachers need to find a way to allow students to engage educational tasks that allow them the opportunity to merge high challenge with high skill. In that spirit, they not only recommended that teachers work to incorporate the core elements of enjoyment into educational tasks—task completion, clear goals, immediate feedback, and skill challenges—but also offered the following three suggestions to teachers:

1. Center students' attention on the challenge and inherent satisfactions of learning something new, rather than on task-linked extrinsic pressures such as grades.

2. Continually challenge and develop one's *own* skills in the academic area and then explicitly communicate to students your personal experiences as to what challenges you find the task has to offer.

3. Develop a flexible teaching style. Sometimes, challenge students' abilities (i.e., work to increase challenge); sometimes, supports their developing skills, as through tutoring and training (i.e., work to increase skill); and at still other times withdraw altogether from students' engagements so they can experience flow for themselves. Essentially, the idea is this: Spend some time trying to increase challenge, some time trying to increase skill, and some time letting students simply enjoy the activity through the balance of skill and challenge.

In the spirit of these suggestions, I would like to add a fourth:

4. Develop a teaching style that focuses students' attention on learning, rather than performance, goals. Learning goals emphasize educational tasks as opportunities to gain in mastery, competence, learning, and growth. Performance goals emphasize educational tasks as opportunities for outcome-oriented situations to define students as winners or losers, passers or failers, worthy of self-worth or of self-shame. With learning goals, students perceive high challenge as potential gain; with performance goals, students perceive high challenge as threat and potential loss. Challenge creates approach motivational tendencies; threat creates avoidance motivational tendencies.

Flow is essentially a state of concentration in which the activity itself is foremost in the performer's mind. Thus, any concern for failing and therefore for looking bad or any concern for succeeding and therefore looking good will more than likely distract one's concentration from the activity per se. Thus, a fifth recommendation for promoting flow would be for teachers to strive to subordinate a task's outcome and its consequences to the immediacy of the experience of recognizing, diagnosing, and meeting its challenges. One pivotal point during task participation comes during the experience of task-generated feedback. When students use that feedback to inform themselves as to how well versus poorly they are doing on the task, then that information helps maintain flow. Alternatively, when students use that feedback to diagnose the consequences of success or failure, then that information disrupts flow. Flow involves being absorbed in the task, not in its consequences.

The Pleasure of Optimal Challenge

To confirm that children do indeed derive maximum pleasure from optimal challenge, Harter (1974, 1978b) gave sixth-graders anagrams of different difficulty levels and monitored each student's expressed pleasure (through smiling) upon solving each anagram. An anagram, by the way, is a common word with its letters scrambled randomly (e.g., an anagram for BOOK would be KOBO). Some anagrams were very easy (three letters), some were easy (four letters), others were moderately difficult (five letters), and still others were very hard (six letters). As expected, as the anagrams increased in difficulty, it took students longer and longer to solve them. The critical measure in the study was expressed pleasure (through smiling) and results showed a curvilinear inverted-U-shaped pattern in which smiling was least following success on the very easy problems, moderate following success on the easy and very hard problems, and greatest following success on the moderately difficult problems. The central point in Harter's program of research is that children experience the greatest pleasure following success in the context of moderate challenge.

A teacher has to wonder, though, why smiling was not greatest following success at the hardest challenge. Apparently, as students worked to solve very hard problems, the worry, anxiety, and frustration they felt upon having their skills stretched beyond current capabilities diluted (rather than intensified) the pleasure they felt upon eventual achievement. Quotations by two of the sixth-graders nicely express the students' relative pleasure following optimal challenge: "The 5's were just right. They were a challenge, but not too much challenge," and "I liked the hard ones because they gave you a sense of satisfaction, but the really hard ones were just too frustrating" (Harter, 1978b, p. 796).

Competence as a Need

An intimate relationship exists among the constructs of enjoyment, challenge, and feedback. To explain *why* these constructs interrelate with one another, however, we must add one final piece to the theoretical puzzle—the notion of competence as a psychological need. *Competence* is the cornerstone construct that unites challenge, feedback, and enjoyment. Optimal challenge relates to the need for competence in that it is the principal environmental event that arouses, or involves, the competence need. Optimal challenge also defines the standard for what constitutes effective performance that will produce the possibility for competence need satisfaction. Positive feedback relates to the competence need in that it supplies the objective performance information on which the person can evaluate whether his or her performance was effective and competent or was ineffective and incompetent. Enjoyment relates to the competence need in that it serves as the emotional marker to signal that competence need satisfaction has indeed occurred.

Consider the following example of how competence unites challenge, feedback, and enjoyment. Young adolescents typically want very much to interact successfully rather than unsuccessfully with their social environment. The need for competence motivates adolescence to seek interaction partners so as to experiment with their communication and relationship skills (e.g., holding another's attention, telling jokes, showing leadership). In exercising such skills, the adolescent discovers that his or her interaction skills win over some peers (easy task), fail with others (hard task), and both succeed and fail with yet others (optimal challenge). People learn that optimal challenge is the arena to refine and master their skills (though easy tasks—loyal friends, in this example—provide a sense of security that is also appealing). In the context of optimal challenge, these interactions produce the feedback that will inform the adolescent of how competent versus incompetent his or her skills prove themselves to be. When skills prove themselves to be competent enough, he or she feels enjoyment, and that feeling emotionally supports a continuing desire to seek additional friends and peers so as to develop and refine his or her skills still further. Such a person also loses inhibitions associated with low skill, as the adolescent seeks rather than avoids social gatherings, parties, blind dates, and so on. Of course, examples other than an adolescent's social skills, such as learning a foreign language or working on computer skills, would be more academic, but the same dynamics would hold true.

We all want to be competent. We have a need to interact effectively with our surroundings. We want to develop skills, and we want to expand our capacities. We feel an energy to improve ourselves beyond our current potential. In other words, we have a need for competence. As for a definition, competence is the need to be effective in interactions with the environment (Deci & Ryan, 1985). To be effective, skills must be exercised, stretched, improved, and refined. It is the need for competence that motivates people to seek out the optimal challenges that provide the soil to exercise, stretch, improve, and refine our skills and capacities.

Competence as Effectance Motivation

At birth, infants explore their environment with only the most basic of skills, such as sucking and grasping. In the first year of life, additional motor competencies emerge, such as shaking, reaching, tossing, and carrying (Gibson, 1988). Soon thereafter, infants experiment with skills related to locomotion and language. In school, elementary school children experiment with skills such as penmanship, reading, and multiplication, while secondary schoolers seek to refine and master skills in how to type, speak to an audience, converse in a foreign language, and perform athletic feats. Throughout high school and college, countless additional skills emerge and undergo refinement.

In exercising one's emerging skills (within the context of a responsive environment), an individual produces discernible effects on the environment. For instance, when a language student says, "*Como se dice en español?,*" another person might very well reply, "Yes, I speak Spanish too." Such environmental responsiveness communicates to the performer that she can alter the environment in a desired way (e.g., she acquires information, the conversation continues, the two exchange feelings of acceptance). When the person perceives that she can manipulate the environment according to personal intentions, such insight cultivates a sense of competence. Over time, an accumulated history of such experiences in different aspects of one's life builds in the individual a personal belief that, yes, she possesses the skills necessary to interact effectively with her environment.

The ongoing process of exercising one's skills effectively in optimally challenging tasks and accumulating a history that one can indeed interact effectively with the world cultivates an inner motivational resource researchers label *effectance motivation* (Harter, 1978a; White, 1959). Figure 4-2 illustrates White's (1959) classic portrayal of how effectance motivation acts as an inner motivational resource to energize and direct (intrinsically motivated) behavior. According to the figure, effectance motivation creates the desire to exercise one's skills and capacities in the first place. When skills are so used, the person's actions produce changes in the environment, some of which are intentional and some of which are incidental. Crawling, for instance, lets the baby leave the room without the toys to go to the room with the toys; making an A on a report card brings a student public recognition and parental praise. Knowing their actions influence the environment, people then begin to attempt to effect purposive change; that is, they attempt to produce intentional, goal-directed adjustments in their surroundings. Some of these intended effects are successful,

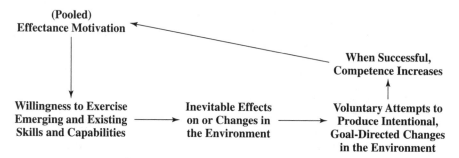

FIGURE 4-2   White's Model of Effectance Motivation

and when the student's skills successfully effect intentional change ("I meant to do that!"), competence increases. Each experience in the self-perception of competence serves to increase the student's pooled reservoir of effectance motivation. Finally, the greater the student's pooled effectance motivation (the inner motivational resource), the greater is his or her desire to seek out and master future optimal challenges.

Effectance motivation is basic to the understanding of human motivation because it reveals that human beings possess a natural, intrinsic motivation to engage environmental challenges. Without effectance motivation, one wonders why a student would read a book, compose an art project, or strive to master a musical instrument. Of course, teachers, parents, and peers can and often do use extrinsic incentives to induce students to perform these actions. But Chapter 1 laid out the argument that extrinsic motivation produces a reliable set of motivationally detrimental side effects. In contrast, effectance motivation is an inner motivational resource that has its origins in the human nervous system rather than in external rewards and pressures. Hence, effectance motivation operates within a self-reinforcement system to produce voluntary, active, and continuous exploration and persistence in the refinement of one's skills and capacities (Harter, 1978a).

Incidentally, this line of reasoning applies as well to teachers as it does to students, in that effectance motivation leads teachers to exercise their existing and emerging capabilities as well (e.g., public speaking, planning and organizing, use of humor). The exercise of such skills in the classroom produces changes in students—perhaps they attend and participate more, or perhaps they attend and participate less. Given positive feedback, the teacher feels an increased competence and such experiences increase the teacher's pooled sense of effectance. Greater effectance motivation, in turn, makes the teacher increasingly willing to exercise and refine additional teaching-related skills in the classroom on future occasions.

Creating Competence-Affirming
Classroom Climates

Competence is a psychological need that provides students with a natural source of motivation to seek out and master challenges that exist in the classroom. Teachers who nurture students' sense of competence gain a wonderful opportunity to develop a classroom full of active, engaged, and intrinsically motivated students. The question then becomes *how* a teacher might create a classroom climate rich in competence-nurturing and competence-affirming experiences. In this section, I offer two interdependent ways to do so: (1) provide the optimal challenges that engage students' competence needs (so as to *involve* the competence need) and (2) provide interpersonal feedback that affirms students' competence and mastery (so as to *satisfy* the competence need).

Involving the Competence Need: Optimal Challenge

Consider two seemingly valid, yet contradictory, strategies for involving students in educational tasks and providing them with feedback that will keep them on task. One approach is the effort to create "schools without failure" (Bloom, 1981; Glasser, 1969); the other is the effort to optimally challenge students (Clifford, 1990).

"Schools without failure" follow the maxim that "nothing succeeds like success." In such a classroom, the teacher attempts to create error-proof learning environments, sets easy standards, and uses minimal performance criteria to pave the road to steady success for all students. Teachers often reduce task difficulty, overlook errors, deemphasize failed attempts, show students models of flawless papers, reduce testing, and reward error-free performances. Although there may be some truth to "nothing succeeds like success," the hard truth is that "schools without failure" have not produced the enthusiastic self-regulated learning that proponents expected (Clifford, 1990). Why not? Easy successes for all students produce only a cheap, watered-down experience that pales in comparison to authentic successes. Easy success does not involve and challenge students' competence needs. Synthetic successes stand in stark contrast to the successes experienced by persons in fields outside of education—athletes, artists and musicians, video arcade players, financial investors, and others who engage tasks that involve their need for competence and sincerely test and challenge their skills.

Optimal challenge follows the maxim "moderate risk-taking is a tonic for achievement" (Clifford, 1988, 1990). Optimal challenge holds that considerable error making is essential to increase learning and optimize motivation. It is only success in the face of optimal challenge that yields the sincere experience of success and achievement. The problem, however, is that students, when faced with moderately difficult tasks, are as likely to experience failure and frustration as they are to experience success and enjoyment. The task of the teacher is to counter the dread of student failure by adopting a classroom climate rich in "failure tolerance" or "error tolerance" (Clifford, 1988, 1990; McCombs & Pope, 1994). According to Clifford, if students are going to engage freely in and persevere at optimally challenging tasks, the social context must adopt a sincere tolerance for (and even a valuing of) failure and error-making. McCombs and Pope (1994) echo this sentiment and identify the qualities that characterize the error-tolerant classroom as interpersonal trust and teacher support.

Academic Risk Taking

Academic risk taking refers to the process by which students select school-related challenges that vary in difficulty with the awareness that teachers and peers will evaluate their performance (Clifford, 1991). I argue that optimal challenge lays the groundwork to cultivate a sense of competence; yet students often go out of their way to choose tasks that are easy or hard. Three factors influence students to pick easy tasks: (1) when rewards are at stake (Shapira, 1976), (2) when others' views of the student's intelligence are at stake (Clifford & Chou, 1991), and (3) when the audience does not tolerate error making (Clifford, 1990). In contrast, the factors that promote students choosing moderately difficult tasks (i.e., academic risks) exist when (1) rewards are not at stake, (2) participants are playing a game, and (3) their audience tolerates (or even supports) error making. Teachers interested in encouraging academic risk-taking and challenge seeking in their classrooms might consider deemphasizing performance consequences, creating a more gamelike atmosphere, and encouraging rather than discouraging error making (experimentation, initiative, guessing, hypothesis testing).

Failure Tolerance

Failure tolerance is the classroom attitude of a teacher who accepts failure and error making as inherent aspects of the learning process (Clifford, 1990). Failure tolerance rests on the belief that "we learn more from failure than we do from success" and emphasizes the constructive aspects of failure—identifying its causes, changing strategies, seeking advice and instruction, and so on (Clifford, 1984).

In offering practical advice for how a teacher might promote students' tendencies to take risks in their school-related activities, Clifford (1990) offered five suggestions for classroom practices:

1. Formative activities should be more plentiful than summative activities. When used, formative evaluation tasks should be scored in a manner that

minimizes ability judgments and maximizes error detection and error correction.

2. Every instructional activity should have at least a moderate percentage of content (e.g., 15%) that poses a challenge to even the best students.

3. Summative evaluation procedures should include "retake exams." Second chances encourage risk taking and create the opportunity for students to identify, rethink, and correct their mistakes.

4. Teachers should encourage improvement scores, voluntary detection of errors, and completion of optional risk-taking activities more than they encourage flawless, error-free performance.

5. Teachers should present optional formative evaluative opportunities, such as incomplete graphs, scrambled outlines, and practice quizzes. These opportunities could take the form of games, cooperative learning, or even competitions that provide nonthreatening feedback.

Fundamental to Clifford's suggestions is the distinction between formative and summative evaluation procedures. Formative evaluation activities are tasks that guide instruction during the learning process to promote learning and skill development (e.g., practice sessions, skill-building activities). Summative evaluation activities (e.g., tests, quizzes) are tasks used to judge level of achievement and determine one's grade.

Satisfying the Competence Need: Feedback

Whether a student perceives his or her performances to be competent or incompetent is often an ambiguous determination. To make such an evaluation, the student needs feedback. Feedback comes from one (or more) of the following three sources: (1) the task itself, (2) comparisons of your current performance with your past performances, and (3) the evaluations of others (Boggiano & Ruble, 1979; Dollinger & Thelen, 1978; Grolnick, Frodi, & Bridges, 1984; Koestner, Zuckerman, & Koestner, 1987; Schunk & Hanson, 1989).

In some tasks, competence feedback is inherent to the task itself, as in jumping over a fence (or not), solving a crossword puzzle (or not), or logging onto the computer (or not). In most tasks, however, performance evaluation is more ambiguous than a right-versus-wrong performance outcome. Consider, for instance, competence evaluations on tasks such as a written essay, social skill, athletic performance, poem, painting, or oral presentation. In performances such as these, our own past performances and the evaluations of other people (rather than the task itself) supply us with the information necessary to make an inference of competence versus incompetence. It is these two sources of informational feedback that I want to examine more closely.

Students almost always have a performance history associated with the task. They therefore use their historical performances as a standard to assess the relative competency of their current performance. The perception of progress is an important signal of competence (Schunk & Hanson, 1989). In the classroom, the perception of progress goes hand in hand with the experience of learning. Schunk and Hanson (1989) demonstrated one way teachers can focus students' attention acutely on their experiences on progess and learning. They videotaped elementary-grade students as each solved a series of difficult fractions (e.g., $11/15 + 37/45 = ?$). The fraction problems appeared on a large chalkboard, and the experimenters asked each child to verbalize aloud all attempts to solve the problems. The children then individually viewed their videotape. Results showed that students' sense of competence increased substantially. Schunk and Hanson argue, however, that viewing such a videotaped performance will not raise competence on tasks the student already performs well. Rather, the videotape would simply confirm what the student already knows. In contrast, seeing oneself *making progress* on a task is the process of learning that boosts competence.

The most ubiquitous source of information students use to evaluate their competence is the evaluation of others. Positive verbal feedback bolsters competence and leads to enjoyment; negative verbal feedback deflates competence and lessens enjoyment (Anderson, et al., 1976; Blank, Reis, & Jackson, 1984; Deci, 1971; Dollinger & Thelen, 1978; Vallerand & Reid, 1984). Consider one study showing that positive verbal feedback breeds a sense of perceived competence (Vallerand & Reid, 1984). These researchers asked undergraduate males to perform the stabilimeter motor task (something like jumping up and down on a pogo stick) while an experimenter verbalized either positive verbal statements (e.g., "It looks like you have a natural ability to balance and it shows in your performance") or negative verbal statements (e.g., "This is an easy task, but your improvement is quite slow; try to perform as well as you can"). After the performance and its feedback, the researchers assessed each person's perceived competence and intrinsic motivation toward the stabilimeter task. Positive verbal feedback increased perceived competence. Further, increases in perceived competence increased intrinsic motivation. Similarly, negative feedback decreased perceived competence, which, in turn, decreased intrinsic motivation.

In summary, informative performance feedback in its various forms—task-generated, self-generated, and other-generated—supplies the information necessary for the individual to formulate a cognitive evaluation of his or her perceived level of competence. When that feedback signals high competence, we enjoy our participation in the task and show high intrinsic motivation toward it (Deci & Ryan, 1980, 1985). Deci and Ryan summarize the vast literature on optimal challenge and perceived competence with the second proposition of their "cognitive evaluation theory":

> *External events will affect a person's intrinsic motivation for an opti-*
> *mally challenging activity to the extent that they influence the person's*
> *perceived competence, within the context of some self-determination.*
> *Events that promote greater perceived competence will enhance intrin-*
> *sic motivation, whereas those that diminish perceived competence will*
> *decrease intrinsic motivation. (Deci & Ryan, 1985, p. 63)*

Conclusion

In structuring a classroom to challenge students optimally, one fundamental is that teachers invite students to select from tasks and materials that vary in their levels of difficulty. In this way, students will be able to match their present skill levels with tasks of various difficulties and proceed in such a way that an ever-increasing sense of competence directs learning. One criticism of inviting students to self-select their own personal challenges (rather than administering a teacher-assigned task), however, is that students might loaf and simply select the task that is easiest for them to do. Indeed, when rewards, grades, and evaluations are at stake, students will more than likely opt for the easiest challenge available. However, when students are offered an array of tasks that differ in difficulty and when no rewards or interpersonal evaluations are at stake, students show a strong preference for optimal (moderately difficult) challenge (Danner & Lonky, 1981; Shapira, 1976). These results encourage the conclusion that an extrinsic motivational orientation (grades, money) engenders challenge avoidance and the pursuit of the easy success, whereas an intrinsic motivational orientation (competence, challenge) engenders challenge seeking and risk taking. In the process of challenging students, the classroom climate is critical. The teacher contributes substantially to students' willingness to seek optimal challenges when he or she gives emphasis to learning goals and communicates a valuing of errors, a tolerance for failure, and an appreciation for academic risk taking.

Half of the equation in the effort to engage students' need for competence is the offering of optimal challenge. But there is a second half to the equation. To continue competence need involvement in the learning enterprise over time, a student needs also to receive informative performance feedback that communicates to him or her the message of a job well done. This feedback can take the form of either task-generated, self-generated, or other-generated information. When such feedback informs students that their performance is a competent rather than an incompetent one, perceived competence increases, as does intrinsic motivation. Overall, the opportunity for optimal challenge essentially activates a student's sense of competence in the classroom, while competence-communicating feedback essentially nurtures a student's competence to ensure its persistence over time. Together, the challenge from an activity, the feedback it and others (i.e., teachers) give, and the feelings of enjoyment from experiences of mastery and personal control interrelate with one another to illustrate how the competence need functions as an inner motivational resource to energize behavior that encourages voluntary attempts at intentional, goal-directed changes in the environment.

Recommended Readings

Clifford, M. M. (1984). Thoughts on a theory of constructive failure. *Educational Psychologist, 19,* 108–120.

Clifford, M. M. (1990). Students need challenge, not easy success. *Educational Leadership, 48,* 22–26.

Csikszentmihalyi, M. (1982). Toward a psychology of optimal experience. *Review of Personality and Social Psychology, 3,* 13–26.

Danner, F. W., & Lonky, E. (1981). A cognitive-developmental approach to the effects of rewards on intrinsic motivation. *Child Development, 52,* 1043–1052.

Harter, S. (1974). Pleasure derived by children from cognitive challenge and mastery. *Child Development, 45,* 661–669.

Harter, S. (1978a). Effectance motivation reconsidered: Toward a developmental model. *Human Development, 21,* 34–64.

Harter, S. (1978b). Pleasure derived from optimal challenge and the effects of extrinsic rewards on children's difficulty level choices. *Child Development, 49,* 788–799.

Shapira, Z. (1976). Expectancy determinants of intrinsically motivated behavior. *Journal of Personality and Social Psychology, 34,* 1235–1244.

Stein, G. L., Kimiecik, J. C., Daniels, J., & Jackson, S. A. (1995). Psychological antecedents of flow in recreational sport. *Personality and Social Psychology Bulletin, 21,* 125–135.

White, R. W. (1959). Motivation reconsidered: The concept of competence. *Psychological Review, 66,* 297–333.

Observational Activities

Observational Activity 4.1: Identifying the Elements of Enjoyment in Common Activities

The purpose of this interview is to investigate and understand how the particular elements of a task influence how enjoyable people experience it to be. You will need to interview two students who are at least in the fourth-grade (because you will being asking about participation in homework). Each interview will last about forty-five minutes. You will be asking each student the same set of questions about three different activities—doing homework, watching television, and engaging in a favorite activity. Let the student pick his or her own favorite activity (such as a sport, musical instrument, or computer game).

To begin, ask the student to recall his or her most recent experience of doing homework. Ask these questions (or modify them to you own liking):

Did you have a clear sense that you could complete the homework?

Did the homework offer clear goals for you to pursue? Did the homework provide you with any immediate feedback as to how well or poorly you were doing?

How challenged—in a good sense—did you feel by the homework?

While you were doing your homework, how competent or skillful did you feel? How able were you to concentrate?

How enjoyable did you find the homework to be? How boring? How worried/anxious did you feel?

After students answer these questions about homework, then ask them to recall their most recent experiences with watching television and ask the same set of questions. Finally, ask them to recall their most recent experience of engaging in the favorite activity and ask the same set of questions.

After you have completed both interviews, answer the following set of questions: Rank order each student's activity preferences from least to most (1) enjoyable, (2) boring, and (3) anxiety-provoking. Did any pattern emerge that would allow you to explain precisely why one activity was enjoyed more or less than the others—completion? clear goals? feedback? challenge? Can Csikszentmihalyi's flow model (depicted in Figure 4-1) explain the students' enjoyment ratings? Can you explain where students' feelings or boredom and/or anxiety came from?

Observational Activity 4.2: Competence-Involving and Competence-Affirming Aspects of Classrooms

The purpose of this observation is to rate classrooms in how rich they are or are not in competence-involving and competence-affirming cues. You will need to observe two classrooms. Gain the permission of each classroom teacher in advance. Once you have received the teacher's permission, sit unobtrusively in the back row of the class, and record these two aspects of the teacher's behavior and of the classroom climate in general.

1. *Encouragement of challenge and risk taking:* Pay particular attention to all instances in which the teacher introduces a task, asks students a question, or encourages them to exert effort. Rate the classroom climate on (a) the extent of the challenge on a scale ranging from "easy task" through "moderately difficult task" to "unrealistically difficult task" and (b) how tolerant the teacher is to failure and error making on a scale ranging from "encourages right answers and flawless performances" to "encourages making errors and accepts failures as inherent in learning."

2. *Feedback:* As students perform (e.g., answer questions, solve problems), observe how involved versus neglectful the teacher is in giving students feedback (e.g., "Very good, that's the best work you've done so far"). For teachers who give frequent performance feedback, also rate the valence of that feedback; that is, rate how often the teacher gives positive verbal feedback versus negative verbal feedback. Notice nonverbal feedback as well (e.g., head nods, marks on papers).

During your observations, also rate two aspects of the students: (1) their emotionality in terms of apathy, boredom, worry or anxiety, and enjoyment, and (2) their engagement in terms of how active and participating the students are as a group.

With your observations complete, describe the teachers in terms of (1) enouragement of optimal challenges, (2) tolerance for error making, and (3) type, frequency, and quality of performance feedback. Relate students' classroom emotionality and engagement to these three teacher characteristics. Also, note the role that the students themselves played in encouraging versus discouraging their peers to accept challenges and to take risks, as well as the role students played in giving performance feedback to their peers. What recommendations could you offer the teachers to make their classrooms richer in competence-involving and competence-affirming cues?

5

Self-Efficacy

It's Friday morning in Mr. Fitzgerald's math class, and that means its time for the week's test on multiplication and division. Two of the test-takers, Sue and Jennifer, are twins with precisely the same natural abilities in mathematics; they even achieved the same score on last October's math aptitude test. Despite their equal abilities, Sue's confidence in mathematics is strong, while Jennifer doubts her capabilities. As the test begins, both quickly solve the first few problems correctly, but as the problems progress in difficulty each begins to run into stumbling blocks. Facing difficulties, confident Sue discards her apparently ineffective problem-solving strategies and generates alternative approaches to rework the unsolved problems. With each false start, Sue maintains her optimism and tries harder than she did before. Jennifer's reaction to each false start, however, is to repeat her inappropriate strategy a second or even a third time. Facing each impasse, Jennifer diminishes her effort a bit, her enthusiasm wanes, and she becomes progressively pessimistic that she will do well on today's test. By the end of the test, Sue has, compared to her twin, solved more problems, returned to and reattempted most of the difficult problems, successfully solved more of the reattempted problems, and retained her positive attitude and expectations toward mathematics in general (based on Collins, 1982).

Self-Efficacy and Competent Functioning

The discussion of self-efficacy as an inner motivational resource revolves around highlighting the difference between merely possessing skills and using them well. Competent functioning requires not only the fine-tuned task-related skills that constitute "ability," but also the cognitive capacity to translate the skills one has into effective performance under trying circumstances. The capacity to use effectively the skills one has under diverse circumstances constitutes the essence of "self-efficacy," which is defined as people's judgments of how well (or poorly) they will perform a task given the skills they possess and the circumstances they face (Bandura, 1986, 1993).

Self-efficacy is just as important a determinant of one's performance as ability itself, because testing situations inherently reek with stress, ambiguity, and unpredictability, and, as one performs, circumstances often change. To perform well, students need not only high ability but also the capacity to manage their fears when their performances break down or bring aversive consequences. For instance, many adolescents have rather sophisticated social skills; they talk, listen, ask and answer questions, hold other people's attention, and use humor with ease, at least in comfortable settings such as hanging out with their friends. During a formal oral presentation at school that uses essentially these same skills, however, adolescents sometimes perform dismally because circumstances change in ways that stress these skills. In this situation, competent functioning requires that the student be aware of and able to enact public-speaking skills in those situations in which they are most called for—communication skills to get, hold, or regain the audience's attention, empathy skills to sense the audience's expressions of confusion or boredom, relaxation skills to keep cool under the pressure of being evaluated by others, and so on.

The opposite of self-efficacy is self-doubt. For the presenter who doubts his or her abilities, unwelcomed surprises, setbacks, and difficulties queue up an avalanche of performance-interfering states of mind, such as anxiety (Bandura, 1988), cognitive confusion (Wood & Bandura, 1989), negative expectations (Bandura, 1983), and aversive physiological arousal and bodily tension (Bandura, Taylor, Williams, Mefford, & Barchas, 1985). Imagine the unfolding of events that might occur when the self-doubt of an otherwise socially skilled presenter comes face to face with situational surprises, setbacks, and difficulties. Perhaps a classmate unexpectedly presents on the same topic, or the teacher calls on the student to go first (surprises); or perhaps the student's co-presenter fails to come to class that day, or the student cannot locate the needed overhead during the talk (setbacks); or perhaps the teacher mentions that, because there is not enough time left, the student will need to go faster and leave some things out (difficulties). Under such trying conditions, doubt can interfere with effective thinking, planning, and decision making so to open the floodgate to anxiety, confusion, arousal, tension, and distressing anticipations that spiral performance toward disaster. Of course, surprises, setbacks, and difficulties need not produce poor performance, any more than skill, talent, and ability will necessarily produce excellent performance. Rather, self-efficacy (or self-doubt) determines the extent to which a performer copes successfully when skills are put to the test.

To help the reader get a more comfortable grasp on self-efficacy's role in competent functioning, imagine performing a variety of life's tasks, such as using a computer to compose, edit, and print out a document; driving a car in the dense highway traffic of a major city; conversing in Spanish with another person; or teaching a class. As you imagine yourself immersed in each performance, let the following set of questions run through your mind:

- As you perform, what specific task-related events do you expect to take place?
- What specific skills will you need to perform well during each of these events?
- How effective do you anticipate each event-related performance will be?
- If things go unexpectedly wrong, could you make the necessary corrective adjustments?
- How do you expect to feel as you perform?

To carry this illustration a bit further, Table 5-1 presents one of these situations—teaching a class—and offers hypothetical answers to these questions. Specifically, the illustration concerns a teacher imagining himself instructing a classroom full of middle school students in a reading strategy referred to as PQ4R (see Thomas & Robinson, 1972, for a discussion of PQ4R).

In this hypothetical situation, the teacher expects that the overall task at hand—instruct a classroom full of middle school students in a reading strategy—will require that he employ a dozen or so skills—small talk, planning, entertainingness, assertiveness, and so on. The teacher also has some expectation of how effectively he will perform each of these skills in the classroom setting, and his performance expectancies range from terrible to excellent. These beliefs of anticipated performance effectiveness—will I perform well or will I perform poorly?—represent the essence of self-efficacy beliefs in this example. The teacher also has some expectation that, if things go wrong, he or she can get the class back on track by initiating the necessary corrective adjustments. These expectations affect the extent and persistence of the teacher's coping efforts to enact corrective adjustments. Finally, the teacher expects to feel a certain way as he or she executes the skills within the demands of this particular middle school classroom. The expected emotions center around a continuum that ranges from doubt to confidence. In glancing down the teacher's expected feelings, perhaps the reader can imagine how the teacher might respond to a general question about how he feels about teaching this particular class (e.g., "It has its ups and downs, but for the most part I feel comfortable and enjoy the class").

Sources of Self-Efficacy Information (Observational Activity 5.1)

The relative strength of an efficacy belief comes from four sources of information. First, past performance accomplishments provide firsthand, performance-

TABLE 5-1 Hypothetical Teacher's Performance Expectations During a One-Hour Class to Teach the PQ4R Reading Strategy

Time	Expected Event	Requisite Skills	Anticipated Performance Effectiveness	Can Make Corrective Adjustments?	Expected Feeling
9:00	Students enter classroom.	Small talk	Awkward	Occasionally	Doubt
9:02	Students chat among themselves.	Planning	Excellent	Certainly	Confidence
9:03	Teacher introduces lesson.	Entertainingness	Excellent	Certainly	Confidence
9:04	...Competes for student's attention.	Assertiveness	Poor	Sometimes	Doubt
9:05	...Defines terms: PQ4R	Oral clarity	Good	Probably	Confidence
9:10	...Gives examples of P, Q, and Rs.	Connection making	Good	Most times	Confidence
9:15	...Demonstrates PQ4R method.	Demonstrativeness	Good	Probably	Confidence
9:17	Students express confusion.	Perspective taking	Poor	Occasionally	Doubt
9:18	Teacher argues PQ4R's relevance.	Persuasiveness	Terrible	Occasionally	Doubt
9:30	Students work individually at desks.	Supportiveness	Excellent	Probably	Confidence
9:35	Teacher competes for students' attention.	Patience	Good	Most times	Confidence
9:38	Students become noisy, disruptive.	Leadership	Terrible	Never	Doubt
9:40	Teacher solves discipline problem.	Assertiveness	Poor	Occasionally	Doubt
9:45	Question and answer dialogue.	Empathy	Excellent	Certainly	Confidence
9:50	Teacher dismisses students.	Small talk	Awkward	Occasionally	Doubt

based information on which to base an efficacy judgment. Second, our observations of another person's performance accomplishments inform us as to our own efficacy ("If he can do it, well, so can I!"). Third, verbal persuasion ("pep talks") can inform efficacy beliefs, as when another person persuades the performer that he or she possesses the skill necessary to perform masterfully. Finally, physiological states such as a racing versus a calmed heart inform efficacy beliefs by signaling how easily versus overwhelmingly performance is proceeding. For teachers interested in facilitating self-efficacy beliefs in students, these four sources of information constitute the means to do so.

Performance Accomplishments

After a student performs an educational task, the quality of that performance provides her with direct mastery experience data. Performances judged as successes raise efficacy beliefs by contributing to an expectation that one's future performances will also be proficient. Performances judged as failures lower efficacy beliefs by contributing to an expectation that future performances will also be inept. Because past performance accomplishments are first-hand mastery experiences, they contribute the most dependable source of efficacy information (Bandura, 1986). This general statements is qualified, however, by several variables such as the perceived difficulty of the task, the amount of physical guidance received, and the temporal pattern of one's record of successes and failures (Bandura, 1986). Specifically, efficacy beliefs strengthen substantially when performance accomplishments occur on difficult tasks, with little assistance or coaching, and relatively early in learning with few early setbacks, whereas efficacy beliefs strengthen only modestly (if at all) on easy tasks, with much assistance from others, with external aids or equipment, and relatively late in learning.

To show that performance accomplishments raises efficacy beliefs, Bandura sought out persons with extraordinary low self-efficacy beliefs—severely phobic individuals (Bandura, Reese, & Adams, 1982). Bandura and his colleagues (1982) guided each phobic through a sequential procedure of performance mastery on progressively more threatening activities. With each successive accomplishment, self-efficacy rose more and more.

In addition to past performance accomplishments, ongoing, concurrent performance accomplishments affect self-efficacy (Schunk, 1989b). That is, as students work on tasks, the appraisal that they are functioning competently and are comprehending the material at hand raises self-efficacy; the appraisal that little progress is being made, however, lowers self-efficacy (Schunk, 1989b).

Vicarious Experience (Modeling)

A second source of information on which people base their efficacy beliefs occurs through a social comparison process with others. When others perform publicly, observers gain the opportunity to observe and judge the effectiveness of their performances on the same task. When one student sees another perform well on a task he or she will soon undertake, personal efficacy expectations increase; when those others perform poorly, personal efficacy expectations decrease. Vicarious modeling experiences always contribute some amount of influence to an observer's efficacy beliefs, but they constitute an especially important source of information when the observer has little experience with the task (and therefore possesses unreliable or nonexistent past performance accomplishments information; Schunk, 1989b).

Observers, especially young ones, do not use vicarious performance information from all the models they see; rather, they emulate peers they believe to be highly similar (Schunk, 1989a) or particularly competent (Brown & Inouye, 1978; Schunk, 1987). Also, efficacy beliefs strengthen more when observers watch models who struggle and cope to overcome task difficulties than they do by watching expert models who perform flawlessly (i.e., coping models are more informative than are mastery models; Schunk, Hanson, & Cox, 1987). In addition, efficacy beliefs strengthen more when observers watch multiple models than when they watch a single model (Schunk, 1987).

In studying vicarious experience information, Schunk and Hanson (1985) created an experimental setting in which children learning subtraction observed either no model, a peer model, or a teacher model doing subtraction problems. The researchers monitored the subtraction-related efficacy beliefs for each child as he or she observed one of the three model conditions. Children who observed the teacher model gained in efficacy, but children who observed the peer model gained the most in efficacy. In a separate investigation, Zimmerman and Ringle (1981) had first- and second-grade students observe a model who verbalized either confident optimism ("I am sure I can . . . I just have to keep trying different ways") or pessimism ("I don't think I can . . . I have tried many different ways and nothing seems to work"). Although the actual performance of each model was the same, the elementary school children who watched and listened to the optimistic-speaking model reported the greater self-efficacy expectations for themselves. Other researchers demonstrate that students also learn low self-efficacy expectations through vicarious experience, if the model's performance comes off as inept (Brown & Inouye, 1978).

Verbal Persuasion

A third source of information on which to base an efficacy belief is the verbal persuasion of others, such as a teacher, parent, peer, coach, employer, therapist, or audience, or even an inspirational poster or a song on the radio. One person can raise the efficacy expectations of another through a successful pep talk that refocuses the performer's attention away from his or her personal deficiencies, past failures, and task obstacles and toward personal strengths, past triumphs, and task vulnerabilities (Schunk, 1983). Of course, the extent to which verbal persuasion attempts translate themselves into bolstered efficacy beliefs is limited by the realistic boundaries of what is possible. Assuming the persuasive information falls within the boundaries of the possible, then the extent of the persuasiveness of the information depends on the credibility, trustworthiness, and expertise of the persuader. The communications of a credible, trustworthy expert carry more persuasive appeal than do the communications of a suspicious, untrustworthy, and inept speaker. In fact, the verbal persuasion of an untrustworthy speaker can backfire (undermine self-efficacy) by coming across as patronizing encouragement or manipulative hype. Verbal persuasion information can also come from oneself—in the form of self-talk. For instance, Schunk and Cox (1986) found that a continuous banter of self-instructive strategy during performance raised efficacy for children solving subtraction problems.

In terms of potency of influence, verbal persuasion is the third most influential source of efficacy information, behind performance accomplishments and vicarious experiences. For instance, failures in actual performances negate earlier gains in self-efficacy via vicarious experiences or verbal persuasions (Schunk, 1989a). That being said, the functional significance of verbal persuasion information is twofold: (1) to provide the student with a temporary, provisional boost in efficacy that enables him to put aside self-doubt enough to at least initiate a task engagement (Schunk, 1991) and (2) to counter the occasional setback that might otherwise instill enough self-doubt to interrupt persistence (Schunk, 1982).

Physiological State

A fourth source of information to inform efficacy beliefs comes from the physiological states one experiences immediately prior to or during task performance. During performance, some degree of autonomic nervous system arousal occurs (e.g., increased heart rate and respiratory rate, trembling hands), as does some degree of somatic arousal (e.g., muscle tension, fatigue, pains and aches) and cortical arousal (e.g., rate of thinking, mental confusion). Heightened arousal confirms stress and unsuccessful coping (unless one interprets the high arousal as being "psyched up"). On the other hand, the perception of having one's autonomic, somatic, and cortical arousal systems under control provides convincing firsthand information that one can indeed cope adequately with the demands of the task.

One academic subject that stirs up its fair share of aversive physiological arousal is mathematics. In one research effort, college students of equal math ability were randomly assigned to perform math problems (e.g., $73 - 15 \times 3 = ?$)

under time pressures that either exceeded or did not exceed their cognitive ability to process the answers (Bandura, Cioffi, Taylor, & Brouillard, 1988). The students with the demanding time pressures reported significantly lower self-efficacy judgments and, as they solved one problem after another, showed significantly higher heart rates. Obviously, the taxing time pressures decreased students' self-efficacy, but the authors argued that the racing heart further contributed to the students' self-doubts (Bandura et al., 1988). Such findings support the idea that the causal direction between self-inefficacy and physiological arousal is bidirectional, as an expectation of math-inefficacy increases arousal while heightened arousal also increases math self-inefficacy. The bidirectionality between inefficacy and physiological arousal is, however, asymmetrical (Bandura, 1983), in that self-inefficacy fuels physiological arousal more than physiological arousal fuels self-inefficacy (because self-efficacy judgments also depend on other sources of information, such as performance accomplishments, vicarious experiences, and verbal persuasions).

One general point about these four sources of information people use to make personal efficacy judgments remains to be made explicit—namely, that efficacy judgments, once formed, vary in how strong and resistant they are to change. Day in and day out, students' competencies are tested, and they continually see the competencies of their peers tested on the same tasks they perform. In the face of such a continuous flow of new information about one's efficacy, efficacy judgments sometimes change markedly, while at other times they change very little, if at all. Efficacy beliefs based on much information and of a sort that has been consistent become firm beliefs and are subject to reanalysis only in the face of compelling disconfirmation. Efficacy beliefs based on little information or on information that has been inconsistent are inconclusive beliefs that are subject to reanalysis. For students, self-efficacy judgments often fall into this latter category of resiliency because it is inherent in the educational process that teachers seek to expand students' skills and employ them in the service of mastering new and challenging activities. Therefore, it might prove a useful heuristic to offer the reader an exemplary comprehensive program targeted specifically at weeding out self-doubts and uncertainties and cultivating in their place positive, resilient self-efficacy beliefs.

Comprehensive Program for Self-Efficacy Training (Observational Activity 5.2)

A comprehensive program for self-efficacy training consists of three parts: (1) identifying the component skills underlying competent functioning in an educational endeavor; (2) measuring self-efficacy expectations for each skill and for the educational endeavor in general, and (3) supplying positive self-efficacy information to the performer, using the four sources of information discussed above. In practice, these three parts of a self-efficacy training program can be realized via the following seven-step procedure:

Step 1: Instructor identifies component skills needed for competent performance. Instructor measures students' self-efficacy expectations on each of these skills.

Step 2: Instructor models each component skill.

Step 3: Following the modeling, students perform each component skill. Instructor supplies corrective feedback until students master each skill.

Step 4: Individually mastered component skills are integrated into competent functioning during a simulation of the task. Instructor graduates the simulations so they consist of a succession of increases in task difficulties and performance obstacles.

Step 5: While one student performs the simulated task, others watch on the sidelines. They offer the performer skill-related tips and motivation-related encouragements.

Step 6: The instructor provides additional instructive modeling, using corrective feedback as needed.

Step 7: Instructor identifies and models confident demeanor and arousal-regulating techniques (e.g., relaxation, imagery) to students.

For illustration, consider how a teacher might apply these seven steps to the task of using a computer to author and print out a two-hundred-word essay. The teacher would first identify the component skills underlying competent functioning. I list next a dozen component skills that leap into my own mind when I think about what actions are necessary to use a computer for such a task. I also list the numbers 1 to 7 to the right of each skill to represent one way to measure self-efficacy expectations for each skill (measuring students' perceptions of self-efficacy is part of step 1). Students' self-reports of self-efficacy inform the instructor as to which skills need the greatest amount of attention (because they generate the strongest sources of self-doubt).

To complete step 2, the instructor would model each component skill as students observe. More than likely, each lesson would focus on only a subset of the component skills. In step 3, students inform their self-efficacy beliefs through performance accomplishments, while the instructor supplies corrective feedback (because McAuley, 1985, showed that aided assistance is superior to unaided assistance). Step 3 continues until students perform each skill—log on, use spell-checker, and so on—masterfully. Step 4 asks students to perform a minimally stressful version of the full activity (e.g., find the computer, log on, type and print out their names, and log off). For part 4, keep in mind that self-efficacy is not so much a question of whether a student can log on the computer, compose an essay, or type 30 words a minute, but, rather, whether a

---

Use the numbers from 1 to 7 to estimate your level of confidence that you can successfully execute each particular action:

	Very Sure		Somewhat Sure			Very Sure	
Find the computer room.	1	2	3	4	5	6	7
Identify a computer that is appropriate for word processing.	1	2	3	4	5	6	7
Log on and log off the computer.	1	2	3	4	5	6	7
Access the word-processing software.	1	2	3	4	5	6	7
Compose a two hundred word essay.	1	2	3	4	5	6	7
Edit that essay on the computer.	1	2	3	4	5	6	7
Use the spell-checker.	1	2	3	4	5	6	7
Save the document on a disk.	1	2	3	4	5	6	7
Print out the document.	1	2	3	4	5	6	7
Type thirty words per minute.	1	2	3	4	5	6	7
Use the mouse.	1	2	3	4	5	6	7
Use a computer reference manual.	1	2	3	4	5	6	7
And, finally, use the computer to write, edit, and print out a two hundred word essay.	1	2	3	4	5	6	7

---

student can use these skills effectively under diverse circumstances. So the simulations should vary in how taxing the performance situation is (i.e., leisurely working alone and at one's own pace versus working under the pressure of a deadline). Instead of having students perform individually, they can practice in small groups so that as one performs the others offer and receive tips and encouragement (step 5). That is, whereas steps 3 and 4 rely on performance accomplishments to boost strong efficacy beliefs, part 5 relies on vicarious experience and verbal persuasion as further sources of positive self-efficacy information. Step 6 is essentially a repetition of step 3, as research finds that additional instructive modeling of troublesome component skills works to prevent lapses into doubt and fear. Finally, step 7 concerns the issue of physiological states as a source of self-efficacy (or inefficacy) and seeks to equip students with the means to exercise control over the aversive arousal that might otherwise breed perceptions of self-inefficacy.

Student Efficacy and Academic Functioning

Efficacy beliefs exert diverse effects on a student's academic functioning (Schunk, 1991). As reviewed in this section, perceptions of efficacy affect (1) choice of activities and selection of environments; (2) the extent of effort and persistence put forth during task performance, (3) the quality of student's thinking and decision making during performance, and (4) emotional reactions, especially those related to stress and anxiety.

Choice

Students continually make (and act on) choices about what activities and what environments they prefer. In general, students seek out and approach with excitement activities and situations that they judge themselves as capable of adjusting to or handling, while students shun and actively avoid activities and situations they see as likely to overwhelm their coping capacities (Bandura, 1977, 1989). Student choice is partly a cost–benefit analysis: "I'll do the assigned homework to learn the material and make a good grade (benefits), though I'll have to miss a favorite television show to do so (costs)." But student choice is further a self-protective action designed to insure against the possibility of being overwhelmed by the demands and challenges of the task. If the student expects homework to lead to cognitive confusion and emotional frustration, then self-doubt works as an additional unseen cost that produces avoidance decisions. Positive self-efficacy beliefs facilitate choice by minimizing students' tendencies to lean toward defensive, self-protective decisions.

Student choices such as whether or not to pursue an elective course of studies (e.g., math, foreign language), to attend or avoid a social function (e.g., the prom), or to volunteer for versus drop out of an organization (e.g., school band) can exert a profound, long-term effect on development (e.g., Bandura, 1986). Strong self-efficacy beliefs set the stage for the student to choose those active engagements that contribute to the growth of competencies; weak self-efficacy beliefs set the stage for the student to shun participating in such activities and therefore to arrested developmental potentials (Holahan & Holahan, 1987). When a student shuns an activity out of doubt over personal competence, then that student participates in the self-destructive process of retarding his or her own potential development. Further, the more the student avoids such activities, the more entrenched one's self-doubts become, because the doubter never gives herself a chance to prove herself wrong. Such a pattern of avoidance effectively narrows a person's range of activities and settings. This line of reasoning applies to students' career choices as well (Bandura, 1982; Betz & Hackett, 1986; Hackett, 1985). Hackett (1985), for instance, explored the idea that females generally avoid math-related majors during college not because of a lack of high school preparation or because they foresee few career opportunities for women but because of perceptions of self-inefficacy in math. Her findings showed that the females who chose to avoid math-related majors were indeed the ones with the lowest efficacy (rather than the lowest ability).

Effort and Persistence

As students perform, self-efficacy beliefs influence how much effort they exert as well as how long they put forth that effort in the face of adversity (Bandura, 1989). Strong self-efficacy beliefs produce effortful and persistent coping efforts aimed at overcoming setbacks and difficulties (Salomon, 1984). The doubt from weak self-efficacy beliefs, on the other hand, leads people to slacken their efforts when they encounter difficulties or to give up altogether (Bandura & Cervone, 1983; Weinberg, Gould, & Jackson, 1979). Self-doubt also leads performers to settle prematurely on mediocre solutions. The contribution that strong self-efficacy beliefs make to effort and persistence is especially important in those domains in which intense effort and enduring persistence are prerequisites to skill development, such as complex activities that require mastery of multiple component skills. In trying to master complex activities, learning is always fraught with difficulties, obstacles, setbacks, frustrations, rejections, and inequalities. Bandura (1989) argues that self-efficacy plays the pivotal role it does in facilitating effort and persistence not because it silences self-doubt following failures and setbacks (because these are expected, normal emotional reactions), but because self-efficacy leads to a *quick recovery* of self-assurance following setbacks. Often, Bandura argues, it is the resiliency of self-efficacy in the face of being pounded by failures that provides the motivational support necessary to continue the persistent effort needed for competent functioning.

Thinking and Decision Making

People who believe strongly in their efficacy to solve problems remain highly efficient in their analytic thinking during episodes of complex decision making, whereas people who doubt their problem-solving capacities are cognitively erratic in their analytic thinking (Bandura & Wood, 1989; Wood & Bandura, 1989). To perform his best, a person must use his memories of past events to generate hypotheses about the most effective course of action to take, he must analyze feedback to assess and reassess the merit of his plans and strategies, and he must reflect upon performances and remember which courses of action proved effective and which did not. Self-doubt deteriorates, and therefore impairs, such thinking and decision-making processes. In contrast, a strong sense of efficacy allows the performer to remain task-involved even in the face of situational stress and problem-solving failures.

Emotional Reactions

Before a student actually begins participating in an activity, she typically spends time thinking about how she will perform. Persons with a strong sense of efficacy attend to the demands and challenges of the task, visualize success scenarios for forthcoming performances; and react to task challenges and feedback with enthusiastic effort, optimism, and interest. Persons with a weak sense of efficacy dwell on personal deficiencies, visualize the formidable obstacles about to be faced, and react to task challenges and feedback with pessimism, anxiety, and depression (Bandura, 1986). When things go wrong, self-efficacy beliefs keep anxiety at bay. People who doubt their skills, however, are quickly threatened by difficulties, react to setbacks with distress, and see their attention drift away from performing the task per se and toward their personal deficiencies and the potential consequences of failure.

School offers students a number of potentially threatening events (e.g., examinations, public performances) and the extent of a student's self-efficacy plays a central role in determining how much stress and anxiety such events bring. Threat itself is not a fixed property of events, as threat always depends on the relationship a person has to the event at hand (Folkman & Lazarus, 1985; Lazarus & Folkman, 1984). That is, events offer potentially aversive experiences and consequences, but performers offer coping capabilities that can effectively counteract the potentially overwhelming aspects of the event. Knowing that one's coping capabilities cannot handle the perceived threats of an event conjures up thoughts of disaster, emotional arousal, and feelings of distress and anxiety (Bandura, 1983; Bandura et al., 1982; Bandura et al., 1985; Lazarus, 1991). On the other hand, when people plagued with self-doubt undergo therapy-like conditions to enhance their coping capabilities, the once intimidating event that conjured up such an avalanche of doubt, dread, and distress no longer does so (Bandura & Adams, 1977; Bandura, Adams, Hardy, & Howells, 1980; Bandura, Reese, & Adams, 1982; Ozer & Bandura, 1990). Put simply, as the strength of one's self-efficacy increases, fear and anxiety slip away.

Teacher Efficacy

Self-efficacy is a valuable inner motivational resource for students, but self-efficacy applies to teachers as well. *Teacher efficacy* is an instructor's belief or conviction that he or she can influence how well students learn, especially students considered to be difficult or amotivated (Ashton, 1985; Guskey & Passaro, 1994). Teacher efficacy is important in the classroom because it influences a teacher's selection of activities, effort, and persistence (Schunk, 1991). Teachers with high efficacy believe they can bring about learning, performance, and achievement in their students (Ashton, 1984; Gibson & Dembo, 1984). To do so, those with high teacher efficacy might develop relatively challenging activities, effortfully assist students as they attempt to learn, and persevere day after day and month after month in helping students learn even when signs of apparent failure mount. When teacher efficacy is low, however, teachers may avoid offering activities that exceed their teaching skills, exert little effort to find learning resources, give up quickly on students who fail to show signs of progress, and forgo the effort to reteach content in a way students might understand it more clearly (Schunk, 1991).

The measurement of teacher efficacy has proved to be a troublesome task (see Guskey & Passaro, 1994). Most researchers nonetheless agree that items such as the following represent the essence of teacher self-efficacy (Teacher Efficacy Scale; Gibson & Dembo, 1984)

1. When I really try, I can get through to most difficult students.
2. If a student did not remember information I gave in a previous lesson, I would know how to increase his or her retention in the next lesson.
3. If a student in my class becomes disruptive and noisy, I feel assured that I know some techniques to redirect him quickly.

Teacher efficacy is an important individual difference because differences among teachers in terms of teacher efficacy explain much of the differences in the quality of the teaching that takes place in the classroom (Ashton & Webb, 1986; Gibson & Dembo, 1984; Trentham, Silvern, & Brogdon, 1985). Compared to those with lower efficacy, teachers with a strong sense of efficacy create positive, responsive learning climates by attending individually to students and by encouraging their enthusiasm for learning (Ashton, 1985). Further, high-efficacy teachers use criticism sparingly and show stronger persistence when students answer questions incorrectly (Gibson & Dembo, 1984). Low-efficacy teachers do not work students toward solutions and correct answers but, instead, simply answer the question themselves, call on another student to answer the question, or allow more knowledgeable students to answer the question posed to the original student.

Teacher efficacy affects student achievement not only through the direct instructional approaches listed in the preceding paragraph but through more subtle ways as well (Brophy & Good, 1974; Dusek, 1985; Good, 1981; Heller & Parsons, 1981; Parsons, Kaczala, & Meece, 1982). For instance, high-efficacy teachers hold more positive expectancies for student achievement than do low-efficacy teachers; when math students transfer (from grade 6 to grade 7) from a high- to a low-efficacy teacher, they see math as more difficult than it seemed before. In contrast, when math students transfer from a low- to a high-efficacy teacher, they see math as less difficult than it seemed before (Midgley, Feldlaufer, & Eccles, 1989). High-efficacy teachers also show more positive affect in the classroom (Ashton & Webb, 1986). Further, when asked whether they would choose teaching as a career if they had the decision to make over again, high-efficacy teachers report the stronger willingness to choose teaching as a career (apparently because they cope more successfully with the demands of the teaching profession; Trentham et al., 1985).

Teachers, like everyone else, overestimate their own efficacy and competencies. I routinely ask the prospective teachers in my own educational psychology courses to judge their teacher efficacy on a scale from 1 (much worse than others) to 5 (much better than others). Year after year, the mean score is an optimistic 4, whether I ask them to use their classmates or currently practicing teachers as their reference (i.e., comparison) group. Of course, the mean on any 1–5 scale should be, mathematically speaking, 3.0, but personal biases skew the mean upward. Even more striking, however, is Trentham, Silvern, and Brogdon's (1985) finding that of 153 teachers they asked to rate their "competence in dealing with life's problems compared to others" as either "above average," "average," or "below average," *none* chose "below average." Fortunately, overestimating one's sense of efficacy and competence is a psychologically healthy habit to develop (Taylor & Brown, 1988, 1994). But there does seem to be an optimal degree of overestimating efficacy; delusions do get in the way of effective functioning (Baumeister, 1989). But from a motivational point of view, it is psychologically productive to see oneself and one's teaching efficacy in a positive light. After all, if self-efficacy beliefs were unbiased and accurately reflected only what people actually can do, then people would routinely do only what they thought they could do and would rarely put forth the effort and persistence needed to exceed their typical performances (Bandura, 1989).

Teacher Education Programs

Some researchers argue that teacher efficacy is the single best teacher characteristic to predict student achievement outcomes (Ashton, 1984). Because teacher efficacy translates into student achievement, teacher education programs might seriously organize their programs around the facilitation of teacher efficacy. Toward that end, Ashton (1984) interviewed dozens of middle school teachers to identify those high versus low in teacher efficacy and to examine the differences between the two groups that emerged. She found that she could distinguish high- from low-efficacy teachers via the following six characteristics: (1) sense of personal accomplishment, (2) positive expectations for student achievement, (3) personal responsibility for student learning, (4) sense of control, (5) sense of cooperative teacher–student goals, and (6) democratic decision making. That is, high-efficacy teachers felt their work was important and meaningful while low-efficacy teachers felt frustrated and discouraged (sense of personal accomplishment); they expected students to progress and fulfill their expectations rather than to fail and react negatively to teacher effort (positive expectations for student achievement); they saw it as their responsibility to see that students learn rather than putting the responsibility (and blame) on the student (personal responsibility for student learning); they were confident that they could influence student learning rather than holding to a sense of futility in working with students (sense of control); they felt immersed in a joint venture with students rather than feeling engaged in a struggle against students whose goals and concerns stood in opposition to theirs (sense of cooperative teacher–student goals); and they involved students in decision making in terms of classroom goals and strategies rather than imposing teacher decisions on students (democratic decision making).

Teacher characteristics such as personal accomplishment, positive student expectations, personal responsibility, sense of control, cooperative teacher–student goals, and democratic decision making are outcomes that are gained only after years of experience. Ashton (1984) believed that these outcomes were possible only after teachers internalized a core set of beliefs about themselves and the teaching profession in general. Specifically, she argued that such teacher outcomes were unlikely to the extent that teachers held firm to beliefs such as these:

1. Intelligence in students is a stable (rather than fluid) trait.
2. There is little causal relationship between teacher behavior and student learning.
3. There is little to be gained from an open, accepting, autonomy-supportive relationship with students, especially students who are hostile and defiant.

In contrast, Ashton argued that teacher education programs should target the development of beliefs that student intelligence is a fluid characteristic teachers enhance through effort and instruction; that there is a causal relationship between instruction and achievement; and that it is important to have a positive, accepting, open, and autonomy-supportive relationship with students, even with students who are hostile and defiant.

Ashton's final point was that teacher efficacy was context-specific such that teachers might feel confident in one setting but doubtful in another. Consequently, students in teacher education programs need training and experience with the a wide range of settings and with the diverse student populations they are likely to encounter as teachers. That is, beginning teachers need experience and training not only in classroom instruction and behavioral management, but they also need training to develop skills in conflict resolution, student motivation, perspective taking, leadership, and so on, and they need experience in working with students who are motivated and unmotivated, compliant and defiant, gifted and disadvantaged, hyperactive and lethargic.

Conclusion

Competent performance requires not only physical, cognitive, social, and behavioral skills (i.e., ability) but the capacity to use those skills well. People have high self-efficacy when they believe they can manage their skills into an integrated, effective course of action to achieve a purpose, even when they face the most difficult and unpredictable of circumstances. People have low self-efficacy when they worry about and expect to struggle in their performances. Of course, we all experience worry, anxiety, and self-doubt in nearly all of our performances, at least to some degree, so the relevance of research on self-efficacy is mostly in the pursuit of enabling people to reduce or minimize the worry, anxiety, and doubt that interfere with the effort to translate personal skills into performance accomplishments.

When I step back and try to see self-efficacy theory and research in the larger picture of education, I think its study is appealing and important for two reasons. The first appeal of self-efficacy is that, as a cognitive belief, it is teachable and trainable. It is clear where self-efficacy beliefs arise from—performance accomplishments, vicarious experiences, verbal persuasions, and physiological states; it is equally clear in specifying how to go about the task of enhancing efficacy beliefs in others. Further, teachers can develop comprehensive self-efficacy programs (as done in the present chapter) for students to build strong efficacy beliefs.

The second appeal of self-efficacy is, I think, that it predicts such an important cluster of educational outcomes—choice, effort and persistence, thinking and problem solving, and emotionality. That is, students with relatively strong and resilient self-efficacy beliefs undertake rather than avoid academic challenges, put forth effortful and persistent coping efforts rather than quit in the face of difficulties, problem-solve in a task-focused rather than emotion-focused way, and approach tasks with optimism and interest rather than with anxiety and fear. Thus, I find it easy to understand why classroom teachers get so excited upon learning about self-efficacy theory and its research—efficacy is both teachable and important.

Students are not the only people who stand to benefit from self-efficacy training programs. The seven-step program for self-efficacy training for effective teaching seems as applicable to teachers as to students. Teacher efficacy, as opposed to various degrees of inefficacy, arms instructors with inner motivational resources that lead to higher expectations for student achievement, more positive emotional tones while teaching, classroom interaction styles that are more student- rather than teacher-centered, and more responsive learning climates for their students. Whether the beneficiaries are teachers or their students, the implementation of comprehensive self-efficacy training programs builds strong and resilient cognitive beliefs that individuals can use to counter the unpredictable, stressful, and difficult tasks and challenges that invade our day-to-day lives.

Recommended Readings

Ashton, P. (1984). Teacher efficacy: A motivational paradigm for effective teacher education. *Journal of Teacher Education, 35*, 28–32.

Bandura, A. (1982). Self-efficacy mechanisms in human agency. *American Psychologist, 37*, 122–147.

Bandura, A. (1983). Self-efficacy mechanisms of anticipated fears and calamities. *Journal of Personality and Social Psychology, 45,* 464–469.

Bandura, A. (1988). Self-efficacy conception of anxiety. *Anxiety Research, 1,* 77–98.

Bandura, A. (1989). Human agency in social cognitive theory. *American Psychologist, 44,* 1175–1184.

Bandura, A. (1993). Perceived self-efficacy in cognitive development and functioning. *Educational Psychologist, 28,* 117–148.

Ozer, E. M., & Bandura, A. (1990). Mechanisms governing empowerment effects: A self-efficacy analysis. *Journal of Personality and Social Psychology, 58,* 472–486.

Schunk, D. H. (1989). Self-efficacy and achievement behaviors. *Educational Psychology Review, 1,* 173–208.

Schunk, D. H. (1991). Self-efficacy and academic motivation. *Educational Psychologist, 26,* 207–231.

Zimmerman, B. J., & Ringle, J. (1981). Effect of model persistence and statements of confidence on children's self-efficacy and problem-solving. *Journal of Educational Psychology, 73,* 485–493.

Observational Activities

Observational Activity 5.1: Sources of Self-Efficacy

The twofold purpose of this interview is to gain an appreciation of (1) the developmental origins of self-efficacy and self-inefficacy beliefs and (2) how self-efficacy judgments affect motivational process such as choice, effort, persistence, thinking patterns, and emotionality before and during task performances.

You will need to enlist the cooperation of one student. The interview will take about one hour. Once you find a volunteer, arrange to introduce him or her to some new skill, academic, social, or physical. An academic skill might be learning to read, use a computer, or converse in a foreign language. A social skill might be public speaking, acting, or interpersonal negotiation during conflict resolution. A physical skill might be hitting a golf ball or learning to play a musical instrument. In deciding which skill to teach, the only restriction is that the student is to be a rank amateur (a novice who is relatively incompetent) at the beginning of your teaching.

The first part is an interview. Before you begin to teach the skill, interview the student about his or her efficacy beliefs with respect to the activity. Ask what the basis is for these performance expectations, and listen carefully for answers you can identify as related to the four sources of efficacy beliefs: (1) performance accomplishments or disappointments, (2) vicarious experiences, (3) verbal persuasions, and (4) physiological states. To get a rich interview, you may need to include prompts (e.g., "What else?"). After the interview, conduct the training session in which you try to teach the person the skills needed to perform competently on the task in question. After the training, interview the student again. Again, ask about the student's efficacy beliefs with respect to the activity.

Ask the basis for these performance expectations, and listen carefully for answers you can identify as related to the four sources of efficacy beliefs.

Finally, answer the following questions:

1. Which of the four efficacy-enhancing strategies were most successful?
2. In your opinion, did his or her efficacy beliefs exceed, match, or fall short of his or her actual abilities?
3. Identify the obstacles you encountered in teaching this skill to the student.
4. Describe the student's self-talk as he or she learned and performed.
5. What emotional reactions or associations to the task does the student now have?
6. Do you sense that the student wants to do this activity in the future, or do you sense that the student would just as soon quit. Why?

Observational Activity 5.2: Developing a Comprehensive Self-Efficacy Training Program

Identify an educational activity in which students doubt their abilities (subtraction, conversing in a foreign language, public speaking, etc.). Choose an activity in which you feel confident in your ability to teach, model, and provide instructional feedback to others.

1. Identify five to eight component skills that you see as basic to competent functioning in this particular activity.
2. Design a brief questionnaire to assess self-efficacy on each component skill and on the task in general. The questionnaire in the section "Comprehensive Program for Self-Efficacy Training" can be used as an example.
3. Administer your self-efficacy scale to at least three students.
4. Compute mean self-efficacy expectations for the group for each component skill and for the educational task overall.
5. Design a comprehensive program for self-efficacy training for this particular educational activity.

You do not have to implement the comprehensive program, just design it. Use the seven-step program in the section "Comprehensive Program for Self-Efficacy Training" as an example. In outlining your self-efficacy program, provide specific illustrations of how you would model specific skills, arousal-regulating strategies, and so on. Also, specify how many students would participate in the small groups, what special equipment (e.g., videotape) you will use, and so on. Overall, your goal is to design a practical, do-able, engaging, age-appropriate, and beneficial program.

6

Personal Control Beliefs

When Marcia began the eighth grade, she was happy, cared deeply about how well she did in school, and participated in several extracurricular activities. But this was a difficult year for her. All year, it seemed as if her new teachers ignored her in the classroom, although she did not know why. Her mother promised her piano lessons in the fall, but the lessons never materialized. She saved up her money to buy a calculator for school, but it was stolen from her locker a week after she purchased it. She tried out for the soccer team, but she was cut because the coach favored another player. Her best friend from the sixth grade was bussed away to another school. Worst of all, she watched and pleaded helplessly as her parents divorced and her father left the house for good. Everywhere Marcia looked, she found an unresponsive world.

Now, Marcia's expectations are not what they used to be. She no longer expects to do well in school, she no longer expects the piano lessons to materialize, she no longer expects to play on the soccer team, she no longer expects to be able to hang out with her best friend at lunch, and she no longer expects to see her father every day. Likewise, her enthusiasm is not what it used to be. She has become passive in her studies, passive about making new friends, passive toward music and sports, and passive at home. Her happiness has turned into depression.

Marcia is a casualty of the loss of personal control, and her depression, demoralization, and underachievement document it.

Personal Control

Personal control revolves around the beliefs each individual holds about the causal impact of his or her actions on gaining desirable outcomes and preventing undesirable ones. When personal control beliefs are strong, the individual feels a sense of mastery over life's outcomes, as she perceives a strong and causal link between the action she initiates and the likelihood of good and bad events happening to her. When personal control beliefs are weak, the individual feels a sense of helplessness, as she believes that good and bad events occur on a random basis, with no causal link between her actions and her outcomes. For Marcia, the eighth grade was a year full of uncontrollable outcomes. Instead of her actions making good events more likely and bad events less likely, life's outcomes followed from the decisions of others, unfortunate circumstances, and just plain bad luck.

Two psychological constructs lie at the heart of understanding personal control: causal attribution and explanatory style. The following paragraphs define and elaborate on these terms. This discussion introduces the two basic phenomena that make personal control beliefs so important—learned helplessness (the phenomenon students show upon losing personal control) and learned mastery (the phenomenon students show upon gaining personal control).

Causal Attributions

A *causal attribution* is an explanation of why a particular outcome came to pass (Weiner, 1986). It is the reason a student uses to explain an outcome (winning or losing, passing or failing, being accepted or rejected). For instance, the statement, "I failed the exam because it was just too difficult," specifies an outcome (failure) and its causal attribution (task difficulty).

Countless reasons explain life's outcomes, but students use five attributions most often: ability, effort, task difficulty, strategy, and luck (Levin & Marshall, 1993). Many additional attributions exist beyond these five (mood; illness or injury; the weather; today's horoscope; the help, hindrance, or bias of others; and so on). Any list of causal attributions can quickly become overwhelming, so researchers organize all possible attributions into three dimensions: (1) internal versus external, (2) stable versus unstable, and (3) controllable versus uncontrollable. The internal-versus-external dimension organizes attributions into those that exist within the person (e.g., intelligence) versus those that exist within the environment (e.g., help from others). The stable-versus-unstable dimension organizes attributions into those that exist on a rather permanent basis (e.g., personality traits) versus those that exist on a transient basis (e.g., moods). The controllable versus uncontrollable dimension organizes attributions into those in which the performer can take personal responsibility (e.g., personal effort) versus those in which he or she cannot (e.g., luck). (Global versus specific is a fourth dimension, but this dimension applies more to the experience of clinical depression that it does to student motivation.)

TABLE 6-1 Ability and Effort Categorized within the Three Attributional Dimensions

Causal Dimensions	Ability	Effort
Internal vs. external	Internal	Internal
Stable vs. unstable	Stable	Unstable
Controllable vs. uncontrollable	Uncontrollable	Controllable

For illustration, Table 6-1 categorizes the two attributions of ability and effort within these three dimensions of causal attribution. Ability and effort are the two attributions students use most to explain their school-related outcomes (Graham, 1994; Weiner, 1979). Perhaps the reader can categorize other attributions along these three dimensions as well (e.g., *strategy* would be internal-unstable-controllable; *task difficulty* would be external-stable-uncontrollable; *racism* would be external-stable-uncontrollable, and so on).

Explanatory Style (Observational Activity 6.1)

Explanatory style is a cognitive personality variable that reflects the habitual manner in which people explain the cause of bad events that befall them (Peterson & Seligman, 1984). Bad events befall everyone, yet people explain life's setbacks with attributions that vary in their internality (internal vs. external), stability (stable vs. unstable), and controllability (controllable vs. uncontrollable). So explanatory style represents a personality characteristic in how individuals typically or habitually explain life's outcomes. A *pessimistic* explanatory style occurs as the tendency to explain bad events with attributions that are internal, stable, and uncontrollable (e.g., "I lost the game because I am an uncoordinated klutz"). An *optimistic* explanatory style occurs as the tendency to explain bad events with attributions that are external, unstable, and controllable (e.g., "I lost because my opponent cheated").

When students face educational frustrations and failures and have a pessimistic explanatory style, they respond to such setbacks in a passive, fatalistic manner (Peterson & Barrett, 1987). Unfortunately for us all, frustrations and setbacks are a part of education as every student runs into his or her share of disappointing grades, uncompleted assignments, confusing and misplaced textbooks, unprepared presentations, writer's block, locked library doors, unintelligible lectures, and so on. Academically successful students react to such difficulties with renewed effort and improved strategies, but academically unsuccessful students react to these same difficulties with a passive listlessness. Pessimistic explanatory style enters into this picture because it is the cognitive personality characteristic that predisposes students to attribute setbacks and failures to factors that are pervasive, far-reaching, and from the self (i.e., internal, stable, and uncontrollable), the pattern of attributions that lead students to a passive approach to studying and learning (Peterson & Barrett, 1987).

Mastery versus Helplessness Orientations

Over time, students' explanatory styles foster in them increasingly distinct motivational orientations. A pessimistic explanatory style leads to a helpless motivational orientation, whereas an optimistic explanatory style leads to a mastery motivational orientation. Mastery-oriented children persist in the face of failure and try to solve difficult problems; helpless-oriented children quit in the face of failure and try to avoid difficult problems (Diener & Dweck, 1978; Dweck & Repucci, 1973). Helpless-oriented children tend to quit in the face of failure because of their pervasive tendency to explain failure with a low-ability attribution. Given the mix of failure and a low-ability attribution (which is an internal, stable, mostly uncontrollable attribution), quitting makes a lot of sense whereas increasing effort does not. When a student lacks ability, failure becomes an insurmountable problem from which the student gains little by trying hard. Mastery-oriented children, on the other hand, resist making low-ability attributions in the face of failure. Instead, they engage in self-instructions that function as strategies to overcome the failure. Mastery-oriented children see their failures as controllable (via increased effort, improved strategies, etc.) and therefore surmountable. In sum, helpless-oriented children focus on the cause of their failures (lack of ability) and give up, whereas mastery-oriented children focus on the remedies for failure (self-instruction and high effort) and try harder (Diener & Dweck, 1978).

Learned Helplessness

When students experience uncontrollable events and when that experience leads to an expectation that future events will also be uncontrollable, potentially profound disruptions in motivation, emotion, and learning occur. This phenomenon is called learned helplessness, because the individual learns through interacting with his environment that he is helpless to influence it. Learned helplessness is the polar opposite of learned mastery (Peterson, Maier, & Seligman, 1993) or learned optimism (Seligman, 1990). Learned helplessness theory consists of three essential components: contingency, cognition, and behavior (Peterson et al., 1993).

Components of Learned Helplessness

Contingency
Contingency refers to the objective relationship between a person's behavior and the outcomes he or she experiences. This term describes a characteristic of

environments (e.g., classrooms, homes) and expresses the extent to which human behavior does or does not influence environmental outcomes, as expressed in the following continuum:

←——→

Uncontrollable Outcomes   Controllable Outcomes
(Outcomes occur on a noncontin-   (Outcomes occur in synchronization
gent, random basis)   with a student's actions)

Take a moment to consider the objective contingencies that exist for the following situations: having a traffic accident, catching the flu, graduating from high school, gaining weight, getting a parking ticket, getting yelled at by a parent, getting a job at the local newspaper, suffering a flat tire, becoming a professional athlete, getting cancer, winning the lottery, winning a tennis match, and being class valedictorian. To understand contingency, ask: "To what extent does a person's intentional actions exert influence over each of these outcomes?" The question asks how much influence the average person's behavior contributes to whether or not she has a traffic accident, whether or not she catches the flu, whether or not she graduates from college, and so forth.

Cognition

The cognitions central to learned helplessness are perceptions, attributions, and expectancies. These cognitions are the mental events that intervene between a person's experiences of actual, *objective* environmental contingencies and his or her *subjective* understanding of those environmental contingencies. A person's mental representation may or may not be the same as the objective environmental contingency; in fact, subjective understanding is always off by some margin of error. Perceptions are inherently incomplete, biased, and distorted; attributions come from perceptions, past experience, and personality characteristics; and expectancies come from attributions and a host of uniquely personal factors (e.g., one's ability, prior experiences, hopes, and fears). Thus, there is a good deal of cognitive intervention between objective environmental contingencies and our subjective understanding of personal control.

Perhaps the best way to illustrate the difference between objective environmental contingencies and subjective personal control beliefs is to ask you to once again consider the examples from the paragraph above. This time, however, generate two sets of expectancies. First, ask yourself what the census data would say about the likelihood for the average American of your age, sex, race, and so on, of being in a traffic accident, catching the flu, graduating from high school, and so on. Census information would correspond, roughly, to the objective contingencies that exist in the world. Next, ask yourself what you believe to be personally true for your odds of a traffic accident, catching the flu, and so on. Your personal expectancies correspond to your subjective personal control beliefs. The point is that these two sets of expectancies would differ on numerous occasions, because people not only use objective information about the world to formulate their person → outcome expectancies, they also rely on their perceptions, attributions, and expectancies. Thus, while the census data might say that one out of 40 college students will have a traffic accident this year, any one driver may optimistically expect the odds on a personal traffic accident to be one in a million (because she believes she drives with greater ability than others, knows more about driving, pays closer attention, has better reflexes, etc.).

Behavior

Learned helplessness–related behavior refers to the student's relative passivity versus activity in coping with situations that are potentially controllable. Coping responses fall somewhere within the following continuum:

←	→
Passive, gives up,	Assertive coping,
withdraws from participation	high activity

Passivity, giving up, and withdrawing typify a listless, demoralized coping effort, whereas assertive coping and high activity typify a planful, optimistic, and mastery-oriented effort. To continue the example of traffic accidents, catching the flu, and the like to its conclusion, I ask you to locate your own probable coping effort in response to each of these possible situations. Imagine yourself trying to find a job, prevent cancer, win a tennis match, or control your body weight, and ask where along the passive-to-assertive coping continuum your behavior falls. Unproductive and exaggerated passivity is the hallmark symptom of learned helplessness. The student who gives up on studying, the adolescent who quits calling people for dates, the job seeker who no longer fills out employment applications, and the teacher who gives up on teaching difficult students all manifest the listless coping behavior that characterizes helplessness.

Learned Helplessness Deficits

Learned helplessness occurs when students experience uncontrollable events and that experience leads them to expect that future events will also be uncontrollable. Once it occurs, helplessness produces potentially profound disruptions in motivation, emotion, and learning.

Motivational Deficit

The motivational deficit of learned helplessness is a decreased willingness to initiate any voluntary response to cope with an allegedly uncontrollable situation. Typically, when people expect that their behaviors influence their outcomes and when they care about those outcomes, they willingly behave to bring those desired outcomes to pass. That is, when students expect that taking notes in class will increase their chance of making a good grade on a test and when they care about the grades they make, then those students will willingly take notes in class. When students come to expect that note taking exerts no control whatsoever over the grades they make, then their willingness to take notes decreases dramatically. Such students ask, "Why try? Why take notes?" When people forfeit their willingness to try to influence life's outcomes, they show learned helplessness' motivational deficit.

Emotional Deficit

The emotional deficit of learned helplessness manifests itself through lethargic, depressive affect in situations that otherwise would call for energy-mobilizing affect. Typically, people react to aversive events with energizing emotions such as anger and frustration. That is, a student who expects that studying produces good grades but then fails the exam will react to the failure with emotional anger and frustration. When so aroused to action, the student channels these emotions into studying twice as hard or thinking of new and improved studying strategies for the next exam. However, when the student becomes convinced that she has little control over upcoming events, then she will react not with anger and frustration but with depression and listlessness. Depression is justifiably a deficit because it is a maladaptive, self-defeating, energy-depleting, cognitively exhausting emotional reaction to potentially controllable environments (Seligman, Abramson, Semmel, & von Baeyer, 1979). When people respond to potentially controllable environments with depressive affect, they show learned helplessness' emotional deficit.

Learning Deficit

The learning deficit of helplessness is the cultivation of a pessimistic learning set that retards (i.e., interferes with) the student's capability to learn new response–outcome contingencies. Typically, when students find themselves in potentially controllable situations, they pay attention to and learn about the extent of their personal control. That is, students who think grades are controllable outcomes pay attention to and readily learn which behaviors lead to good grades: Does studying help? Does being nice help? Does class participation help? Does turning in one's homework help? When a student comes to expect little control over an outcome, however, a pessimistic learning set interferes with new learning about how he might effectively exert control in that situation. A pessimistic learning set is essentially an assumption that no matter what one does, control will not be possible. With such a pessimistic assumption, students dismiss instances of apparent control as "a fluke," or a "happy accident." That is, the student with a pessimistic learning set fails to notice when studying, being nice, participating in class, and turning in homework influence his grading outcomes. When people show a delayed or retarded ability to learn how to influence controllable environments, they show learned helplessness' learning deficit.

Learned Helplessness as a Process

Students do not suddenly become helpless. Rather, learned helplessness occurs as a process over time. Figure 6-1 illustrate's Wortman and Brehm's (1975) model of how helplessness occurs over time. When students enter a new, potentially controllable environment, they invariably have some expectation of control over the outcomes in that situation (point a). Upon encountering a first experience of no control, students still hold fast to their prior expectation of control and feel an increased motivation to exert control in the situation. That is, after a first encounter of no control, students typically try harder than they did before. Upon encountering a second consecutive experience of no control, students continue to hold fast to their prior expectations of control; continue to feel a strong motivation to exert control; and show active, assertive coping behaviors. Wortman and Brehm (1975) refer to this phenomenon of increased motivation in the face of uncontrollable events as *reactance,* as in reacting against

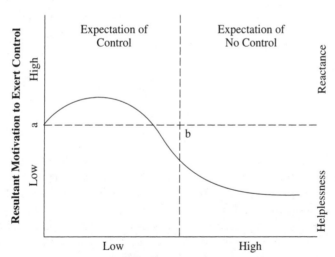

FIGURE 6-1   Illustrative Model of Learned Helplessness as a Process

Source: Adapted with permission from Wortman, C. B., & Brehm, J. W. (1975). Responses to uncontrollable outcomes: An integration of reactance theory and the learned helplessness model. In L. Berkowitz (Ed.), *Advances in experimental social psychology* (Vol. 8, pp. 277–336). New York: Academic Press.

the loss of personal control. After some number of experiences of no control, however, people's expectations of control, their motivation to exert control, and their assertiveness in coping reach a plateau, level off, and eventually decline. If the experiences of no control continue, then, at some point (point b), the student will lose his or her expectation of control and start to endorse an expectation of no control. When one's expectation shifts from control to no control, then motivation to exert control decreases and coping behaviors become increasingly passive and listless. After the expectation of no control replaces the expectation of control, the experience of learned helplessness begins.

To understand the essence of Figure 6-1, consider the example of a mathematics teacher who tries to teach a middle school class how to solve geometry problems. The teacher begins the semester expecting to be able to influence control over whether or not the students learn geometry (point *a*). Upon receiving the first bit of information that his teaching goes for naught as students fail to show any learning of geometry, the teacher holds fast to his expectation of control and feels an increased motivation to teach geometry. After receiving a second bit of information that his teaching goes for naught, he will continue to hold fast to his expectation of control; will want to teach; and will do so in an active, assertive, mastery-oriented fashion. But after he receives a continuous flow of information that his teaching goes for naught, his expectations are in jeopardy of changing from control to no control. If the uncontrollable outcomes continue, his expectation slides into one of no control, his motivation to influence students' learning wanes, and his teaching efforts slacken and become increasingly passive (point *b*).

Mikulincer (1988) demonstrated such a scenario of events experimentally. Mikulincer first gave undergraduate students (in an experiment) differential amounts of experience with uncontrollable outcomes (to manipulate their expectancies of control). One group of students experienced one unsolvable problem, a second group experienced a series of four consecutive unsolvable problems, and a control group received no problems. Mikulincer then gave each group one potentially solvable problem. The students who first had one unsolvable problem performed best on the solvable problem, the students who had no unsolvable problems performed next best, and the students who had the series of unsolvable problems performed the worst. The S-shaped curve in Figure 6-1 illustrates this pattern. A small dose of uncontrollable outcomes increases motivation to exert control and enhances performance, but a large dose of uncontrollable outcomes decreases motivation and impairs performance.

Attribution Theory of Learned Helplessness

Repeated experience with uncontrollable outcomes is one fundamental cause of learned helplessness (Seligman, 1975). That is, persistent experience with uncontrollable outcomes leads people to develop an expectation of *non*control, and this expectation produces learned helplessness deficits. But, people do not *always* develop helplessness after learning there is nothing they can do to exert control over life's outcomes (Tennen & Eller, 1977). The causal attribution the student makes following a lack of control is a second crucial determinant of helplessness (Peterson et al., 1993). For helplessness to occur, it is not enough that one expect outcomes to be uncontrollable; one must also perceive an inability to surmount the uncontrollable outcomes. In a school setting, for instance, many students experience failure, but it is only those students who perceive themselves unable to triumph over those failures that experience helplessness. Students who fail but believe that they can eventually surmount failure do not show helplessness deficits (Dweck, 1975).

Reformulated Model of Learned Helplessness

In the "reformulated model of learned helplessness," the individual's causal analysis of why outcomes are uncontrollable is just as important as is the experience of uncontrollability (Abramson, Seligman, & Teasdale, 1978). That is, helplessness has two necessary causes: (1) experience with uncontrollable outcomes and (2) a pessimistic explanatory style. This reformulated model of helplessness speaks to teachers, because although a teacher often can do little about a student's experience with uncontrollable outcomes, she often can do relatively much about how the student comes to understand and interpret why those outcomes occur.

When people experience outcomes to be beyond their personal control, they ask themselves why the environment is unresponsive. When such an analysis leads them to internal, stable, and uncontrollable attributions for a lack of personal control, then they stand at risk of suffering learned helplessness. For instance, a student who explains his poor academic performance by saying he is not clever enough makes an internal-stable-uncontrollable attribution that makes him vulnerable to helplessness. A student who explains his poor performance because of temporary family problems and distractions, makes an external-unstable-somewhat controllable attribution that, in effect, exempts him from suffering helplessness, because he can expect to perform well once the family solves its temporary problems. Internal-stable-controllable attributions for a lack of control send the message that failures and setbacks are the student's fault, that a lack of control will continue into the future, and that there is little the student can do about it. External-unstable-controllable attributions for a lack of control, on the other hand, send the message that failures and setbacks follow from unfortunate environmental forces, will not continue into the future, and are subject to potential adjustment.

Attributional Retraining Programs

Students learn attributions. Because students learn attributions, it stands to reason that anyone who learns to make maladaptive attributions to explain life's outcomes (i.e., pessimistic explanatory style) can also learn to make adaptive attributions (i.e., optimistic explanatory style). Educators refer to the therapy-like process of teaching students to consider a more adaptive at-tributional analysis to explain school's aversive events as "attributional retraining."

The goal of attributional retraining programs is to alter the student's understanding of why failures and setbacks occur (Andrews & Debus, 1978; Craske, 1988; Dweck, 1975; Zoeller, Mahoney, & Weiner, 1983). One attribu-tion for failure is, of course, a lack of ability (or intelligence). An ability attribution for failure, however, has the disadvantage of interfering with the student's future effort and performance, because ability attributions are both stable and uncontrollable. Attributions of low ability therefore leave the student asking herself, "Why try?" because if one is incapable of success (because of low ability) then she will fail whether or not she exerts effort. Further, low-abil-ity attributions instigate a self-defeating cycle in which perceptions of inability both precede and follow from reduced effort and poor performance levels (Butkowsky & Willows, 1980).

Fortunately, other valid attributions for failure exist that can explain failure equally well, if not better. Lack of effort (Dweck, 1975), lack of an effective strategy (Anderson & Jennings, 1980), and lack of experience (Wilson & Linville, 1982) are all attributions that are unstable and under volitional control. Once students understand failure is both unstable and under voluntary control, then failure is no longer an insurmountable, uncontrollable ogre of an obstacle. Retraining students to make nonability attributions for their failures leads them to improvements in task persistence and performance (Anderson & Jennings, 1980; Dweck, 1975; Wilson & Linville, 1982).

One academic difficulty is poor grades, a difficulty that sometimes leads to the extreme in listless coping—academic truancy and dropping out. Wilson and Linville (1982, 1985) initiated an attributional retraining program with college students who performed poorly in their first semester in college. The researchers divided their pool of first-year college students into two groups—one group received the attributional retraining program (experimental group) and the other did not (control group). In the attributional retraining program, the researchers showed the first-year students GPA information and videotaped testimonial interviews from upperclass students that confirmed that GPAs increase systematically each year in college. The information pointed out that all students experience academic problems, but these problems get easier to solve for upperclass students as they learn the ropes, adjust to work demands, schedule study time, overcome homesickness, learn where the library is and what its resources are, and so on. The researchers trusted that this information would lead students to infer that the obstacles to their academic difficulties were temporary rather than permanent (i.e., unstable rather than stable). In contrast, students in the control group who did not receive the attributional retraining were prone to blame themselves (i.e., their lack of ability and intelligence) for their troubles. The researchers followed all of the first-year students until the end of their sophomore year. As the researchers suspected, attributionally retrained students were more likely to stay in school, expected to do better academically, and improved their GPAs (Wilson & Linville, 1982).

Another researcher instigated an attributional retaining program for primary-grade children who showed a substantial deterioration in performance following failure (Craske, 1988). In the attributional retraining program, Craske encouraged students to view failures as the result of a lack of effort and to view subsequent successes as more likely with increased effort. The task was mathematics (computing sums), and the researcher measured the success of the program by observing each student's effortful versus quitting response to a failure experience as well as by listening to their attributions as to why they failed. For students in the attributional retraining program, they were less likely to invoke a low-ability attribution for their failures, and the effect of failure was significantly less disruptive than it was for students not experiencing the retraining program. In fact, the attributional retraining students actually showed *improved* performance following failure. This latter finding is particularly impressive because it implies that the attributional retraining not only inoculated students against failure's demoralizing effects, it even produced a flair of positive motivation (Craske, 1988).

Perhaps the most ambitious attributional retraining effort to date attempted to reduce the peer-directed aggression of preadolescent boys (Hudley & Graham, 1993). Hudley and Graham reasoned that much of preadolescent boys' aggression occurred because of a sense that a peer inflicted harm "on purpose." For example, a fight might start after one boy gets bumped while standing in line and assumes that the bumper meant to do the act. Being harmed is a social outcome; when a boy cites the hostile intent of other boy as the cause of his injury, then he uses a controllable attribution to explain the harm done. The researchers had a group of aggression-prone boys participate in an intervention program designed to alter their biased attributions of controllability. Through role playing, group discussions, and other exercises, the researchers trained the children to discriminate between accidental, ambiguous, and hostile peer intent. The training also featured developing the ability to make causal attributions of nonresponsibility (i.e., uncontrollability) when appropriate. Following six weeks of training, the experimenters presented the aggression-prone boys with a series of peer provocation scenarios (e.g., another kid steps on and tears your homework paper) and assessed perceived intentionally, anticipated anger, and likely behavioral response to the harm done. Compared to the aggression-prone boys in the control group (who did not participate in the training), the attributional retrained aggression-prone boys made more uncontrollable attributions, felt less anger, and preferred less hostile behavioral responses to these interpersonal conflicts.

Learned Mastery

Since a person with a pessimistic explanatory style underestimates the extent of her personal control, it stands to reason that a person with an optimistic explanatory style overestimates her personal control. Overestimating personal control does indeed occur in students (Voelkl, 1993; Illardi, Reeve, & Nix, 1994), and it leads to a full range of positive outcomes, including a positive self-view (Voelkl, 1993), high academic performance (Illardi et al., 1994), and an optimistic view of the future (Taylor & Brown, 1988).

Over time, a student's patterned history of taking too much credit for successes (via internal-stable-controllable attributions) and too little blame for failures (via external-unstable-uncontrollable attributions) breeds a self-conception that she has more control over outcomes that is actually the case. Of course, self-serving attributions are not an inherited gift. Rather, students learn to be biased and to make self-serving attributions. When they do so, they show *learned mastery*.

There are numerous psychological processes at work in learning mastery beliefs (Taylor & Brown, 1988), but two are essential. First, when a person expects to produce a certain outcome and that outcome then comes to fruition, then that person typically overestimates the degree to which he or she was instrumental in bringing the outcome to pass (Miller & Ross, 1975). For instance, victorious athletes are notorious for their sweeping attributions of personal control (i.e., effort, ability), even when logic dictates that the performance of one's opponent contributed at least half of the outcome's explanation (Spink, 1978). Second, people seem to arm themselves with a repertoire of excuses, denials, and self-deceptions that allow them to discount, or even ignore, life's failures (Lazarus, 1983; Sackeim, 1983; Tennen & Affleck, 1990). If sufficiently immunized against failure, then all that is left for the person to pay attention to—and take credit for—are life's successes. Though such learned mastery carries an air of delusional optimism, it does exert positive effects on students' motivation. That is, students with inflated beliefs of personal control work harder and persist longer than do their peers (Felson, 1984). Working harder and persisting longer do pay off in terms of academic success, so an optimistic view of personal control actually produces the behaviors and successful outcomes that eventually confirm the validity of the student's optimistic mastery beliefs (Illardi et al., 1994).

In thinking about the educational implications of learned mastery, we might wonder if the belief in extreme personal control is better than the belief in moderate personal control (Taylor & Brown, 1994). Some studies show that the more optimistic students' personal control beliefs are, the better they perform in school (Illardi et al., 1994; Voelkl, 1993). Yet, I cannot help think there must be an "optimal margin of illusion" in personal control beliefs (Baumeister, 1989). Teachers, like environments in general, tolerate (and encourage) strong personal control beliefs, but they draw the line on and sanction overly optimistic, delusional beliefs (Taylor, 1989).

Suggestions on Preventing and Reversing Learned Helplessness

Learned helplessness is both preventable (Altmaier & Happ, 1985; Hirt & Genshaft, 1981; Jones, Nation, & Massad, 1977) and reversible (Klein & Seligman, 1976; Miller & Norman, 1981; Orbach & Hadas, 1982). To prevent or reverse helplessness, teachers must first understand its causes. Students experience helplessness because (1) the environment is nonresponsive to their behavioral initiatives and (2) the student uses a pessimistic explanatory style to explain classroom frustrations and failures (Peterson et al., 1993). These causal dynamics suggest two major avenues of reversing helplessness: Change the responsiveness of the environment, and change the pessimistic attributions one makes following school's negative and uncontrollable outcomes.

Changing a Nonresponsive Environment to a Responsive One

Occasionally, students find themselves in a nonresponsive classroom, school, relationship, or home environment. That is, sometimes the outcomes students seek are truly outside their realm of influence and control (e.g., a student trying to earn a high grade from a prejudiced teacher, a child who gets sick riding the school bus each morning and afternoon, or a child who wishes her parents would quit fighting). In such cases, the student's efforts are best directed not so much at changing personal behaviors as they are at changing the environment itself. In such situations, the situationally appropriate action would not necessarily be greater effort to enhance performance as it would be an attempt to restructure his or her surrounding environment through negotiation, bargaining, confrontation coping, help seeking, coalition formation, and the like.

Changing Attributional Style: Attribution Training and Retraining

Attribution training involves the cultivation of optimistic attributions, such as making internal-stable-controllable attributions for successes and external-unstable-uncontrollable attributions for failure. Students who hold optimistic attributional styles, are somewhat immunized against the demoralizing effects of life's failures (Seligman, 1990). Immunization against helplessness is the attempt to prevent helplessness before it occurs. Immunization is a developmental process in which parents and teachers "raise" students to experience early control and mastery over their environments. It often involves giving students small doses of early failure experiences that are quickly followed up by training and coaching that enables them to cope successfully with and therefore overcome the failure. The focus of such immunization is the effort to encourage people to see connections between their behaviors and their outcomes (Klein & Seligman, 1976). The logic of early immunization is to foster personal control beliefs that are strong enough to prevent the onset of learned helplessness, even in the face of nonresponsive environments in the future. Research confirms that providing people with early experiences with controllability immunizes them against the effects of uncontrollable environments (Altmaier & Happ, 1985; Dyck & Breen, 1978; Eckelman & Dyck, 1979; Hirt & Genshaft, 1981; Jones, Nation, & Massad, 1977; Thornton & Powell, 1974).

Sometimes, however, students do make pessimistic attributions for their difficulties, pessimistic attributions that leave them vulnerable to helplessness. Attributional retraining programs act as therapeutic attempts to reverse helplessness that has already occurred. Next, I discuss such therapy within a two-part strategy to retrain students' pessimistic attributions: First, extend the range of possible attributions students make for their failures. Second, persuade students to change their original, pessimistic attribution for a revised, optimistic attribution.

Extending Students' Limited Range of Possible Attributions

The first step in reversing students' pessimistic attributions is to extend the range of possible attributions that explain the problematic academic setback or failure. For instance, after a failed exam, a student might say "it's because I can't read as fast as everyone else." Given such pessimism, the teacher might suggest alternative, yet equally valid, rival attributions, such as an ineffective strategy, insufficient effort, lack of proper training or experience, high task difficulty, and so on. Earlier in the chapter's discussion on attributional retraining programs, several studies relied on extending the attributional possibilities of troubled students, as in the Wilson and Linville (1982) study with first-year college students learning to attribute their poor first-year academic performances to temporary adjustment problems.

Retraining Unnecessarily Pessimistic Attributions

In practice, the fundamental objective in attributional retraining programs is to undermine students' tendencies to make stable, uncontrollable attributions for their academic difficulties and to encourage students' tendencies to make unstable, controllable attributions. Stability and controllability attributions allow students to predict the future of their academic difficulties, "Will these failures continue, or are they only a temporary phenomenon? And if they continue, how much influence to affect the outcomes can I exert?" Stable, uncontrollable attributions lead to the conclusion that failure is a permanent, irreversible condition; unstable, controllable attributions lead to the conclusion that failure is a temporary, reversible condition. Encouraging students to attribute setbacks to temporary, reversible causes increases future performance expectancies, decreases anxiety and helplessness, and ultimately leads to better academic performance (Wilson & Linville, 1982).

Forsterling (1985) reviewed the procedural techniques used in fifteen different attributional retraining programs and concluded that researchers accomplish retraining in one of three ways:

1. *Persuasion:* First, a student performs a task, and then an expert commentator verbalizes the desired attribution (e.g., Zoeller et al., 1983). Persuasion enters into the picture as the expert tries to convince the student of the validity of the desired attribution.
2. *Behavior modification:* In this method, desired responses are reinforced. In the attributional retraining version of behavior modification, the teacher encourages students to make attributions of ability, effort, task difficulty, and luck for a failure but verbally reinforces only the unstable, uncontrollable attribution (i.e., luck; Andrews & Debus, 1978).
3. *Information:* The previously discussed studies by Wilson and Linville (1982, 1985) in which the researchers informed first-year students that most students increased their GPAs over the years exemplify informational methods for attribution retraining.

Each technique has proved successful in attributional retraining, but it remains an open question whether one technique works better than another (Forsterling, 1985).

Protecting the Ability Attribution by Avoiding Inadvertent Communications of Low-Ability Cues

Students perceive a strong link between their abilities and how much control they can exert over their environments. To infer whether they have high or low ability, students rely on information from prior performance history ("I've made all Cs in the past, so my ability must be about average.") and social normative information ("Compared to my classmates, I am doing well above average—so I must be smart"; Kelley & Michela, 1980). In addition, students use a third source of information to infer their level of ability: teacher-provided feedback (Graham, 1994). Some teacher feedback is direct and transparently obvious ("Oh, you are just so talented!). Other teacher feedback, however, occurs more subtly. Graham (1994) conducted a program of research to investigate how teachers (unintentionally) communicate messages of low ability to their students through their verbal responses, facial expressions, and postural gestures. For Graham (1994), teachers communicate low-ability messages to their students by (1) communicating pity following failure; (2) offering praise following success, particularly at easy tasks; and (3) providing unsolicited offers of help (Graham, 1990, 1994).

Pity Following Failure as a Low-Ability Cue

Teachers show pity and sympathy to students who fail because of a lack of ability, but they show anger to students who fail because of a lack of effort (Weiner, Graham, Stern, & Lawson, 1982). Once students catch on to this pattern, they use the teachers emotional displays to infer the cause of their own failures. Graham (1984) demonstrated this experimentally by having sixth-grade students fail at a puzzle-solving task while a female teacher communicated pity to one group of students and anger to a second group. The experimenters then asked the puzzle-solvers individually why they thought they were unsuccessful. When the teacher expressed anger, children attributed their failure to a lack of effort; when the teacher expressed pity, children attributed their failure to a lack of ability.

Praise Following (Easy) Success as a Low-Ability Cue

Teachers give high praise and low blame when students expend high effort, whereas teachers give low praise and high blame when students expend low effort (Weiner & Kukla, 1970). In another of her studies (Barker & Graham, 1987), Graham had a pair of students solve relatively easy math problems while a teacher enthusiastically praised one student but not the other. A second pair of students failed the easy math problems, and the teacher criticized one student but not the other. All these performances were on videotape, so the experimenter showed the videotapes to elementary-aged children and asked them to rate the ability and effort of the four students they observed. Students rated the praised student as having lower ability than the nonpraised student and the noncriticized student as having lower ability than the criticized student. These results were particular true for the older children.

Provision of (Unsolicited) Help as a Low-Ability Cue

Students believe that people need more help when the cause of their need is an uncontrollable factor (e.g., low ability) than when the cause is a controllable factor (e.g., low effort) (Schmidt & Weiner, 1988). Graham conducted yet another study to determine whether or not a teacher's unsolicited help to a student who is trying to solve a problem communicates a message of low ability (Graham & Barker, 1990). The researchers had two students work to solve a set of math problems and arranged for a teacher to circulate around the room, moving from desk to desk as she might in a typical classroom. For one student, the teacher stopped and offered help ("Let me give you a hint. Don't forget to carry your tens."). For the other student, the teacher stopped, glanced over the student's shoulder, but did not provide a helpful hint. The experimenter then asked a group of elementary school children to infer each student's ability. Regardless of age, elementary school children rated the helped student as having lower ability than the nonhelped student. Of course, teacher assistance, sympathy, and praise are positive instructional behaviors, but the point here is that well-intentioned teacher feedback *can* communicate low ability cues and thereby undermine one of the core attributional beliefs on which students base their beliefs of personal control (Graham, 1990, 1994).

Conclusion

Personal control beliefs explain instances in which students show strong, active, and assertive behavioral effort and persistence. Personal control beliefs also explain times when students throw up their hands in exasperation, turn markedly passive, and give up trying to cope. Learned mastery beliefs produce the former reaction; learned helplessness beliefs produce the latter reaction.

Two chief skills a teacher can posses for diagnosing students' vulnerability to helplessness are the abilities to recognize when a classroom situation is or is not controllable (from the students' point of view) and when students posses a relatively pessimistic explanatory style. To make their classrooms responsive and controllable environments, teachers can begin by asking questions such as these: On what basis do students receive good grades? On what basis do students get my attention? On what basis do students receive praise or punishment? On what basis do student receive help and assistance? Because a difference exists between actual and perceived control, teachers might also consider explicitly communicating to students exactly how they can control such outcomes (i.e., explain which behaviors do and which do not produce desirable outcomes). As for explanatory style, there are interesting ways teachers can develop the ability to hear, interpret, and classify students' attributions as optimistic and pessimistic (e.g., Winter & Healy, 1981). People reveal their explanatory styles literally everyday as through the letters they write, the excuses they offer, and how they interpret the events around them. One way to develop the ear of the clinician is to listen carefully to the explanations people offer in the newspaper's editorials, advice columns, or personal advertisements. Musicians offer numerous explanations in the lyrics of their songs. Politicians offer interesting explanations in the speeches they make. Athletes give interesting interpretations for their sporting outcomes, as when asked "So, why did you lose this time?" Autobiographies are another rich source of understanding the reasons people offer to explain the events that life brings. The skills to learn are the abilities to translate the explanations people offer into (1) the attributional dimensions of internality, stability, and controllability (e.g., in an autobiography, a woman might explain her divorce by saying, "because for twenty years, he was a lazy, drunkard, do-nothing with his own stubborn mind!" which I hear as an external-stable-un-controllable attribution) and then (2) into general attributional styles (this example suggests a rather optimistic explanatory style).

A final point is that students give up for two, not just one, essential reasons. Students become passive and give up when they come to perceive a lack of personal control. Students also give up trying because they believe themselves to be incapable of executing the behaviors they know control the outcomes they desire (e.g., I know that if I told jokes and became the life of the party then people would like and accept me, but I lack the confidence—i.e., self-efficacy—to do those sorts of extraverted behaviors). These two separate sources of helplessness have different causes and carry different remedial implications (Bandura, 1982, 1986). To change efficacy-based helplessness requires building in the student particular skills, competencies, and resilient perceptions of self-efficacy. That is, the target for change is some aspect of the person, not the environment. To change personal control–based helplessness typically requires changing some aspect of the social environment (or changing some aspect of the person such as a pessimistic explanatory style). In instigating any remedial effort, however, a teacher notices the interdependent relationship that exists between self-efficacy expectations and personal control expectations. That is, most efforts to increase self-efficacy also produce increases in personal control because the skillfulness with which one interacts with any particular setting correlates with how responsive and benevolent that setting is. Thus, self-efficacy beliefs and personal control beliefs combine to empower students with the motivational resiliency to cope effectively and persistently with a world all too often characterized by biases, uncontrollability, and unresponsiveness.

Recommended Readings

Abramson, L. Y., Seligman, M. E. P., & Teasdale, J. D. (1978). Learned helplessness in humans: Critique and reformulation. *Journal of Abnormal Psychology, 87,* 49–74.

Andrews, G. R., & Debus, R. L. (1978). Persistence and the causal perception of failure: Modifying cognitive attributions. *Journal of Educational Psychology, 70,* 154–166.

Diener, C. I., & Dweck, C. S. (1978). An analysis of learned helplessness: Continuous changes in performance, strategy, and achievement cognitions following failure. *Journal of Personality and Social Psychology, 36,* 451–462.

Dweck, C. S. (1975). The role of expectancies and attributions in the alleviation of learned helplessness. *Journal of Personality and Social Psychology, 31,* 674–685.

Forsterling, F. (1985). Attribution retraining: A review. *Psychological Bulletin, 98,* 495–512.

Mikulincer, M. (1988). The relationship of probability of success and performance following failure: Reactance and helplessness effects. *Motivation and Emotion, 12,* 139–152.

Peterson, C., & Barrett, L. C. (1987). Explanatory style and academic achievement among university freshmen. *Journal of Personality and Social Psychology, 53,* 603–607.

Weiner, B. (1979). A theory of motivation for some classroom experiences. *Journal of Educational Psychology, 71,* 3–25.

Wilson, T. D., & Linville, P. W. (1982). Improving the academic performance of college freshmen with attributional techniques. *Journal of Personality and Social Psychology, 42,* 367–376.

Zoeller, C. J., Mahoney, G., & Weiner, B. (1983). Effects of attribution training on the assembly task performance of mentally retarded adults. *American Journal of Mental Deficiency, 88,* 109–112.

Observational Activities

Observational Activity 6.1: Understanding Explanatory Style

The purpose of this interview is to gain an understanding of explanatory style and how it affects students' voluntary coping efforts. Before you begin, you will need to read Peterson and Barrett's article on explanatory style in the *Journal of Personality and Social Psychology* (see Peterson & Barrett, 1987).

Interview two students separately. Each interview will last between thirty and forty minutes. During the first part of each interview, ask questions that allow you to assess each person's explanatory style. Before your first interview, prepare a list of possible educational outcomes that are appropriate for that student (something along the lines of Peterson and Barrett's situations listed in their Table 1). For a college student, for instance, I might ask questions like these:

1. Imagine you just failed a final examination in a course within your major. Why do you think you failed?
2. Imagine you just received a letter from a scholarship committee announcing they selected someone else for the academic scholarship you very much wanted. Why did you get turned down?
3. Imagine you had a paper due on a particular date. When that date came, you did not hand the paper. Why not?

During the second half of each interview, assess each student's coping efforts and coping style. Repeat the above questions, but instead of asking students for an explanation for the outcome, ask them for their way of handling the situation ("What would you *do* if you failed the final examination?"). Also, ask about their emotional reactions ("How would you feel about failing the examination?").

With your interviews completed, answer the following questions for each student: Describe the student's explanatory style. Describe its dimensionality (internal/external, stable/unstable, controllable/uncontrollable). Describe the student's typical coping responses to failure. How consistent is the link for each student between explanatory style and willingness to exert coping responses? Does the person show any signs of learned helplessness? If so, why? If not, why not?

Observational Activity 6.2: Attributional Retraining

The twofold purpose of this interview is to (1) assess how easy or how difficult it is to change a student's outcome attribution and (2) gain experience using the techniques to do so. You will need to interview two students, and each interview will last about thirty to forty minutes.

Ask the student about his or her recent performance outcomes in school. Listen for both successes and failures, but mostly you will be probing for recent setbacks, disappointments, rejections, and failures—disappointing test scores, interpersonal rejections, athletic defeats, and the like. Ask why students believe they experienced one of the negative outcomes ("Johnny, why do you think you made such a low grade on Mr. Mudd's test last Friday?"). Listen carefully to the student's explanations and reasons. Listen for any instance of a pessimistic attribution (i.e., one that is internal-stable-uncontrollable), such as low ability or a performance-debilitating personality trait.

In the second part of the interview, try to attributionally retrain students to view the failure as a function of a more optimistic attribution (i.e., one that is external-unstable-controllable), such as low effort, poor strategy, or insufficient preparation. There are three major methods of attributional retraining, as discussed in the chapter: persuasion, behavior modification, and information. Pick out the two methods you think work best, and then try to attributionally retain the first student with one of the techniques and try to attributionally retrain the second student with a different technique.

After the interviews, answer the following questions: How common were pessimistic attributions? How common were optimistic attributions? How resistant were students to your attempt to change their attributional understanding of why they failed? Did one of the techniques seem to work better than the other? If so, why? All things considered, do you think attributional retraining is a good idea? Do you think attributional retraining can produce long-term changes in students' attributional styles, or do you think the effects are only for the short term?

7

Achievement Strivings

It's early evening and Kip weighs the pros and cons of working on his term paper, due in three days. On his desktop lie the term paper (a challenging task) and the television's remote control (a distractor task). As the night progresses, Kip contemplates which task to begin and how long to keep doing that task before switching to the other one (e.g., Blankenship, 1992). If Kip is achievement-oriented, once he begins the challenging term paper he will persist for a long duration of time, perhaps switching to television only upon completing the paper. If he does begin watching television, Kip will likely tire of its lack of challenge and return his attention to something more challenging. If Kip's motivation is to avoid failure, however, any beginning of the term paper will be interrupted quickly by the anxiety about failure and by the attraction and security of the distracting TV. Once he begins television viewing, Kip will watch for a long time, partly as a means to keep away from the challenging term paper. As we shall see, educational challenges put students into a risk-taking dilemma in which they must ask themselves, "What should I do—work hard and approach success or withhold effort and avoid failure?

Achievement Strivings

Achievement Motivation Defined

Achievement motivation is the driving force to do well relative to a standard of excellence (McClelland, Atkinson, Clark, & Lowell, 1953). *Standard of excellence* is a broad term that encompasses task-related, self-related, and other-related challenges (Heckhausen, 1967). A task-related standard of excellence involves performing a task well, such as writing a persuasive essay, painting a convincing landscape, or solving a math problem. A self-related standard of excellence involves performing better than done previously, as in exceeding last semester's GPA, improving one's typing speed, or running a mile quicker than ever before. An other-related standard of excellence involves performing better than another person or a group of others, as in making higher grades than your older brother, beating a tennis opponent, or becoming the school's valedictorian.

When facing standards of excellence, students' emotional reactions vary. Sometimes, students anticipate feeling pride and gratification from a job well done. Anticipating pride and gratification leads students to approach standards of excellence. Other times, however, students anticipate negative emotional reactions such as anxiety (Sarason, 1984; Schlenker & Leary, 1982), fear (Birney, Burdick, & Teevan, 1969), and defensiveness (Covington, 1984a). Anticipating anxiety, fear, and defensiveness leads students to avoid or withdraw from standards of excellence. Thus, *standards of excellence are double-edged swords,* as part of the student might cognitive and emotionally welcome an opportunity to seek out and persist after a standard of excellence while some other part of the student might simultaneously cognitive and emotionally fear such a threatening occasion. Thus, the teacher's attempt to facilitate achievement strivings in students is twofold: Encourage the tendency to approach a standard of excellence as well as overcome the tendency to avoid it.

Facilitating the Tendency to Approach Success

Before 1980, personality psychologists conducted most of the research on achievement strivings. Personality researchers conceptualize achievement strivings as a stable individual difference variable in which some people are dispositionally high in achievement motivation while others are dispositionally low (though most people lie somewhere in between; Atkinson, 1964). This research literature produced (and continues to produce) a wealth of knowledge about the antecedents, measurement, and behavioral implications of personality-based achievement strivings (for a review, see McClelland, 1985). By about 1980, however, educational researchers became dissatisfied with the portrayal of achievement motivation as a traitlike dispositional characteristic. Instead, educators focused on the achievement-related thoughts and beliefs (i.e., cognitions) people have in a particular social and cultural setting (i.e., school; Ames & Ames, 1984). Soon, educators embraced the idea that all students could show strong achievement behavior, provided they acquired achievement-related cognitions (i.e., perceptions of high ability, adoption of learning goals, high expectancies for success, strong values for achievement tasks, an optimistic attributional style, all discussed later). For educators, the critical objective was not to cultivate high need for achievement within the personality but, rather, to teach students ways of thinking that encourage their willingness to put forth high (rather than low) effort in achievement settings. So, in education, the focus of facilitating achievement strivings became the task of trying to promote high and persistent effort.

Perceptions of Ability

An intimate relationship exists between the perception of high ability and students' willingness to exert effort. Compared to students with a perception of low ability, students with a perception of high ability hold higher expectations for success (Eccles-Parsons et al., 1983; Volmer, 1986; Weiner & Potepan, 1970), persist longer on tasks in that domain (Felson, 1984; Phillips, 1984), experience greater intrinsic motivation (Harter, 1981), and perform more competently (Hansford & Hattie, 1982; Marsh, 1990; McCombs, 1986). Because students understand their ability levels in part from their performance accomplishments, a self-perpetuating cycle emerges in which high-ability perceptions fuel the beliefs and behaviors that cultivate high-ability perceptions (i.e., expectations for success, high persistence, intrinsic motivation, and competent performance).

The problem with perceptions of ability is that trying to perceive your own ability is like trying to see your reflection off the surface of a rippling pond. Ability is an elusive, fuzzy characteristic that each person knows only indirectly. Performances and accomplishments are indirect representatives of ability. Young children are particularly amateurish in perceiving their level of ability (Nicholls, 1979; Stipek, 1984). I call them amateurs because they not only have unrealistically lofty ability beliefs, but also because they fail to lower their ability beliefs after failure (Parsons & Ruble, 1977) and fail to consider their performances in relation to those of others (Ruble, Parsons, & Ross, 1976). By the third or fourth grade, however, children become more realistic in their perceptions of ability, largely because they pay increasing attention to objective indicators of their ability. After the third grade or so, all students rely on four sources of ability-knowing information: self-evaluations ("How much ability do I think I have?"), teacher evaluations ("How much ability does my teacher think I have?"), peer evaluations ("How much ability do my classmates think I have?"), and parental evaluations ("How much ability do my parents think I have?"). Together, personal, teacher, peer, and parental evaluations provide the student with the perspective she seeks to perceive her level of abilities (Felson, 1984; Rosenholtz & Rosenholtz, 1981).

In many classrooms, students, teachers, and classmates come to a collective consensus about an *ability hierarchy* in which they understand a clear rank order of ability levels among the students in the class. That is, teachers and students alike understand which student has the most ability, which student has the next most ability, and so on, all the way down to the student with the least ability.

Even among third-graders, practically all students agree with the statement, "Some kids are just smarter at most things than other kids are" (Simpson, 1981). In other classrooms, however, such an ability hierarchy is more ambiguous and less salient, to the point where it is not clear who are the high-ability students and who are the low-ability students. In such classrooms, some students seem to have the highest ability on one day while others seem to have the highest ability on another, just as some students seem to have the highest ability in one skill or subject while others seem to have the highest ability in another. When present, clear ability hierarchies produce debilitating and demoralizing effects on (perceived) low-ability students. Students with high ability experience little harm in such classrooms, but it is a motivationally disruptive experience for the low-ability students. Such students expect to fail on tasks of at least moderate difficulty, and more often than not wind up showing avoidance behaviors in classrooms with clear and salient ability hierarchies (Nicholls, 1984).

Research shows that three variables explain when ability hierarchies are most likely to emerge in any particular classroom (Rosenholtz & Rosenholtz, 1981; Rosenholtz & Simpson, 1984):

- Task differentiation
- Student autonomy
- Comparative assessment

Task differentiation exist on a continuum from unidimensional to multidimensional and refers to the number of different skills teachers ask students to perform and recognize as important. For instance, in a reading instruction classroom with low task differentiation, all students read and the teacher emphasizes the skill of reading; with high task differentiation, students read but they also perform and value other abilities, such as listening, speaking, imagining, and paraphrasing. *Student autonomy* refers to the freedom and flexibility each student senses in his or her decisions related to choice opportunities to pursue different tasks. In a low-autonomy classroom, all students work with a single reader; in a high-autonomy classroom, each student makes frequent decisions on which tasks and which skills to pursue ("What will I read?" "What skill will I work on—comprehension, oral production, vocabulary, reading speed?"). *Comparative assessment* refers to the extent to which teachers group students as a whole (or by ability level) to perform a single task and judge students' performances with frequent, visible, and comparative procedures such as letter grades. Alternatively, other classrooms feature individual work and rely on individually referenced standards (e.g., portfolios). In the first case, ability differences are visible, perhaps even obvious; in the second case, ability differences are less discernible, even to the point that students refrain from comparative assessments because of a feeling of "comparing apples to oranges."

When a teacher maximizes task differentiation, maximize student autonomy, and conducts assessments via individually referenced standards, she is working to minimize the probability that some of her students will develop the belief that they possess relatively low ability. On the other hand, when a teacher minimizes task differentiation, miminizes student autonomy, and relies on comparative assessment practices, then she works to maximize the probability that students come to understand a clear ability hierarchy among the members of the class.

In addition to these three general aspects of classroom structure, teachers further engage in (at least) eight specific behaviors that send students' information they use to infer high versus low ability (Rosenholtz & Simpson, 1984). That is, teachers give high-ability students (1) more opportunities to perform (the teacher calls on the smart kids for the answers to questions and passes over the not-so-smart kids), (2) less assistance (high help means low ability), (3) high choice of activities (high-ability students read what they want, low-ability students read what the teacher says they need to read), (4) less supervision, (5) greater time allocation (low-ability children get less time to respond to a question and get asked to turn in incomplete assignments), (6) faster pace of work, (7) more difficult materials and more special assignments, and (8) less negative feedback. All this is to say that while the perception of ability begins in a fuzzy, indirect, ambiguous way, specific classroom behaviors supply students with the information from which to infer their ability levels and to infer their place in the classroom's ability hierarchy. When ability inferences occur in a normative, comparative way, it must follow that some students find places near the top of the classroom ability hierarchy and therefore show approach-oriented behaviors while other students find places near the bottom of the classroom ability hierarchy and therefore show avoidance-oriented behaviors. If all students are to understand they possess high ability, then classroom structures have to encourage ability inferences that are individually based rather than comparatively based, and the means to do this is through a classroom structure rich in multidimensional task differentiation, student autonomy, individual assessment, and a teaching style favoring the eight specific ability-implying teacher behaviors listed above.

Achievement Goals

Factors other than ability perceptions also influence students' achievement strivings—whether they seek out or avoid academic challenges, exert or withhold effort, persist or give up in the face of failure, and work to develop skills efficiently or not (Dweck, 1986). Such behavioral differences stem from adopting adaptive versus maladaptive patterns of motivation. Dweck (1986; Dweck & Leggett, 1988; Elliot & Dweck, 1988) termed the adaptive motivational pattern *mastery-oriented* because such students appear to enjoy the pursuit of task mastery and show volitional challenge seeking and persistence even in the face of obstacles. Likewise, Dweck termed the maladaptive motivational pattern *helpless-oriented* because such students experience anxiety and distress when forced to pursue achievement situations and show challenge avoidance and a lack of persistence in the face of difficulty and failure. (On page 99, Chapter 6 also discussed Dweck's distinction between adaptive and maladaptive patterns of motivation under the title "mastery versus helplessness orientations.")

Level of ability, or intelligence, does not explain why some students adopt the adaptive, mastery-oriented motivational pattern and why others adopt the maladaptive, helpless-oriented pattern (Dweck, 1986). Rather, motivational patterns come from the goals students adopt in achievement settings (Dweck, 1986; Dweck & Leggett, 1988; Elliot & Dweck, 1988). *Learning goals* in the classroom lead students to approach academic challenges with the desire to increase their competence, gain task mastery, improve knowledge and skill, and understand something new. *Performance goals* in the classroom lead students to approach academic challenges with the desire to gain favorable and to avoid unfavorable evaluations of their competence (Dweck, 1986; Nicholls, 1984). For instance, while painting a picture, a student with a learning goal seeks to enhance painting skills and master the use of a paintbrush; a student with a performance goal seeks to use painting as a means to prove her competence and personal worth to an audience of others.

Table 7-1 outlines the classroom implications of how perceptions of ability combine with these two goal orientations to produce various levels of achievement behavior. With performance goals, the student's achievement behaviors depend on his perception of ability. The combination of a performance goal and a perception of high ability leads to a mastery-oriented approach. The combination of a performance goal and a perception of low ability leads to a helpless-oriented behavioral pattern. With a learning goal, on the other hand, all students—high- and low-ability alike—tend toward strong achievement behaviors and toward a willingness to accept mistakes as an inherent part of the learning process. Elliot and Dweck's (1988) laboratory research with fifth-graders confirms the assertions summarized in Table 7-1. They showed that children with *low ability* and *performance goals* reacted to their mistakes by reducing effort, blaming themselves, and expressing negative affect (helpless response to difficulty) as well as by passing up opportunities to discover ways of overcoming their mistakes (helpless task choice); children with *high ability* and *performance goals* reacted to their mistakes by showing persistent effort to find solutions, not blaming themselves, and not expressing negative affect (mastery response to failure), although they did pass up opportunities to learn about the task in which their mistakes would be known by others (helpless task choice); and all children with *learning goals,* irrespective of their perceptions of ability, reacted to their mistakes in a mastery-oriented fashion by persisting and experimenting with their problem-solving strategies until they

TABLE 7-1 Effect of Learning and Performance Goals on Patterns of Classroom Achievement Behavior

Goal Value	Confidence (Perceived Level of Ability)	Predicted Achievement Pattern	
		Task Choice	Response to Difficulty
Perform-ance goal	High	Sacrifice learning and choose moderate or moderately difficult task to display competence	Mastery orientation of effective problem solving
	Low	Sacrifice learning and choose moderately easy task to avoid display of incompetence	Learned-helpless response of deterioration in problem solving and negative affect
Learning goal	High or low	Choose learning at risk of displaying mistakes to increase competence	Mastery-orientation of effective problem solving

Source: Elliot, E., & Dweck, C. (1988). Goals: An approach to motivation and achievement. *Journal of Personality and Social Psychology, 54,* 5–12. Copyright 1988 by the American Psychological Association. Adapted with permission.

improved (mastery response to difficulty) and by choosing challenging tasks (mastery task choice).

Why Do Students Adopt Learning or Performance Goals?
There are two reasons that students adopt either learning or performance goals. The first is a classroom factor, as the structure of some classrooms promote learning goals while the structure of others promote performance goals. Some classrooms tolerate error-making while others value flawless performances (Clifford, 1990). Some classrooms operate with a competitive reward structure while others use an individualistic structure (Johnson & Johnson, 1985). Some classrooms present academic tasks as tests and ability evaluations while others present them as games and learning opportunities (Entin & Raynor, 1973; Ryan, 1982; Ryan, Mims, & Koestner, 1983). Finally, some classrooms emphasize performance in a public domain and draw attention to the student's worth in the eyes of an audience, while others allow students to perform in private and to focus their attention on the task (Anderman & Maehr, 1994; Carver & Scheier, 1981). Classrooms that are intolerant of error-making, are competitive, present academic tasks as tests, and feature public student performances orient students toward adopting performance goals. Classrooms that encourage error-making, are individualistic, present academic tasks as games, and feature private student performances orient students toward adopting learning goals.

The second reason is a personal factor, as students differ in their beliefs about the *nature* of ability (Dweck, 1986). Some children understand ability as a fixed, stable, and unchanging trait they possess to some degree. The belief that ability is a fixed trait leads students to adopt performance goals because they strive to prove to others that they do indeed possess this laudable personal characteristic. Other children understand ability as a gradually escalating, forever-changing quality they possess at some present level, yet will also possess at some greater level in the future. The belief that ability is an escalating quality leads students to adopt learning goals because they view tasks as opportunities to increase an ever-malleable quality in themselves (Dweck, 1986). Think about your own belief system—do you see ability and intelligence as a fixed characteristic, like eye color, or as an ever-accumulating characteristic, like experience? After answering this question for yourself, reflect whether and to what extent your belief about the nature of ability and intelligence affected your own academic choices ("I'm bad in math; I'll pick a college major that doesn't require math courses") and reactions to failures ("I'm bad in math, so why should I study harder for the second test to pull up my low grade?").

Expectation of Success

Students enter achievement situations with some expectation that their performance will be successful. When expectation of success is low (and therefore expectation of failure is high), students' achievement behaviors drop. With low expectancy of success, students feel a reluctance to engage in a task they suspect will bring only shame and embarrassment. How students come to hold general expectancies for success (and failure) is an interesting developmental phenomenon (Heckhausen, 1982; Parsons & Ruble, 1977; Stipek, 1984; Weiner, 1979), one that holds important implications for students' achievement strivings.

Almost without exception, young children embrace extremely high performance expectancies for themselves (Parsons & Ruble, 1977; Stipek, 1981, 1984). Expectancies for success are so high among young children because the information they rely on comes very much from parental and teacher praise and very little or not at all from task-generated failure feedback. First-graders just do not seem to notice when they fail or that their performance is markedly worse than others. By about the second grade and throughout the remaining elementary grades, children's expectancies for success become increasingly congruent with their teacher's (Nicholls, 1978, 1979) and peers' (Ruble, Crosovsky, Frey, & Cohen, 1992) expectations for them. Late-elementary-grade children do attend to normative information ("How well did I do compared to others?") and objective past performance feedback (success/failure) in formulating their performance expectancies. By adolescence, students are mostly realistic in their expectancies for success, as they pay a good deal of attention to reliable predictors of future performances, namely peer comparisons and past performance outcomes. Thus, by adolescence, a student's performance history of task successes and failures and of relative accomplishments compared to her peers builds in that student a general expectation of success (or failure).

Value of Achievement-Related Activities

Students also enter achievement settings with some value for academic achievement. In math class, for instance, some students value the study of mathematics while others see it as pointless and valueless. High value fosters high achievement-related behavior in that domain. Just as expectations of success undergo a clear and interesting developmental pattern, achievement values too follow a developmental course.

According to Stipek (1984), early-elementary-grade children care little about academic achievement per se. Instead, first- and second-graders see high value in nonacademic, approval-based concerns, such as "being good." Some preadolescents and adolescents show a strong valuing of academic achievement for its own sake, most of which arises from parental attitudes that place a high value on academic achievement (Eccles-Parsons, Adler, & Kaczala, 1982). In the absence of strong parental valuing of academic achievement, adolescents tend toward a strong valuing for peer approval and physical prowess. Values for approval and prowess often overshadow and even compete against the valuing of academic achievement. Older teenagers often value academic achievement only when they begin to see an occupational value in it. Occupational utility can therefore create meaning and valuing in academic achievement (Marcia, 1966, 1980; Waterman, 1988). Whether rooted in parental valuing, occupational utility, or both, valuing of achievement-related activities is a learned process. One learns to value achievement-related activities through internalizing the values of socializing agents and through understanding the meaning and utility of various domains of achievement.

Both expectation of success and valuing of achievement-related activities predict achievement in the classroom. These two beliefs, however, predict different manifestations of achievement behavior. An expectation for success predicts performance measures such as grades in the relevant academic domain; a value for that academic domain predicts persistence measures such as intentions to take more courses in that academic subject (Eccles, 1984a, 1984b; Ethington, 1991). Thus, the teacher interested in increasing student performance wants to concentrate on facilitating students' expectancies for success; the teacher interested in increasing student persistence wants to concentrate on facilitating students' valuing of achievement in that domain. For all its merit, however, such research does leave open the question of *how* a teacher might go about facilitating high expectancies and high task values in students. For this task, we need to add to the discussion of expectancies and values Weiner's (1986) attributional theory of achievement motivation.

Attributional Theory of Achievement Motivation

Chapter 6 introduced *causal attribution,* the reason the student gives to explain a particular outcome. Causal attributions influence both future expectancies for success as well as future sense of value in that particular academic domain. Specifically, the stability (stable vs. unstable) dimension of an attribution affects changes in expectancies, while the internality (internal vs. external) dimension affects changes in value.

Stable–Unstable Attributions Affect Changes in Expectancy

Attribution theory addresses the question of how one person might change another person's expectation of success. According to Weiner's (1985, p. 559) expectancy principle, "Changes in expectancy of success following an outcome are influenced by the perceived stability of the cause of the event." Thus, an outcome attributed to a stable cause increases a student's future expectation of success, whereas an outcome attributed to an unstable cause does not affect expectations. That is, success attributed to a stable cause (e.g., ability, or ease of subject matter) builds a relatively stronger expectation for future success. On the other hand, success attributed to an unstable cause (e.g., effort, strategy, luck) leaves future expectations unchanged. In addition, failure attributed to a stable cause builds a relatively stronger expectation of future failures. Failure attributed to an unstable cause, on the other hand, leaves future expectations unchanged. In practice, then, a teacher can influence students' expectation of success in a favorable (i.e., effort-promoting) direction by pointing out the stable causes for successes and the unstable causes for failures.

Internal–External Attributions Affect Changes in Value

Attribution theory also addresses the question how one person might change another person's value for a particular achievement domain. According to Weiner (1985, 1986), value is affected by the internal–external attributional dimension. That is, success attributed to some aspects of the self (an internal cause, such as ability, effort, or personality) produces the emotion of pride and bolsters self-esteem. On the other hand, success attributed to some aspect outside the self (an external cause, such as the difficulty of the task or assistance from the teacher) produces non-self-related emotions and feelings. Likewise, failure attributed to some aspect of the self produces shame and erodes self-esteem (Stipek, 1983), whereas failure attributed externally produces non-self-related emotions and feelings. It is feelings of pride and self-esteem, Weiner argues, that contribute positively to a valuing of one's achievement strivings in a particular domain, and it is feelings of shame and negative self-esteem that erode a valuing in that domain. In practice, then, the teacher can influence students' valuing a particular domain in a favorable (i.e., effort-promoting) direction by pointing out the internal causes for successes and the external causes for failures.

Overcoming the Tendency to Avoid Failure

During the middle elementary school years, children begin to compare their performances with those of their classmates, and, in doing so, begin to compromise some of their wild optimism about how academically able they are (Stipek, 1984). During adolescence, self-consciousness hits its peak as students care deeply about how they compare with their peers and what their peers think of them and their abilities (Gray & Hudson, 1984; Riley, Adams, & Nielsen, 1984). As a consequence, students gradually accumulate inhibitions against achievement efforts as they progress from one grade to the next—inhibitions such as concerns to preserve self-worth, motives to present themselves to others in a positive light, and fears of being evaluated (Baumeister, 1982). Thus, students acquire motives that we will discuss, in turn, as self-worth protection, self-handicapping, and achievement anxiety. These three motives manifest themselves as the dark side of the achievement dilemma, in which some part of the student wants to risk putting forth the high effort necessary to approach success (thereby enhancing the self) while some other part wants to play it safe and withhold effort in the name of avoiding failure (thereby protecting the self).

The Problem of Underachievement

In a typical classroom, some students overachieve while others underachieve. A teacher begins to sense whether a student is over- or underachieving when he becomes aware of discrepancies between the student's actual abilities and his or her classroom performances. Of course, many factors help explain why students do not perform up to their potentialities—learning disabilities, cultural influences, lack of experience, and mismatches between students' instructional needs and teacher's classroom presentations. From a motivational perspective, however, the root cause of underachievement is low effort. Sometimes, students become so fearful of the emotional and social consequences of failure (e.g., shame, criticism, embarrassment, loss of status) that they would rather withhold effort to protect against such consequences than put forth effort to avoid failing in the first place. When a student decides that preserving self-worth in the eyes of others is more important than achievement per se, then withholding effort makes sense and fulfills personal priorities ("If I fail and don't try, who can blame me, but if I succeed and don't try, it will be clear just how smart I am"). Given these same priorities, putting forth high effort does not make sense and contradicts personal priorities ("If I fail and try hard, it will be clear how dumb

I am; if I succeed and try hard, everyone can discount my ability because my effort was so strong"). Thus, from the student's point of view, withholding effort becomes an attractive and rational strategy (because low effort protects the self). The following paragraphs trace the underlying causes of the motivation to protect the self and suggest some ways out of the problem of intentional underachievement.

Self-Worth Protection

According to self-worth theory, a student's sense of worth versus worthlessness emanates from three achievement-related factors—performance accomplishments, perceptions of ability, and extent of effort (Covington, 1984a, 1984b). Early-elementary-school children (grades K–3) give the highest worth to those persons (and the self) who demonstrate successful accomplishments, high ability, and high effort. For young children a person is good and worthy of praise if he or she performs successfully, shows high ability, or shows high effort. For older students, however, high ability becomes the dominant determinant of self-worth. Performance accomplishments add somewhat to self-worth, but high effort becomes the billboard for shame. Older students come to the understanding that people who try hard—regardless of whether they eventually succeed or fail—must have tried so hard because they lacked enough ability to breeze through the task (Nicholls, 1978). In effect, expending effort puts the student's self-worth at risk in that it becomes a telltale sign that the performer lacks high ability.

Many post-elementary-grade students enter achievement situations more concerned about preserving their self-worth than about achieving their task-related goals. Preserving self-worth means guarding yourself against the possibility that others will infer you possess low ability. When self-worth concerns dominate achievement strivings, then students prefer failure-avoiding strategies over success-approaching ones. One prototypical failure-avoiding strategy is procrastination (Covington, 1984a). With procrastination, a student might study only the night before a test and therefore tip the balance of the achievement risk-taking dilemma in his favor—"If I fail, then who can blame me (because I didn't try very hard)? And if I succeed despite such a carefree effort, then I must surely be highly able!" With strong preparation, however, the balance of the achievement risk-taking dilemma does not fall in the student's favor, as failure with high effort confirms low ability, while success with high effort leaves ability inferences ambiguous. For these reasons, procrastination functions as a defensive self-worth protecting strategy to effectively immunize the self against potential self-worth-belittling experiences of failure. Of course, procrastination is self-defeating in the long run because reducing effort undermines performance potential and increases the probability of failure. That is the essential problem with a self-protection strategy—the student focuses on remedying the aversive consequences of failure rather than on working to increase her chances for success. After all, the best way to remedy the aversive consequences of failure is to work so hard that one does not experience failure in the first place.

Self-Handicapping

Self-handicapping is a defensive, self-presentational strategy that involves intentionally interfering with one's own performance in such a way as to provide a face-saving excuse for why one failed (Jones & Berglas, 1978). More often than not, high-ability students are the ones who use self-handicapping strategies. Their essence is this: "Before I perform, I will find or create an obstacle to good performance; then, if I perform poorly I can convince others that the obstacle caused my failure, but if I perform well I can convince others that my ability caused not only the success but my triumph over the obstacle as well." Researchers have put forth many viable explanations of why students handicap themselves (see Jones & Berglas, 1978; Riggs, 1992), but the primary motivation is the preservation of high self-esteem (Arkin & Baumgardner, 1985; Baumeister, 1982; Frankel & Snyder, 1978). For instance, in their original work, Berglas and Jones (1978) found that individuals who experienced a "lucky success" were quick to handicap themselves before beginning their second performance. That is, students do not expect lucky successes to repeat themselves consistently, so the student stands to lose the self-esteem gained from the first success. Thus, when students acquire a positive identity in the minds of others but feel uncertain about their chances to maintain that positive identity in the future, then self-handicapping becomes an expected strategy to pull out of the bag of face-saving tricks (Pyszczynski & Greenberg, 1983).

Three classroom conditions increase students' proneness to self-handicap (Riggs, 1992). First, students must experience success before they contemplate using a self-handicapping strategy, because success gives life to the positive self-image the student needs to protect. Second, a lack of confidence in perceived ability increases the motivation to self-handicap, mostly because low confidence feeds doubt as to whether the success will repeat itself. Third, self-handicapping is more likely in evaluative contexts, because evaluation announces that successes and failures will be forthcoming and therefore so will inferences about students' abilities. In addition, the motivation to self-handicap increases so dramatically during adolescence that adolescence acts as a fourth facilitating condition (Riggs, 1992).

The obstacles students conjure up to use as self-handicapping strategies take a variety of forms, including use of the sick role (Smith, Snyder, & Perkins, 1983), excuses (Snyder & Higgins, 1988), drugs and alcohol (Jones & Berglas, 1978), lack of sleep, lack of practice, a bad mood (Baumgardner, Lake, & Arkin,

1985), reduction of effort (Covington & Omelich, 1979), and perhaps others as well. In attempting to deal with self-handicapping strategies, it helps to appreciate both the pros and the cons of such strategies. The beneficial consequence of using a self-handicapping strategy is that the self is protected, or immunized, against potential humiliation. The harmful consequence is that failure (or underachievement) is made a more likely outcome than it otherwise would be. The task of the teacher is to find a way to combine sheltering the self from harm with encouraging high effort in achievement settings. The pivotal means of integrating these two objectives is for the teacher (or parents) to communicate clearly an unconditional positive regard to students as learners. If acceptance and positive regard are contingent on the display of high ability, then it makes a good deal of sense from the students' point of view to stage performances in such a way that blame for a potential failure will be externalized to some handicap other than a lack of ability (Jones & Berglas, 1978; Riggs, 1992). But, the student who fears exposing his lack of competence must protect his self-image not only in the eyes of his teachers but also in the eyes of his classmates as well. To head off exaggerated peer-related self-presentational concerns, a teacher can foster a classroom environment rich in the tolerance for errors (Clifford, 1990) and unconditional positive regard (Rogers, 1969) as well as one that features noncompetitive reward structures (Johnson & Johnson, 1985) and individualized rather than normative performance feedback.

From the student's point of view, the motive to self-handicap boils down to one fundamental question: What will others think of my ability when they see me put forth a great deal of effort on an achievement task? To the extent that the student believes that others will use his high effort as a cue to infer low ability, the motivation to use self-handicapping strategies will be strong. To the extent that the student believes that others will use high effort as a cue to infer a mastery orientation, the motive to self-handicap will be weak.

Achievement Anxiety

Anxiety in school settings, often referred to as *test anxiety,* refers to the unpleasant, aversive emotional state students experience in evaluative settings such as formal testing or public speaking (Dusek, 1980). Anxiety motivates escape and avoidance behaviors in students (pleas, excuses, not participating, skipping school; Smith, Snyder, & Handelsman, 1982) and it produces debilitating effects on academic performance through cognitive disruption, poor decision making, emotional pressure, and a distracting and preoccupying attentional shift to the threat of failure and its consequences (Dusek, Kermis, & Mergler, 1975; Dusek, Mergler, & Kermis, 1976; Janis, 1982; Keinan, 1987). Consider once again that in all achievement settings there is a risk-taking dilemma: Should I try hard and approach success, or should I withhold effort and avoid failure? Achievement (or test) anxiety makes students especially sensitive to failure and therefore especially likely to work to avoid failure (rather than work to approach success). This sensitivity to the negative aspects of the achievement dilemma increases with age, as anxiety exerts a negligible effect on students' academic performance during the early elementary grades, a moderate effect during the middle elementary grades, a robust effect during the late elementary grades, and a downright debilitating effect among junior and senior high school students (Hill & Sarason, 1966). Further, this progressive relationship between anxiety and debilitated performance holds across factors such as gender and race (Hill, 1980; Willig, Harnisch, Hill, & Maehr, 1983).

High anxiety originates from a self-perception that the student is unable to cope in achievement settings (Lazarus & Folkman, 1984). Failure feedback, when experienced, sends an objective message to the student that he is not coping successfully with the demands placed upon him. The anticipation of a negative evaluation makes students fearful of future testing situations. Parents sometimes add to students' anticipation of negative evaluations by communicating and imposing unrealistic performance demands on the student. When the student's performances show themselves to be short of parental expectations, then the parent's negative reaction to these shortcomings generates in the child a fear of future evaluations in achievement settings (Hill, 1980). In addition, students feel performance demands and pressures from their peers. Competition and pressure to do as well or better than classmates lead students to become fearful of future evaluations in achievement settings (Hill, 1984). Anxiety also originates from generalized school-based performance demands, as children experience an ever-increasing number of evaluations as well as an ever-increasing formality to the evaluation process as the grades advance (Eccles et al., 1984). Thus, anxiety grows as failures mount and as evaluations—from tests, parents, teachers, peers, and the school culture in general—increase in number and in importance.

What Can Be Done to Reduce Anxiety?

Three recommendations speak to a teacher's attempt to reduce anxiety in students: A teacher can (1) provide performance information rather than evaluation; (2) create testing situations in a way that minimizes evaluative pressures, and (3) equip students with the coping skills they need to deal effectively with evaluative pressure (Hill & Wigfield, 1984).

The most popular way to communicate to students their level of achievement is to assign their performance a letter grade. In a competitive school culture and in a competitive society in general, the standard of excellence for a letter grade is typically designated an A, a lofty standard that understandably induces a good deal of stress and anxiety. The anxiety makes sense because the coping efforts of most students are doomed to failure, or at least doomed to being unable to live up to their own and their parents' expectations of an A. As an alternative to normative grading, Hill and Wigfield (1984) tested the effectiveness of documenting achievement progress by way of using individualized comments from the teacher. Such new "grade cards" featured teachers' written comments of the student's achievement, effort, and especially strengths and weaknesses. Informative (rather than evaluative) reports on how the student might improve and on his strengths and weaknesses reduce anxiety (Hill, 1980; Hill & Wigfield, 1984).

As to creating optimal testing situations, three conditions determine most of the evaluative pressure students experience—time limits, ego-involving instructions, and sequencing of easy and difficult questions (see Hill & Wigfield, 1984). Time limits create an evaluative pressure and a source of cognitive and emotional distraction in anxious students with which nonanxious students do not have to contend. Thus, when time limits are stressed, anxious students perform worse than nonanxious students, but when students can take as much time as they need to complete a test, then anxious students perform just as well as do nonanxious students (Hill, Wigfield, & Plass, 1980). Test instructions can be highly ego-involving ("This test measures your ability") and therefore threatening, or test instructions can be not at all ego-involving ("This test contains some items that are quite difficult, but don't worry about missing them") and therefore nonthreatening. With ego-involving instructions, anxious students perform worse than nonanxious students, but with less threatening instructions anxious students perform just as well as do nonanxious students (Williams, 1976). Finally, teachers can organize tests to alternate easy and hard questions in order to balance students' success–failure experiences during the evaluative process. Many tests present a group of easy questions and then a group of difficult questions, which can be a problem for anxious students because a cluster of difficult questions can precipitate a prolonged period of repeated failures. A history of repeated failures is perhaps the most nutritious soil possible for worry and doubt to grow. One way around this problem of successive failures would be to intentionally alternate easy and difficult questions in the effort to balance students' failures and anxiety with successes and confidence.

Finally, teachers can work to equip students with the coping skills necessary to deal effectively with school's evaluative pressures. Here, the teacher recognizes that students will experience anxiety when evaluated, especially under unusual circumstances such as time limits, difficult material, and public presentations. When teachers recognize the role that anxiety plays in affecting student performance, they tend to have open minds about devoting class time to equipping students with test-taking coping skills. In one anxiety-reducing program (outlined in Hill & Wigfield, 1984), teachers gave students test-taking strategies ("Answer the questions you know first"), advice on self-regulating aversive emotions ("Don't worry if some problems are too hard"), test-taking tips ("If you finish a section before time is called, go back and check your answers"), and a series of practice tests followed by informative rather than evaluative feedback. When teachers take the time to prepare students with an armament of coping skills to handle the evaluative pressures they will encounter, student achievement does increase, most notably for highly anxious students (Hill & Wigfield, 1984). Further, teachers' efforts to equip students with coping skills to handle evaluative pressures show the greatest gains if implemented early in the academic year (Hunsley, 1985).

Failure Avoidance via Overachievement?

In addition to the set of failure avoiding strategies discussed here—self-worth protection, self-handicapping, and achievement anxiety—there remains yet another way to avoid failure, namely through effort that is so intense and so persistent that failure becomes a next to impossible outcome. Such supereffort might be termed *overachievement*. For instance, people high in the fear of failure often work twice as hard as others on achievement-related tasks, at least on those occasions on which they feel threatened by the possibility of failure (Birney et al., 1969). Much work remains to be done on this coping strategy to deal with the negative psychological consequences of failing, but it is clear that achievement behavior that is full of pressure, stress, and the ideology of work is psychologically less healthy than is achievement behavior that is full of volition, enjoyment, and the ideology of play (Ryan, Connell, & Grolnick, 1992).

Conclusion

This chapter revolved around the theme that achievement situations put students into an approach–avoidance risk-taking dilemma in which they must decide: "Should I work hard and put forth high effort to approach the possibility of success, or should I slacken off and withhold my effort to avoid the possibility of failure?" Educators are more interested in encouraging high effort and the approach of success, but educational tasks and classroom climates are rich both in characteristics that heighten the tendency to approach success and in characteristics that heighten the tendency to avoid failure. Factors that contribute to the motivation to approach achievement-related tasks and situations include perceptions of high ability, learning rather than performance goals, high expectations for success, a valuing of the achievement domain, and an optimistic attributional style. Factors that contribute to the motivation to avoid achievement-related tasks and situations include self-worth protection, self-handicapping strategies, and achievement anxiety. All these factors combine together into a mixture of approach versus avoidance tendencies to result in the most basic and important of all educational concerns—the student's willingness to exert high effort in the classroom.

A final question is: "What does it mean to achieve?" This chapter took a narrow view of achievement and conceptualized it as success on academic challenges. People of different genders, ages, and cultures, however, define achievement in different terms. Consider, for instance, the following four domains of potential achievement, from Salili (1994): (1) academic and career (e.g., schoolwork, career achievement); (2) personal social life (e.g., getting married, developing a good personality); (3) extracurricular activities (e.g., sports, community service); and (4) family life (e.g., parenting, family relations). When Salili (1994) asked people to rate the importance of these aspects of achievement, most people did not value academic and career achievements most highly. Rather, people valued success in personal social life and in family life most highly. Further, what aspects of success and achievement people valued varied with their gender, with their age, and with their culture. This point makes it apparent that individuals might not all be oriented toward achieving in just one area of their lives (i.e., school). Rather, people seek achievement in multiple areas of their lives at the same time. Thus, the achievement risk-taking dilemma extends beyond deciding between high effort to approach success versus low effort to avoid failure in that it further includes effort to achieve in one area versus effort to achieve in another area. I point this out because diversity of achievement goals underscores the need to promote a student-centered, rather than a teacher-centered, view of what constitutes achievement in each student's life.

Recommended Readings

Brophy, J. (1986). Teacher influences on student achievement. *American Psychologist, 41,* 1069-1077.

Covington, M. (1984). The self-worth theory of achievement motivation *The Elementary School Journal, 85,* 5–20.

Covington, M., & Omelich, C. (1979). Effort: The double-edged sword in school achievement. *Journal of Educational Psychology, 71,* 169–182.

Pyszczynski, T., & Greenberg, J. (1983). Determinants of reduction in intended effort as a strategy for coping with anticipated failure. *Journal of Research in Personality, 17,* 412–422.

Rosenholtz, S. J., & Simpson, C. (1984). The formation of ability conceptions: Developmental trend or social construction? *Review of Educational Research, 54,* 31–63.

Smith, T. W., Snyder, C. R., & Handelsman, M. M. (1982). On the self-serving function of an academic wooden leg: Test anxiety as a self-handicapping strategy. *Journal of Personality and Social Psychology, 42,* 314–321.

Stipek, D. (1981). Children's perceptions of their own and their classmates' ability. *Journal of Educational Psychology, 73,* 404–410.

Stipek, D. (1983). A developmental analysis of pride and shame. *Human Development,* *26,* 42–56.

Weiner, B. (1979). A theory of motivation for some classroom experiences. *Journal of Educational Psychology, 71,* 3–25.

Weiner, B. (1980). May I borrow your class notes? An attributional analysis of judgments of help-giving in an achievement related context. *Journal of Educational Psychology, 72,* 676–681.

Observational Activities

Observational Activity 7.1: Achievement-Related Beliefs and Behaviors

The purpose of this interview is to examine the relationship between achievement-related beliefs and achievement-related behaviors. You will need to solicit the voluntary participation of two students. Interview each student separately; each interview will last between fifteen and thirty minutes. Make sure that at least one of your interviewees is past the third grade; it would be informative if one interviewee was past middle school. These ages are important because achievement-related beliefs undergo significant and interesting changes during the early elementary grades and during adolescence.

Begin by asking what subjects the student is currently taking (math, English, social studies, etc.). Ask the student in which subject he or she puts forth the most effort and in which subject he or she puts forth the least effort. After you identify one high-effort and one low-effort subject area, ask the student about his or her performances (i.e., grades) in that subject and his or her willingness to take future courses in that subject area. Next, ask the student about five achievement-related beliefs reviewed in the chapter: (1) perception of ability, (2) learning versus performance goal, (3) ability as a fixed trait versus an escalating quality, (4) expectation of success versus failure, and (5) value of the subject matter. In addition, you might want to ask about some general classroom factors (e.g., ability hierarchies, teacher expectations). You will need to ask these questions in creative, age-appropriate ways. For instance, a question to assess learning versus performance goals might ask, "When you're reading your social studies textbook, what would you say is your number one priority to accomplish?"

Once you complete the two interviews, see if there is any systematic relationship between the students' achievement-related beliefs on the one hand and their willingness to exert effort in that subject area on the other hand. Which particular achievement-related beliefs seem best to explain high and low effort. Did one belief or another best predict effort? Grades? Willingness to take future courses in the area? Detail the relationships you found (or failed to find) between the students' beliefs and their effort in each class.

Observational Activity 7.2: Behavioral Manifestations of the Tendency to Avoid Failure

The purpose of this observation is to become aware of how students express the tendency to avoid failure through self-worth protection, self-handicapping, and achievement anxiety. Begin by thinking about the best age for the student you will invite to participate; then pick a task that the two students will find relatively difficult. For instance, you might pick a Rubik's cube, a difficult crossword puzzle, or a sophisticated athletic skill (e.g., hitting a golf ball). Once you select your activity, invite two students to participate in performing the task for you. Create a time in which the students talk to you before they perform (e.g., while you explain the task), a time in which they talk as they perform (e.g., you will be the audience), and a time in which they talk after they perform (e.g., a postgame interview).

Pay particular attention to each student's emotional expressions at each stage of the performance (before, during, and after). Unobtrusively write down any and all instances in which students express a concern to protect their self-worth, use a self-handicapping strategy, express achievement anxiety, or manifest fear over failing or being evaluated. Pay particular attention to whether the student emotions are approach-oriented or avoidance-oriented.

Following your observations, answer the following set of questions. How difficult was the task for the two students? Did the students feel that their performances were successes or failures? Describe their emotions before, during, and after their performance. How rare versus how common were each of the three face-saving strategies of self-worth protection, self-handicapping, and achievement anxiety? What function did these three strategies seem to serve when students used them? Do you think students' use of these three strategies was good and desirable, or do you think their use of these strategies was undesirable and self-defeating? Why?

8

Healthy Sense of Self

It is recess time and the sun is warm and inviting, so you decide to accompany your students to the playground for an afternoon lunch. As you witness the chaos that is the playground, the actions and expressions of one second-grade boy capture your attention. As he wanders about, you imagine what he is thinking and what he is wanting. First, he approaches a group of older children playing around the monkey bars. You can tell he is trying to fit in and be invited to join a game, but he gets a cold reception as the older kids tell him subtly that he is not "one of them." You notice a bit of fear in his face as he looks over the perilous monkey bars, which seem to say to him, "You can't do this." Suddenly, one of his classmates screams that it is his turn at kickball. He quickly runs to take his turn, as he soaks in the message that he is indeed "one of them." As he watches the ball rolling slowly toward him to be kicked to high heaven, the emotion on his face is an anticipation of great things to come. The rolling ball seems to whisper, "You can do this." As recess ends, you understand that this boy's essential concerns for the last thirty minutes have revolved around the struggle to answer a question something like, "Who am I and what can I do?" (Wigfield & Karpathian, 1991).

"Who am I and what can I do?" is a question we all ask of ourselves frequently, in one form or another. We wonder about who we want to be, how we want to relate to others, what values we wish to guide us, and what place we wish to occupy in the social world.

Students face three basic problems pertaining to the self: (1) defining or creating the self, (2) relating the self to society, and (3) understanding the potential of the self and fulfilling it (Baumeister, 1987). Defining the self is the attempt to answer the question, "Who am I?" Some aspects of self-definition are simply ascribed to the individual (e.g., gender), but other aspects must be gained through achievement and acts of choice (e.g., career, friends, beliefs, values). The answer to the question "Who am I?" is the student's *self-concept*, the first topic of the chapter.

Relating the self to society is the individual's struggle to define his or her relationship to others. In some respects, society is rigid in the roles it encourages or even allows individuals to pursue, but in other respects society is flexible in that it gives the individual some degree of personal choice and responsibility in determining the self's relationships to others and to society (e.g., partners, careers). The individual's relationship to society bestows the student with *identity,* the second topic of the chapter.

The problem of understanding the potential of the self and fulfilling it is the student's struggle to establish meaning and purpose in his or her life. It is simplistic to reduce meaning and purpose to two factors, but the student's success in school and work on the one hand and the student's success in love and friendship on the other hand capture much of the meaning and purpose at stake, at least during the school years. Fulfilling the self's potential is the process of *ego development,* the third topic of the chapter.

Self-Concept

The first aspect of the self is *self-concept*, the set of beliefs the individual uses to conceptualize or understand his or her *self.* To conceptualize the self (its attributes, characteristics, roles, preferences, and interests), students pay attention to the wealth of self-related information that daily experience provides. Sue, for instance, can look back on her week to recall that she made a good grade on her English test, easily understood a schoolbook she read, and heard special praise from Mr. Marlow for the poem she wrote. Eventually, if Sue's experiences in her English classes are consistent and frequent enough, she will come to the generalization that, for the most part, she is smart (at least in English). This general conclusion constitutes a critical component of her self-concept. In another domain, such as athletics, however, Sue might look back on her past experience to recall that she consistently strikes out in softball and that she came within an eyelash of drowning when she last tried to swim. Based on such experience, Sue will likely conclude that she is, for the most part, unathletic. These generalizations ("Intellectually, I am smart" and "Physically, I am unathletic") constitute *self-schemas* (Markus, 1977), as will be discussed. An individual's collection of self-schemas (in different life domains) constitutes the components of the self-concept (i.e., a student has many self-schemas that make up a general self-concept).

Self-Schemas (Observational Activity 8.1)

Formally stated, self-schemas (or *self-schemata*) are cognitive generalizations about the self, derived from past experience, that organize and guide the processing of self-related information contained in the individual's social experience (Markus, 1977). Self-schemas are important because students do not readily recall every life experience they have in a particular domain. Rather, they evaluate and interpret their wealth of experience in a systematic and organized way that enables them to construct generalizations. These generalizations, which are the self-schemas, are domain-specific in that a student comes to an understanding of herself in English, in math, in athletics, in social situations, in music, and in the other domains that are important to her.

Development of Self-Schemas in Children
(Observational Activity 8.1)
Self-recognition begins to appear at about the age of two (Bertenthal & Fischer, 1978; Lewis, 1987) and develops gradually thereafter as language and cognitive processes develop and mature. One interesting way to tap into children's increasingly sophisticated self-views at different ages is to follow Observational Activity 8.1 and ask children to answer the question "Who am I?" with twenty different statements (Bugental & Zelen, 1950; Kuhn & McPartland, 1954; Montemayor & Eisen, 1977). The self-descriptive statements/answers that students of different ages provide to this simple question generally document three reliable developmental tendencies: Self-schemas develop (from one grade to the next) toward realism, toward abstraction, and toward differentiation.

Realism.   The self of early childhood is wildly optimistic as children learn about the self mostly from wildly biased parents. The self of early childhood is a self still very much under construction. During middle childhood, children gain new perspective and information about the self via increased social opportunities and an increased number of experiences with peers and teachers (Markus & Nurius, 1986). That is, during middle childhood, the self receives information not only from parents but also from peers, teachers, task feedback ("I couldn't solve the problem; maybe I'm not so good in math"), and social comparison ("Everyone else solved that math problem, except me"). As a consequence, late-elementary-grade children are more accurate or realistic in their self-constructions than are early-elementary-grade children. Interestingly, gains in accuracy of self-understanding bring not only increased realism but also, typically, increased negativism (Nicholls, 1979; Stipek & MacIver, 1989), as the self comes to realize that it is probably not the fastest, smartest, prettiest, and strongest self in the history of the world (as parents sometimes would have the self believe). During adolescence, students begin in earnest the lifelong task of integration in which they try to take the vast amount of information they receive about the self and come to an understanding of their "true self" (Harter, 1990).

Abstraction.   Self-concept change proceeds in a way that follows changes in cognitive development (Harter, 1990; Piaget, 1963), such that elementary-grade children focus mostly on concrete, observable aspects of the self, middle school children focus mostly on psychological traits, and high school students focus mostly on abstract qualities and unobservable psychological processes (Harter, 1990). Thus, elementary-grade (preoperational) children typically describe themselves (in answering "Who am I?") by listing physical characteristics ("I have brown eyes") and behavioral skills ("I can run fast"). Middle school (concrete-operations) students typically list trait labels ("I am friendly, smart, helpful to others"). And high school (formal operations) students typically list abstract qualities ("I am moody"), personal beliefs ("I am a democrat"), and resolutions of personal struggles and crises ("I want to marry, but have a career too"). From one grade to the next, the trend is toward an increasingly abstract view of the self.

Differentiation.   The self of the preschooler advances from an undifferentiated self to that of the adolescent, whose self is differentiated into complex characterizations and attributes such as its emotionality, spirituality, honesty, and the like (Harter, 1990; Marsh, 1989; Marsh, Parker, & Barnes, 1985; Marsh & O'Neil, 1984; Montemayor & Eisen, 1977; Rosenberg, 1986). First-graders show the beginnings of a differentiated self-concept by noticing distinctions in their competence and achievement in domains such as math and English (Marsh, Barnes, Cairns, & Tidman, 1984). Throughout the elementary grades, children's self-conceptions continue to differentiate into at least three distinct domains— social, academic, and physical (Harter, 1983, 1986; Marsh & Shavelson, 1985) and sometimes into six—math, reading, physical abilities, physical appearance, relationship with peers, and relationship with parents (Marsh, 1989; Marsh et al., 1984; Marsh, Smith, & Barnes, 1983). With adolescence comes increased differentiation as self-characterizations expand to include internal, private attributes of the self, sometimes termed the *psychological interior* (Harter, 1990, p. 207). Among high school students, the self differentiates even within a single domain (e.g., in English: "I'm good in reading; so-so in poetry; bad in writing; excellent in the works of Mark Twain").

Gender and Ethnicity Identities in the Classroom
Gender and ethnicity are two core aspects of students' self-conceptualizations. Genders and ethnicities that are relatively rare (i.e., in the minority) become especially salient in the classroom, a process referred to as *distinctiveness theory* (McGuire, 1984). The self is a highly complex cognitive structure, and those aspects of the self that stand out as different from other people tend to get noticed in a salient, attention-getting way. For instance, when asked to complete a version of the Twenty Statements Test ("Tell me about yourself"), members of the minority group, in terms of both ethnicity and gender, are significantly more likely to report their ethnicity or gender (Cota & Dion, 1986; McGuire, McGuire, Child, & Fujioka, 1978; McGuire, McGuire, & Winton, 1979). This

gender salience and *ethnicity salience* occurs in schools (McGuire et al., 1978), at home (McGuire et al., 1979), and in the experimental laboratory (Cota & Dion, 1986). Hence, the rarer the student's personal characteristics (gender, ethnicity), the more likely they are to become salient aspects of his or her self-conceptualization.

Stability versus Change in Self-Schema

Dependent on how consistent or inconsistent the student's experience in a particular domain is, the stability of that self-schema varies. In those domains in which the student has relatively rich and consistent experience, self-schemas are relatively stable and not susceptible to change; but in those domains in which the student has relatively little experience or has contradictory experience, self-schemas exist in a state of developmental flux and are susceptible to change (Swann, 1983, 1985). So a key variable in determining self-concept stability versus change is how confident a person is that his or her self-schemas are valid and true, a variable called *self-concept certainty* (Harris & Snyder, 1986).

From one schoolday to the next, students receive feedback consistent with their self-conception ("I think I have art talent, and, sure enough, the teacher said I drew well") as well as feedback discrepant with their self-conception ("I think I have art talent, but, surprisingly, the teacher didn't pick my drawing for the school exhibit"). For students with high self-concept certainty, consistent feedback simply increases the certainty of their self-schemas while discrepant feedback serves only as one piece of information within the context of a lifetime of historical information ("True, this particular drawing is poor, but it is also true that I have other drawings that are excellent"). In effect, self-concept certainty *anchors* stable self-schemas. When self-concept certainty is high, discrepant feedback never changes a self-schema but, rather, leads only to a slight lowering of self-schema certainty (Swann, 1983). When self-concept certainty is low, however, discrepant feedback can indeed instigate a change in the self-schema. The student who holds an uncertain self-schema focuses on making sense of discrepant feedback, as conflict within an uncertain self-schema (via discrepant feedback) instigates a "crisis self-verification" (Swann, 1983). The self-verification crisis essentially asks, "How do I verify the accuracy of my self-view, given this contradictory feedback?" Students resolve the self-verification crisis, Swann (1983) argues, by seeking out and attending to additional domain-relevant feedback. If the additional feedback is self-confirmatory (e.g., friends assure her that she is indeed a fine artist), then the crisis resolves itself toward self-concept verification and confirms or increases self-concept certainty. But if the additional feedback is self-discrepant (e.g., friends fail to assure her that she is a fine artist), then the student's self-conception is vulnerable to change. In summary, two events must occur before self-concept change is likely:

(1) self-concept certainty must be low and (2) self-discrepant feedback must be unambiguous, potent, and consistent—that is, difficult to discredit (Swann, 1983, 1985, 1987).

In practice, research on how and when self-schemas change implies that teachers should resist arguing against a student's negative self-view (because when the self-view is highly certain, then the self will most likely reject the teacher's discrepant feedback). Rather the most promising route the teacher has to begin the process of self-concept change is through the attempt to undermine the student's certainty of a negative self-view. That is, for a math teacher instructing a student with a negative self-view (in math), her attempt at self-schema change will go smoothly if she adopts as her goal to decrease the student's *certainty* of his or her negative self-view (via discrepant feedback and other means; see Jussim, 1986). In contrast, her attempt at self-schema change will go roughly if she attempts to challenge, contradict, or otherwise change the student's self-view directly.

Possible Selves

Discrepant feedback is not the only means by which self-schemas change. Self-schema change also occurs through an intentional and deliberate effort on the student's part to move the "present self" toward a future "possible self." Possible selves represent a student's ideas of what he would like to become, what he might become, and what he is afraid of becoming (Markus & Nurius, 1986). Possible selves are mostly social in their origin, as the student observes others and makes inferences such as "what she is now, I could soon become" (Markus & Nurius, 1986). For instance, a student might listen to a classroom visitor talking about her job as a lawyer and say, "I could become a lawyer myself." Possible selves are not always positive, however, as a person might watch a friend fail out of school and say, "I could become a dropout too."

Adding the notion of possible selves to that of self-schemas ("actual selves"), presents teachers with a more dynamic image of students' selves—one that is active and capable of intentional change. Such a dynamic view of the self has important implications for motivation, because possible selves function as incentives to direct the student's future behavior (Cantor, Markus, Niedenthal, & Nurius, 1986; Markus & Nurius, 1986; Markus & Wurf, 1987). A possible self represents a goal to be approached (or perhaps avoided) and motivationally links thoughts ("I could become a lawyer") to motivation (energy devoted toward accomplishing that goal). When a student pursues a possible self, he or she relies relatively little on present actual self-schemas and relatively greatly on possible hoped-for selves to translate aspirations into behavioral strategies and intentions: "If I am going to become my possible self, then how should I behave, what activities should I pursue, and what courses should I take?" (Cantor et al., 1986).

The notion of possible selves rejects the idea that the self is a product of past experience only and, instead, argues for the portray of the self as a dynamic entity with a past, present, and future (Cantor et al., 1986; Day, Borkowski, Punzo, & Howsepian, 1994). In education, possible selves effectively build a motivational bridge between a student's current self and the future outcomes he desires (Cross & Markus, 1994; Nurius, 1991; Oyserman & Markus, 1990). According to Cross and Markus (1994), the student without a possible self in a particular academic subject will lack an important cognitive basis to develop and use his abilities and skills in that subject. On the other hand, a student who can bring to mind a vivid and elaborate possible self in the academic subject is more likely to be energized and motivated during that course (Cross & Markus, 1994). Perhaps the reader can look back at the energy he devoted to his college-level courses and ask, "To what extent did my possible self of 'teacher' affect my motivation in each course I took, each book I read, and each lecture I attended (or skipped!)?"

Social Comparison Processes

Another source of information students rely on to define the self is social comparison, the practice by which a student compares his or her personal characteristics and abilities to those of others (Pyszczynski, Greenberg, & LaPrelle, 1985; Ruble, 1983; Ruble & Frey, 1991; Wheeler & Miyake, 1992; Wood, 1989). Without other people around, it is difficult to know whether or not you are smart, attractive, athletic, emotionally sensitive, or whatever. In the attempt to define the self, it is handy to have other people around so you can compare how smart, attractive, and so on you are with how smart, attractive, and so on everyone else appears to be. Social comparison processes inform students' self-evaluations as they work on abilities about which they are unsure and then make relative comparisons: Am I artistic? A good speaker? A good reader? Early-elementary-grade children do not to use social comparison information to diagnosis their abilities (instead, they rely on information from parents and teachers), so social comparison processes are important only from the third grade on and reach their peak in importance during adolescence.

Most of the time social comparison is an active rather than a passive process, as students make social comparisons for a purpose. Three such purposes exist: (1) to diagnosis an accurate self-view; (2) to construct a favorable self-view; and (3) to learn what excellence—the best—is. When students want to self-diagnose (to construct an accurate self-view), they compare their characteristics, attributes, and abilities to those of peers who are similar and share with them other qualities such as age, gender, or physical characteristics (Zanna, Goethals, &

Hill, 1975). When students seek to construct a favorable self-view, however, they engage in a self-enhancing strategy called *downward social comparison* (Pyszczynski et al., 1985; Taylor & Lobel, 1989; Wills, 1981), in which they compare themselves to others who they suspect to be less smart, less talented, and the like (so the student comes out looking most favorable). Downward social comparisons serve a self-protective (rather than a self-diagnostic) purpose, and they occur mostly after experiences that threaten the self, such as failure and rejection. Finally, when students seek to learn what excellence, or the best, is, they engage in *upward social comparison,* in which they intentionally compare themselves to others who they suspect to be more able to define what excellence is on some particular ability (e.g., experts, professionals, gifted students; Gibbon, Benbow, & Gerrard, 1994). Upward social comparisons help the student formulate and judge the viability of a possible self.

Identity

The second aspect of the self is *identity*. Identity refers to who or what one is within a cultural context (Gecas & Burke, 1995), which is another way of saying that identity emerges from the meanings the culture attaches to the roles the individual inhabits. Who one is, for instance, might be *teacher* (your role, or meaning, to students), *mother* (your role to your own children), *rich tourist* (your role to a San Francisco taxi driver), and so on. Identity emerges from social interaction and interpersonal relationships and therefore gives the self a highly social face. Of the three topics discussed in the present chapter (self-concept, identity, and ego), identity is the self's most public aspect.

Roles (Observational Activity 8.2)

A role consists of cultural expectations for behavior from persons who inhabit a particular position in a societal structure (Gross, Mason, & McEachern, 1958). The self inhabits different positions in the societal structure (i.e., roles), depending on which situation the self is in and depending on with whom the self is interacting. For instance, during the class you are taking and while talking with your professor, you inhabit the role of *student*. When you leave this class, drive a few miles down the road to the school, and begin to interact with your class of fifth-graders, you inhabit the role of *teacher*. When you go home at the end of the day and interact with your family, you may inhabit the roles of *spouse* and *parent*. While you occupy one role rather than another, your social interaction behaviors vary systematically—the topic of your conversation, the vocabulary you use, your tone of voice, and so forth. Compare the social interaction styles of an adolescent who, in school, occupies the role of *student,* but with friends after school occupies the role of *leader*.

Our social interaction behaviors vary to such an extent from one role to the next that it makes sense to speak of *identities* in the plural rather than *identity* in the singular. Thus, we possess a full repertoire of identities, and the self presents to others the identity that is most appropriate for a particular situational context. Identities are, therefore, the social positions students inhabit.

Affect Control Theory

Anytime you participate in social interaction, your chief task is to figure out who you are and who the other people are. Perhaps that sounds silly, but deciding how to act and what to say is difficult when the identities of the self and others remain in question. Knowing what roles the self and others occupy in a given situation tells you which behaviors and which ways of interacting are most and least appropriate. According to affect control theory (Heise, 1979, 1985; MacKinnon, 1994; Smith-Lovin & Heise, 1988), people act differently with one another because different identities have different sentiments—or feelings—associated with them. Affect control theory expresses the meanings a culture attaches to its identities numerically along the three independent dimensions of evaluation (how good?) (E), potency (how powerful?) (P), and activity (how lively?) (A) (after Osgood, May, & Miron, 1975; Osgood, Suci, & Tannenbaum, 1957). Taken together, these dimensions are abbreviated EPA. Each of the three EPA scores ranges from a mathematical low of –4 to high of +4 and uses the following bipolar descriptors: evaluation (–4 = bad, mean; +4 = good, nice); potency (–4 = weak, powerless; +4 = strong, powerful); and activity (–4 = slow, old; +4 = fast, lively). For illustration, the left-hand side of Table 8-1 lists some teacher-related and student-related identities with their associated EPA meanings, as rated by U.S. college students. According to the table, the EPA meaning of a teacher is (approximately) +1, +1, 0 (which is somewhat nice, somewhat strong, and neither active nor passive), and the meaning of a student is +1, 0, +2 (which is somewhat nice, neither strong nor weak, and highly active). The right-hand side of Table 8-1 lists some typical classroom behaviors with their associated EPA meanings to illustrate that behaviors, like identities, also have EPA meanings.

Affect control theory labels the identities shown on the lefthand side of Table 8-1 as *fundamental sentiments*. Fundamental sentiments represent how a culture understands its identities. A culture understands and expects a teacher to be someone who is somewhat nice, somewhat strong, and neither active nor passive (i.e., EPA = +1, +1, 0). Once in a particular setting, however, events create *transitory impressions* of persons whose meanings (EPA scores) might or might not be different from the fundamental sentiment. All this is simply to say that if a teacher (EPA = 1, 1, 0) controls (EPA = –1, 2, 0) students, then the act of control creates a transitory impression that stand at odds with the fundamen-

TABLE 8-1   EPA Meaning of Classroom Identities (on Left) and Behaviors (on Right)

EPA Meanings of Classroom Identities				EPA Meanings of Classroom Behaviors			
Identity	E	P	A	Behavior	E	P	A
Teacher-Related Identities:				*Teacher-Related Behaviors:*			
Boor	-1.61	-0.99	-1.01	Confuse	-0.90	0.58	0.77
Boss	0.28	1.81	-0.26	Control	-1.42	2.23	0.03
Disciplinarian	-0.62	1.02	-0.93	Humor	0.38	0.69	-0.11
Expert	1.40	1.70	0.84	Ignore	-1.53	-0.20	-0.19
Instructor	0.80	1.44	0.14	Interest	1.71	1.23	0.28
Killjoy	-1.63	0.19	-0.28	Neglect	-2.00	-0.24	0.13
Ogre	-2.28	1.99	0.40	Praise	1.68	1.69	0.30
Slavedriver	-2.37	1.80	1.39	Support	1.64	2.20	0.17
Teacher	0.93	1.22	0.03	Teach	1.91	2.21	-0.27
Windbag	-1.37	-0.67	0.41	Thank	1.91	1.69	-0.45
Student-Related Identities:				*Student-Related Behaviors:*			
Brat	-2.04	-1.33	2.58	Answer	1.43	0.78	-0.13
Bully	-2.23	1.29	1.86	Cheat	-2.13	0.02	0.77
Clown	1.44	-0.40	1.30	Disrespect	-2.32	-0.49	1.17
Devil	-2.65	1.82	1.44	Fight	-1.20	0.66	1.87
Dropout	-1.10	-1.38	1.12	Interrupt	-1.29	0.40	1.68
Pest	-1.94	-0.70	1.65	Listen to	1.72	0.73	-0.95
Scholar	1.56	0.83	-0.34	Obey	0.52	0.40	-0.38
Student	1.35	-0.12	2.10	Outwit	0.64	1.53	0.72
Troublemaker	-2.17	0.29	1.54	Question	0.58	1.17	0.98
Whizkid	0.91	1.23	1.80	Refuse	-0.59	0.79	0.13

Note. E = Evaluation, P = Potency, and A = Activity; each scale has a possible range of -4 to +4.
Source: Adapted with permission from Heise (1991).

tal sentiment associated with teacher (at least with respect to goodness and power). We call this discrepancy between a culturally defined identity versus a behaviorally implied identity a *deflection*. Deflections range from nonexistent (identity-confirming behavior) to very large (identity-violating behavior). When they occur, deflections motivate behavior (MacKinnon, 1994), and once energized, behavior takes a specific direction as the self tries behaviorally to restore its original, culturally defined fundamental sentiment (Smith-Lovin, 1990; Smith-Lovin & Heise, 1988). To restore a fundamental sentiment, the individual must engage in an *identity-restorative* act. This, then, is the affect control principle: Students engage in social interactions in order to minimize affective deflection (MacKinnon, 1994). Hence, much classroom behavior occurs as identity maintenance and as identity restoration.

This is the vocabulary of affect control theory: fundamental sentiments, transitory impressions, deflections, and identity-restoring behaviors. The society defines the fundamental sentiments associated with each of its identities (e.g., "I am a teacher; the culture therefore sees me as somewhat nice, somewhat strong, and neither active nor passive"). Situational events create transitory impressions (e.g., "a student brings the teacher an apple; this implies that the teacher is very—rather than only somewhat—nice."). Discrepancies between fundamental sentiments and transitory impressions create deflections (e.g., "My identity suggests I am somewhat nice, but the student's gift suggests I am very nice"). Finally, identity-restoring behaviors follow from felt discrepancies, a process that we will discuss shortly.

At this point, let me say explicitly *how* identities motivate behavior. Once a student occupies a given identity, a teacher can predict his or her ensuing behavior. That is, a student in the role of *troublemaker* (EPA = –2, 0, 2, in Table 8-1) fights (–1, 0, 2) and disrespects (–2, 0, 1); a student in the role of *scholar* (2, 1, 0) answers (1, 1, 0) and listens (2, 1, –1). The meaning is this: Nice identities lead students to behave in nice ways, powerful identities lead students to behave in powerful ways, passive identities lead students to behave in passive ways, and so on.

Consider the classroom applications of fundamental sentiments, transient impressions, and identity-restoring acts. In U.S. culture, we expect a "teacher" (0.9, 1.2, 0.0) to behave in a mostly nice, fairly powerful, and neither active nor passive way, and we expect a "student" (1.4, –0.1, 2.1) to behave in a positive, neither powerful nor weak, and very active way. Given the EPA profiles of teacher and student, affect control theory uses its mathematical equations and computer software program to predict that teachers should "greet, compliment, speak to, and praise" students, who in turn, should "dazzle, amaze, and entertain" the teacher. When a teacher "teaches" and "inspires" students, both teacher and students maintain their fundamental identities and can continue identity prototypical acts. When a teacher "neglects" a student, however, affect control theory predicts one of three events will occur: The student either (1) acts to restore her identity as a student (and therefore will "confront or disagree with" the teacher), (2) reevaluate her identity away from "student" and toward an identity of one who is neglected, or (3) reevaluate the teacher away from "teacher" and toward an identity of one who neglects. Notice that when a teacher fails to behave in an identity-confirming way (for both teacher and student identities), only ill-fated results follow—the student either (1) behaves in a nonstudent way, (2) reidentifies the self away from "student," or (3) reidentifies the teacher away from the "teacher."

Above all else, affect control theory is an identity maintenance theory (Robinson & Smith-Lovin, 1992). That is, teachers and students behave in identity-consistent ways. In addition to performing identity-consistent behaviors, people have additional ways to maintain or to restore their identities (i.e., fundamental sentiments). Teachers and students can maintain their identities through a strategic emotion display (Robinson, Smith-Lovin, & Tsoudis, 1994) as well as through selectively choosing who they do and do not want to interact with (Robinson & Smith-Lovin, 1992). As to displays of emotion, a "teacher who ignores a student" can show a sorrowful facial expression to send an identity-restoring message that says to the student, "I did a bad behavior to you, but since you can see that I feel bad about it then you should still see me as an overall nice person." Emotion displays create transitory impressions just as behavioral acts do, and these transitory impressions act as identity cues such that good people who act badly should show a sorrowful emotion if they are truly good people (just as bad people who act badly should show no such sorrowful emotion if they are truly bad people).

As for selectively choosing whom you want to interact with (a process referred to as *selective interaction*), students can seek those interaction partners who they think are most likely to confirm, or verify, their identities (Robinson & Smith-Lovin, 1992; Swann, 1987, 1990). Students who occupy a positive identity seek interaction partners (friends, roommates, tutors, teachers, spouses, teammates, etc.) who will treat them in a positive way. Students with negative identities seek interaction partners who will treat them in a negative way. Similarly, students with a powerful identity seek people who will treat them in a power-confirming way. That is, as a rule, people seek out interaction partners who confirm their identities—regardless of whether that identity is a culturally positive and valued one or a culturally negative and devalued one (Swann, Pelham, & Krull, 1989). You might ask, "Why would a student with a negative identity (e.g., *bully* or *troublemaker*) intentionally seek out and prefer to interact with fellow-students who they know will treat him in a negative and critical way?" The answer lies in the identity negotiation process, in which people use others to provide self-verifying feedback that maintains their identity (Swann, 1987).

All this research on identity-maintaining behaviors, emotion displays, and interactions partners offers a clear message to teachers—namely, that students behave in a way that is consistent with the identity they occupy. If teachers want students to behave in a way that is positive, powerful, and active, then teachers need to allow students the opportunities to occupy identities that are positive, powerful, and active—identities such as *leader, captain, tutor, explorer, researcher, detective, artist, instructor, athlete, scientist,* and *whizkid*—rather than identities that are negative, weak, and passive. One way a teacher might accomplish this objective would be to structure a classroom so students occupy roles such as detective (here is a mystery, see if you can figure it out) and teacher (break students into dyads for reciprocal teaching in which each student tutors the other on a lesson). A second way a teacher might accomplish this objective would be to offer positive, powerful, and active possible selves for student to emulate. A classroom guest, a model on a videotape, or some other means of introducing possible selves to emulate can create the opportunity for students to occupy positive, powerful, and active identities.

Ego Development

The third aspect of the self is *ego.* Defining ego is difficult because ego is not so much a thing as it is a developmental process. The essence of ego development is the self's progression toward what is possible in terms of psychological growth, maturity, adjustment, competence, and autonomous functioning (Deci, 1980; Loevinger, 1976). Perhaps the best way to introduce the concept of ego is to overview its typical stages of development (from Loevinger, 1976):

- Symbiotic
- Impulsive
- Self-protective
- Conformist
- Conscientious
- Autonomous
- Integrated

During the (infantile) symbiotic stage of development, the ego is extremely immature and exists only in a dependent relation with its caretaker. With language, the symbiotic ego differentiates itself from the primary caretaker but remains terribly immature. In the impulsive stage, external forces (parental constraints, rules), not the ego per se, curb the child's impulses and desires. Self-control begins to emerge when the child learns to anticipate consequences (i.e., punishments) and understands that rules exist. The main rule during the self-protective stage is, however, "Don't get caught," as getting caught (an external, rather than an internal, standard) defines an act as wrong. During the conformist stage, the ego accepts group-accepted rules, and the threat of group disapproval functions as a potent sanction that curbs the child's impulses. The conscientious ego has a "conscience," as define by an internalization of rules and a sense of responsibility to others, in which internal standards curb the student's impulses even in the absence of other people. The conscientious ego is the modal ego stage for adults (Loevinger, 1976). The autonomous ego is one in which activity stems from within the self; that is, the emergent center of one's activity is the self, rather than societal pressures, rules, and constraints (Ryan, 1993). Finally, the integrated stage (which is the rarest ego stage) is essentially what Maslow (1987) termed *self-actualization,* an all-encompassing term that defines all those aspects of the ego that contribute to what is possible in terms of psychological growth, maturity, adjustment, competence, and autonomous functioning.

Perhaps no theory better communicates the role that teachers and schools can contribute to students' ego development than Erik Erikson's (1963, 1964, 1968). Erikson describes eight ego developmental turning points, the approximate age at which each turning point occurs, the social agents who influence the outcomes at stake during each turning point, and the inner resource (i.e., "ego virtue") acquired upon a successful resolution of each turning point. Erikson argued that ego development "has a ground plan" in which ego development proceeds naturally through a series of eight consecutive turning points. With each developmental turning point, the ego moves either in a direction of increased strength and adaptation or in a direction of increased weakness and maladaptation. Erikson's life span theory outlines the developmental turning points people face during eight phases of their lives: infancy, early childhood, preschool years, elementary grades, secondary grades, young adulthood, adult-hood, and older age. Human beings pass through all eight stages, but stages 3, 4, and 5 emerge during the K–12 years and therefore deserve our special attention.

Influence of Preschool Education on Ego Development: Initiative versus Guilt

The chief ego characteristic preschool teachers can promote is *purpose,* or self-determination (Chapter 2). The ego-developmental turning point pre-schoolers face is that of moving toward initiative versus guilt. Four- and five-year-olds become increasingly experimental and increasingly capable in physical, language, and imagination skills, their curiosity is untiring, and as-similation and learning are vigorous (Erikson, 1959). Equipped with such skills, curiosity, and vigor, children test the limits adults impose on them to learn what is and is not permissible. When adults support and encourage pre-schoolers' curiosity and vigor, children develop initiative and a tendency to explore; when adults ridicule and suppress preschoolers' curiosity and vigor, children develop guilt and a tendency to live within the narrow limits others impose on them.

The teacher's task during initiative support is to find the means to nurture students' zest for initiative while, at the same time, communicating clearly classroom limits that presuppose that all childhood desires and impulses cannot be enacted. The balance between initiative support and limit setting is indeed a fine line to walk, but Table 2-1 (in Chapter 2) outlined five essential elements of autonomy-supportive classrooms: Acknowledging the child's point of view; encouraging choice and initiative; communicating rationale for social control; acknowledging that negative emotion is a valid reaction to social control; and relying on noncontrolling, positive feedback.

Influence of Elementary Education on Ego Development: Industry versus Inferiority

The chief ego characteristic elementary-grade teachers can promote is compe-tence (Chapter 4). The ego-developmental turning point elementary-grade students face is that of moving toward industry (or competence) versus inferiority. Children aged six to eleven engage themselves in the learning of all those tasks necessary for "entrance into life," such as social skills and the ability to work cooperatively with others, but Erikson stressed one task that occupies elementary-grade children's ego development more than others—learning the pleasure of work and of a job well done. When episodes of challenge seeking and performance outcomes produce positive feedback and completed tasks, children develop industry and a sense of competence; when challenge seeking and performance outcomes produce negative feedback and consistently unfinished tasks, children develop inferiority and a sense of incompetence.

The teacher's task during industry support is to provide students with developmentally appropriate challenges, positive feedback that communicates a job well done, and discussions about the relationship between perseverance and the pleasure of a job well done. In addition, Woolfolk (1995) offered the following three guidelines:

1. Give students a chance to show their independence and responsibility (e.g., delegate to students tasks like watering plants, collecting and distributing materials).
2. Invite students to set and work toward realistic goals (e.g., begin with short assignments, then move on to longer ones).
3. Provide support to discouraged students (e.g., keep samples of earlier work so students can see their improvements).

Influence of Middle and High School Education on Ego Development: Identity versus Role Confusion

The chief ego characteristic middle and high school teachers can promote is identity (as discussed earlier in the chapter). The ego-developmental turning point secondary-grade students face is that of moving toward identity versus role confusion. Adolescents struggle with the transition from childhood to adulthood, and they use their sense of self-determination and competence to direct their initiative and industry toward specific adult endeavors and societal roles that are available to them (Baumeister, 1986, 1987). When they search for, find, and eventually commit to a particular "strategy for life," adolescents develop an identity and gain the ego virtue of fidelity (or loyalty); when they fail to search for, find, or commit to adult roles, adolescents develop role confusion and a sense of ego uncertainty (Meilman, 1979).

The teacher's task during identity support is to create classroom opportunities in which students test their aspirations, possible selves, and personal beliefs and explore the aspirtions, possible selves, and beliefs of others. This information allows adolescents the opportunity to make deliberate choices in various aspects of their lives, such as vocation and personal values. Woolfolk (1995) offered the following guidelines for teachers to encourage identity exploration and formation:

1. Give students many models for career choices and other adult roles (e.g., invite guest speakers of all kinds to describe how and why they chose their professions).
2. Be tolerant of teenage fads as long as they don't offend others or interfere with learning (e.g., don't impose strict dress or hair codes).
3. Help students find resources for working out personal problems (e.g., discuss potential outside services, such as career counselors).

The Problem with Self-Esteem

It hardly seems appropriate to close a chapter on the self without at least a brief discussion of self-esteem. The problem with including self-esteem in the study of motivation is that research shows "there are almost no findings that self-esteem causes anything at all. Rather, self-esteem is caused by a whole panoply of successes and failures. . . . What needs improving is not self-esteem but improvement of our skills [for dealing] with the world" (Seligman, quoted in Azar, 1994, p. 4).

Two questions in particular occupy the attention of educators:

1. Where does self-esteem come from (and how does it change)?
2. Do increases in self-esteem produce contingent increases in school achievement?

In effect, the first question asks, "Why do some students have relatively high self-esteem while others have relatively low self-esteem?" The second question asks, "What is the causal relationship between self-esteem and achievement?" As to the first question, the ontological roots of self-esteem are multidimensional and include the following five sources (Crocker, 1994; Crocker, Luhtanen, Blaine, & Broadnax, 1994): secure attachments in one's interpersonal relationships; positive reflected appraisals of how others see and evaluate us (e.g., "Others think highly of me"); positive social comparison outcomes (e.g., "Compared to everyone else, I have many fine attributes"); specific competencies valued by both self and society (e.g., "I am a highly skilled teacher"); and positive social identities (e.g., the person occupies identities that score high on the E, or goodness, dimension). As to the second question, the causal role that self-esteem plays in enhancing academic achievement is this: Increases in self-esteem do not produce increases in academic achievement; rather, increases in academic achievement produce increases in self-esteem (Byrne, 1984; Marsh, 1990; Scheier & Kraut, 1979; Shaalvik & Hagtvet, 1990). The causal arrow linking self-esteem and academic achievement is as follows: Academic achievement → increases in self-esteem.

If self-esteem is not the royal road to enhancing academic achievement in students, then what is? There are several aspects of self-functioning that are empirically validated means to enhance academic achievement—self-schemas, possible selves, self-efficacy, ability beliefs, personal control beliefs, and so on. I suggest that proponents of self-esteem enhancement programs consider diverting some of their effort toward encouraging students' inner resources that researchers find link more directly to academic achievement. Some educators agree. Beane (1991), for instance, argues that schools should emphasize promoting self-functioning over promoting self-esteem. Specifically, Beane (1991) recommends schools emphasize authentic participation, collaborative action, a problem-centered curriculum, and interdependent diversity as well as work to remove practices that detract from self-functioning such as tracking, autocratic classroom climates, a unicultural curriculum, and competition. It is self-functioning, not self-esteem per se, that promotes the energetic and directed behavior that leads to healthy personal development.

Conclusion

I would like to conclude by addressing the chapter's title directly and asking, "What qualities characterize a healthy sense of self?" The attempt to characterize those qualities that define a healthy self is both important and presumptuous. Personal bias and subjective criteria act as a couple of bogeymen in any effort to say what qualities of the psyche are its healthiest. That notwithstanding, I think the exercise is time well spent. Before reading further, pause and brainstorm two or three qualities of the self that your own experience and perspective lead you to characterize as healthy. Notice how difficult it is to articulate (and defend) qualities of the healthy self.

I will use the contents of this chapter to offer the following three aspects of the healthy self: A self-view that is authentic, realistic, and well articulated (healthy self-concept), a self characterized by positive identities within the social milieu (healthy identity), and a self characterized by agency and a growth-oriented developmental trajectory (healthy ego). The healthiest outcome of discovering and defining the self-concept is to conceptualize a self that is authentic, realistic, and well articulated. Authenticity, which is the opposite of defensiveness and deception, involves discovering and accepting all aspects of oneself. Realism involves an accurate, honest self-appraisal. A well-articulated self is one that both differentiates itself into new life domains as well as integrates that ever-emerging complexity into an overall, coherent self-view (Deci & Ryan, 1991). The healthiest outcome of relating the self to the social world is finding places in the social hierarchy in which the self inhabits positive identities (perhaps powerful and active ones too). That is, identities such as teacher, valedictorian, and athlete are social roles with positive identities that promote health and well-being, while social roles such as unemployed, dropout, and criminal correspond to negative identities that detract from health and well-being. The healthiest outcome of ego development is a self that is both agenetic and hardy. Agency captures the initiative and personal strivings qualities of the ego, as the agenetic self is a self capable of tapping into its own needs and interests (i.e., inner motivational resources) to generate motivation of its own. A hardy self is one that problem-solves in a way that is adaptive rather than maladaptive.

Certainly, we can debate the extent to which these particular aspects of the self characterize its healthiness, but perhaps we can agree that selves do indeed differ in how healthy versus unhealthy they are and this degree of healthiness determines the extent to which the self functions as an inner motivational resource to generate motivation of its own and to face successfully the challenges inherent in personal understanding, social interaction, and competent functioning.

Recommended Readings

Baumeister, R. F. (1987). How the self became a problem: A psychological review of historical research. *Journal of Personality and Social Psychology, 52,* 163–176.

Harter, S. (1985). Processes underlying the construction, maintenance, and enhancement of the self-concept formation in children. In J. Suls & A. Greenwald (Eds.), *Psychological perspectives on the self* (Vol. 3, pp. 132–182). Hillsdale, NJ: Erlbaum.

Loevinger, J. (1976). Stages of ego development. In *Ego development* (Chap. 2, pp. 13–28). San Francisco: Jossey-Bass.

Markus, H. (1977). Self-schemas and processing information about the self. *Journal of Personality and Social Psychology, 35,* 63–78.

Markus, H., & Nurius, P. (1986). Possible selves. *American Psychologist, 41,* 954–969.

Marsh, H. W., Barnes, J., Cairns, L., & Tidman, M. (1984). Self-Description Questionnaire: Age and sex effects in the structure and level of self-concept for preadolescent children. *Journal of Educational Psychology, 76,* 940–956.

Robinson, D. T., & Smith-Lovin, L. (1992). Selective interaction as a strategy for identity maintenance: An affect control model. *Social Psychology Quarterly, 55,* 12–28.

Rosenberg, M. (1986). Self-concept from middle childhood through adolescence. In J. Suls & A. G. Greenwald (Eds.), *Psychological perspectives on the self* (Vol. 3, pp. 107–136). Hillsdale, NJ: Lawrence Erlbaum.

Swann, W. B. (1987). Identity negotiation: Where two roads meet. *Journal of Personality and Social Psychology, 53,* 1038–1051.

Wigfield, A., & Karpathian, M. (1991). Who am I and what can I do? Children's self-concepts and motivation in achievement situations. *Educational Psychologist, 26,* 233–261.

Observational Activities

Observational Activity 8.1:
Twenty Statements Test—"Who Am I?"

The purpose of this interview is to assess the developmental changes that occur in students' self-conceptualizations as they progress from one grade to the next. You will need to solicit the cooperation of at least three students, all of different ages. Try to invite one student from each of Piaget's stages of cognitive development (i.e., preoperational, aged 2–7; concrete-operations, aged 7–11; and adolescents in the formal-operations stage). You might add a fourth student from post–high school adults, if possible. This diverse sample might be difficult to attain, but the goal is to do what you can to obtain a sample of students who vary in their ages.

To complete this interview, ask each student to complete the Twenty Statements Test, a questionnaire that takes about 5 to 10 minutes to complete. You can have all of the students complete the questionnaire simultaneously. To construct the Twenty Statements Test, give each student a separate piece of paper with the numbers 1–20 listed down the left-side margin of the page. Incidentally, I find that primary grade children have a difficult time generating twenty statements; so use a Fifteen Statements Test if your sample involves one or more primary grade student. At the top of the page write the question, "Who am I?" Also, before students begin, include these verbal instructions: "I am going to ask you a question and I want you to write 20 answers to it on the piece of paper. The question is 'Who am I?' and your answers can be anything you want: words, phrases, sentences, or anything at all, so long as you feel satisfied that you have answered the question, 'Who am I?' Answer as if you were giving the answers to yourself, not to somebody else."

To score students' responses, categorize each statement into one of the following categories (which proceed from relatively concrete to relatively abstract): gender, age, name, race, religion, possessions, physical characteristics, family role, student role, social role, occupational role, judgments such as likes and tastes, membership in a group, membership in an abstract category, ideological beliefs, sense of morality, interpersonal style, strivings and motivations, and abstract personality characteristics. You may need to add an additional category or two. To report your results, list the three age groups (preoperational, concrete operations, and formal operations; and maybe adults, too) in columns along the top of the page, and list the fifteen or so categories down the left side of the page in rows. Enter, using either frequencies or percentages, the number of students in each Piagetian stage that describe themselves as within each category.

Once you construct your table, answer the following questions:

Did you see any evidence that as students increased in age their self-concepts became less concrete (i.e., more abstract)? Describe the trends that emerged in the data (e.g., linear or curvilinear). Also, glance back over each student's Twenty Statements and ask, "Are the first few answers (i.e., 1–5) more informative or less informative than the last 15 or so answers?" Do you think the Twenty Statements test is an effective or ineffective tool to give you a sense of the child's self-concept?

Observational Activity 8.2: Identities in the Classroom

The purpose of this observation is to understand teachers and students in terms of the roles they occupy during a typical classroom experience. You will be observing two students and their teacher in the classroom. You will need to gain the permission of the teacher before you begin. During your observation, simply sit where you can easily see both the teacher and the two students. Whatever the class size, focus your attention on just three people—the teacher and the two students. In picking which two students to observe, select two students who seem very different from one another (in gender, race, personality, academic abilities, etc.).

In your observation, identify all the roles the teacher and the two students occupy during the class period. Be imaginative in labeling the roles you see, most of which will be only implicit in nature. For example, if a student intensely volunteers to read aloud, *whizkid* might be an appropriate label; if a student jokingly strives for attention, *clown* might be appropriate. After your observation, make a list of all the identities occupied by the teacher and the two students. Next, list the frequencies associated with each identity. For example, the teacher might occupy the role of *instructor* 22 times but occupy the role of *disciplinarian* only once. Finally, rate each different identity you observed in terms of affect control theory's EPA meanings. That is, rate each identity in terms of evaluation (bad-to-good), potency (weak-to-strong), and activity (slow-to-lively).

Your summary sheet should list each person's various identities, the frequency of those identities, and estimated EPA sources for each identity. Use your rating sheet to answer the following questions. Summarize the collection of identities occupied by the teacher—was the teacher mostly an instructor? A facilitator? A friend? A disciplinarian? Summarize the collection of identities for each student. Overall, how positive, powerful, and active were the identities of the teacher? of each student? Finally, describe each instance (if there were any) in which the teacher tried deliberately to bestow a student with a particular identity (e.g., "Mary, would you be the leader in charge of your table of students?").

9

Curiosity and Interest

Let me begin this chapter with a confession—I recall few of the lectures I heard during my college years back in Tennessee. I can, however, still remember the details of one lecture in particular given by my introductory psychology professor. The title was "Women—The Stronger Sex." I felt confused upon hearing such a nonsensical title and wondered what in the world Dr. Troelstrup had up his intellectual sleeve to justify such a contradiction. (Recall that the cultural context of the past was more chauvinistic than today's.) Dr. Troelstrup informed us that women, compared to men, have a longer life expectancy, are more likely to survive infancy, have a higher tolerance to pain, and are less susceptible to all sorts of psychological disorders (e.g., mental retardation, conduct disorder); men are also more likely, he said, to die of heart attacks, strokes, cancer, respiratory diseases, accidents, liver cirrhosis, suicide, and homicide.

I'll spare you the details of the lecture, but I wonder how much of this information I would have remembered twenty years later had Dr. Troelstrup not first aroused my curiosity via contradiction. (The contradiction is, of course, "You think men are stronger, but the evidence says that women are the stronger sex"). Dr. Troelstrup simply could have listed the biological differences between men and women in a dry, uninspiring way and concluded that research shows that women, compared to men, "live long and prosper." Instead, he began with a contradiction and reiterated it with tantalizing questions throughout ("O.K., which sex do you think is more likely to die of heart attacks?"). I recall that the class discussion was unusually lively that day, and that the person sitting next to me showed her only signs of interest and asked her only questions of the semester on that day. I remember sensing that the class cared about this information, mostly because we wanted our curiosity satisfied. Twenty years later, in retrospect, I can see that some serious, long-lasting learning took place that day. There is something special about how curiosity and interest facilitate learning; pinpointing that *something* is the point of this chapter.

A similar, though more trivial, incident occurred to me just this week to remind me of how curiosity generates a motivational appetite for learning. Lunching at a popular fast-food restaurant, I read this question typed on my tray's cover sheet: "Which came first, dinosaurs or grass?" As I imagine most people would, I guessed grass. But the napkin informed me that dinosaurs had been extinct for 15 million years before the first grass ever grew. Curious, I asked myself some questions: "Well, where did grass come from?" "Where did seeds come from?" "Where did topsoil come from?" Five minutes into my trancelike struggle to figure out the origins of grass, I realized what had happened. The question's surprising answer revealed a gap in my knowledge that I simply could not explain, and my five minutes of cognitive problem solving represented an attempt to reconcile this knowledge gap. Hours later, when I got home, I went straight to the bookshelf to look up the origins of grass in a turfgrass book (I actually had one!). I am sure I would still be in the dark about the origins of grass, seeds, and topsoil had that question about dinosaurs and grass not piqued my curiosity. Because education is about encouraging students to gain knowledge about all sorts of objects and events in the world, curiosity's motivational power to facilitate students' information-seeking efforts is not to be taken lightly.

Curiosity

Curiosity is a cognitively based emotion that occurs whenever a student perceives a gap in his or her knowledge (Loewenstein, 1994). That is, when a student recognizes a discrepancy, or conflict, between what she believes to be true about the world and what turns out actually to be true, curiosity occurs. We feel curious about events that we can neither make sense of nor explain, such as lectures that tell us that women are the stronger sex and pieces of paper that tell us that grass is relatively new to the earth. In addition, curiosity occurs when students encounter unexpected, novel, strange, and unpredictable objects (e.g., the teacher fails to show up for class, brings in a guest speaker, hands out a pop quiz) (Berlyne, 1966).

Curiosity motivates exploratory behavior—the search for information. Exploration is approach behavior aimed at sources of stimulation capable of supplying the information necessary to make sense of the world. When a student asks a question, looks for a book, reads an article in the newspaper, or seeks out a knowledgeable expert in an effort to gain information necessary to clarify a knowledge gap, then that student shows curiosity-inspired, educationally relevant exploratory behavior. (Exploration also occurs covertly via self-directed questioning and thinking [Day, 1982], as with my questions about the origins of grass, seed, and topsoil.) So exploration is the behavioral bridge that links a student's emotional curiosity with her eventual acquisition of the information necessary to reconcile the uncertainty that caused the curiosity in the first place.

The Cause of Curiosity

Two theoretical traditions organize our understanding about the cause of curiosity (Voss & Keller, 1983; Spielberger & Starr, 1994). The first way of understanding curiosity emphasizes the cognitive effects of information and environmental stimulation. The cognitive-developmental theorist Jean Piaget (1952, 1969) exemplifies this research tradition. The second way of understanding curiosity emphasizes the physiological, arousal-based effects of environmental stimulation. The motivational theorist Dan Berlyne (1960, 1966) exemplifies this second tradition.

For Piaget (1969), an expectancy violation ("I expected X, but Y happened") creates the cognitive disequilibrium that gives life to curiosity (in the form of a desire to make sense of the world). That is, cognitive conflicts produce cognitive disequilibria, which in turn produce emotional desire (i.e., curiosity), which initiates our attempts to assimilate new information into existing cognitive structures or to accommodate existing cognitive structures to align themselves with a new way of understanding the world. As a point of illustration, consider that, generally speaking, people presume they understand the world fairly well (Getty, Pliske, Manning, & Casey, 1987). Through personal experiences, conversations with others, and contact with the media, we learn what to expect from any of number of life's activities. In the classroom, students learn what to expect from an algebra class, a visit to the principal's office, a book by Dr. Seuss, an hour spent with a particular teacher, and so on. Expectancy violations tell the student that she might not understand the world (i.e., algebra class, visits to see the principal, Dr. Seuss books, a particular teacher) as well as she thought she did (Mandler, 1982). The new information (and the cognitive conflict the expectancy violation forces upon us) does three things:

1. It points to the inadequacy of our existing cognitive structures.
2. It generates an emotional state of curiosity.
3. It fuels the cognitive processes of assimilation and accommodation—that is, learning (Berlyne, 1960, 1978; Bruner, 1962; Hunt, 1965; Kagan, 1972; Mandler, 1982; Piaget, 1969).

So there is an intimate link between learning and curiosity in that they share a common cause—cognitive conflict—and relate to one another—curiosity motivates learning.

According to Berlyne (1967), human beings seek to establish and maintain a preferred level of arousal. An optimal level of arousal, which varies from one person to the next, feels pleasurable, while too little or too much arousal feels psychologically unpleasant. When a person is underaroused, the feeling of unpleasantness encourages the person to seek out environmental change, novelty, and variety to increase arousal. When a person is overaroused, the feeling of unpleasantness encourages the person to minimize environmental stimulation by inhibiting activity to decrease arousal. Berlyne's theory of curiosity emphasizes that curiosity is only one of the possible emotional reactions students have to various levels of classroom information, stimulation, and challenge. Too little information, stimulation, and challenge cultivates emotional indifference, apathy, or boredom. We will address strategies to overcome such negative emotional reactions in the section titled "Getting Boredom Out of the Classroom." Too much information, stimulation, and challenge, on the other hand, typically cultivates emotional stress, fear, or anxiety, and we will address strategies to overcome these negative emotional reactions as well. In brief, Berlyne's idea is this:

1. Environments vary in how informative, stimulating, and challenging they are.
2. People react emotionally to environmental stimulation by feeling underaroused, optimally-aroused, or overaroused.
3. Underarousal and overarousal are psychologically unpleasant experiences, while optimal-arousal is psychologically pleasant.

Spielberger and Starr (1994) offer a theoretical integration of these two research traditions. Figure 9-1 plots a pair of complex graphs to illustrate the theoretical basis for the relationship between classroom stimulation and students' emotionality. Figure 9-1's lefthand panel plots four variables—emotional reaction (y-axis), arousal potential of the environment (x-axis), curiosity curve, and anxiety curve. *Emotional reaction* refers to Berlyne's three emotional states: indifference, pleasantness (i.e., reward), or unpleasantness (i.e., aversion). *Arousal potential* makes the point that classrooms vary in how informative and stimulating students experience them to be. Sitting alone in the time-out room might typify an environment with little arousal potential, whereas speaking in front of the classroom while being graded might typify an environment rich in arousal potential. A synonym for arousal potential is stimulus intensity (Berlyne, 1960). *Curiosity curve* (or *curiosity drive*) shows that as an environment gains in arousal potential, curiosity increases rapidly up to a point and then levels off as the environment become increasingly informative and stimulating. Finally; *anxiety curve* (or *anxiety drive*) shows that as an environment gains in arousal potential, anxiety increases gradually. The curiosity and anxiety curves show that students experience both positive (approach-oriented) and negative (avoidance-oriented) emotions in the face of increasing arousal potential, although the relationship between curiosity and

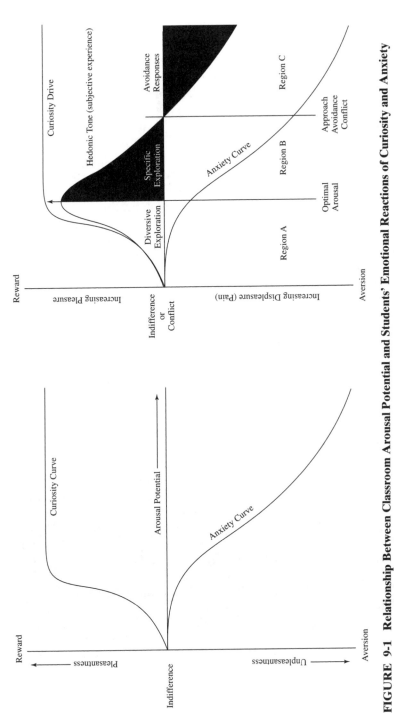

FIGURE 9-1 Relationship Between Classroom Arousal Potential and Students' Emotional Reactions of Curiosity and Anxiety

Source: Adapted with permission from Spielberger, C. D., & Starr, L. M. (1994). In H. F. O'Neil, & M. Drillings (Eds), *Motivation: Theory and research* (pp. 221–243). Hillsdale, NJ: Lawrence Erlbaum.

anxiety to arousal potential differs (notice that the curves have different shapes).

Figure 9-1's righthand panel integrates these four variables into a single schematic representation, the *dual-process theory* (Spielberger & Starr, 1994). These authors contend that curiosity and anxiety are dual, antagonistic emotional processes that interact with each other to produce the motivation underlying approach (exploration) versus avoidance behavior. The wavelike curve between the curiosity and anxiety curves is the mathematical difference between two curves (the avoidance tendency subtracted from the approach tendency). Spielberger and Starr divide this *difference curve* into three regions—A, B, and C. The leftmost part of the curve (region A) shows that when environments offer a mild arousal potential, the resulting motivation is increasingly pleasant (because curiosity is high and anxiety is low). High curiosity with low anxiety produces *diverse exploration,* general stimulus-seeking behavior that people use to raise their emotionality from a state of indifference upward to a state of pleasure and reward. An example of diverse exploration is flipping through the table of contents of a book for something interesting to read or flipping the television's remote control in hopes of discovering something stimulating. The centermost part of the curve (region B) shows that when environments offer a moderate arousal potential, the resulting motivation decreases from very pleasurable to a state of indifference (or conflict between pleasure and displeasure). Throughout region B, curiosity is at its maximum while anxiety continues to increase in proportion to the environment's arousal potential. High curiosity and moderate anxiety produce *specific exploration,* goal-directed information seeking that people use to lower their emotionality from a state of stress and fear downward to a state of pleasure and reward. An example of specific exploration is conducting a goal-directed search through the pages of a book to find a particular topic or scanning the television's remote control to find a particular program. Finally, the rightmost part of the curve (region C) shows that when environments offer dense arousal potential, the resulting motivation is increasingly displeasurable. High curiosity and high anxiety combine in a way that the unpleasantness of anxiety overwhelms the pleasantness of curiosity. Under these conditions, a teacher can expect students to show escape and avoidance behaviors. *Escape* (e.g., withdrawing participation) and *avoidance* (e.g., finding an excuse to skip class) make sense in the context of extreme arousal potential because these behaviors effectively minimize the arousal the student experiences.

Taken as a whole, Figure 9-1 shows how the curves for curiosity and anxiety originate from the arousal potential of an environment and interact with each other to produce the emotional states (reward-aversion) that motivate exploratory and avoidance behaviors. Figure 9-1 presents a pair of complicated graphs, which carry with them a wealth of practical application for the classroom teacher. In making the transition from theoretical graphs to practical application, keep in mind four fundamentals:

1. All classrooms vary in how informative, stimulating, and challenging they are.
2. The teacher exerts a strong influence over the classroom's arousal potential.
3. Arousal potential determines the extent of felt curiosity and anxiety.
4. The particular pattern of curiosity and anxiety determines students' approach versus avoidance tendencies.[1]

We can use Figure 9-1's four fundamentals to offer a number of insights as to how the teacher might go about facilitating curiosity in the classroom. At one end of the continuum, the teacher has the goal of getting indifference and boredom out of the classroom (by increasing arousal potential). At the other end of the continuum, the teacher has the goal of keeping anxiety out of the classroom by not increasing arousal potential too much. The following suggestions seek to increase curiosity to a high level in such a way that anxiety will not piggyback onto student's emotional reactions.

Facilitating Curiosity in the Classroom

The first step in facilitating curiosity is to get boredom out of the classroom. One technique for doing this is to introduce stimulus change. Stimulus change works to counteract students' boredom and indifference, mostly by promoting diverse exploration in students. Most of the time, however, the sort of curiosity and exploration teachers' desire to promote is a learning-specific curiosity that motivates specific exploration. Each strategy to facilitate curiosity discussed after stimulus change aims to produce the kind of curiosity that leads not only to attention and alertness but to learning and intellectual growth as well. Each of these strategies gives rise to a curiosity in which students feel a dissatisfaction with the current state of their knowledge. The specific exploration functions to remedy the perceived gap in their knowledge that the curiosity-facilitating strategy revealed. These curiosity-facilitating strategies are suspense, guessing and feedback, playing to students' sense of knowing, controversy, and contradiction.

Getting Boredom Out of the Classroom

A starting point in the effort to facilitate curiosity is to overcome student indifference and boredom. Boredom is all too often present in the classroom

(Csikszentmihalyi & Larsen, 1984), especially in high school classrooms (Kline, 1977). A teacher works to overcome boredom and indifference by increasing the classroom's arousal potential. When classrooms offer minimal arousal potential, students are inattentive; they daydream and may actually fall asleep (Heron, 1957). Inattentativeness, daydreaming, and falling asleep are all escape behaviors in that the student seeks to remove himself from a psychologically unpleasant situation and move into a more psychologically pleasant situation (e.g., a daydream). A more active student reaction to understimulating class-rooms is to find or create attention-diverting behaviors (e.g., talking, rough-housing, doodling, drawing). Students are not simply passive recipients of whatever stimulation the classroom offers. Rather, students react to impover-ished, understimulating, uninformative classrooms either through psychological escape (e.g., looking out the window) or through creating more stimulating surroundings (e.g., talking).

As a way of thinking about the goal of getting boredom out of the classroom, visit one of the following settings and ask yourself: What could be done to make this a more stimulating, enriching environment?

- Zoo animals in cages
- Inmates in prison cells
- Elderly persons in a nursing home
- Long-term patients in hospital wards
- College students enduring monotonous lectures

As I write this, I recall a recent visit to a zoo in which I observed an elephant just swaying back and forth continually for about an hour. To me, the elephant looked autistic, so much so that I had to ask the zoo attendant what in the world the elephant was doing. He told me that elephants in the wild routinely walk fifteen miles a day; this elephant's swaying was simply an active effort to produce his usual daily exercise, which otherwise was not possible in his single acre of living space. As I remember that elephant, I try to image what my behavior would be like if I were penned up for the rest of the semester in the small office where I sit writing at the moment, or what my attitude toward college would be if I had to sit still and listen passively to a series of lectures day after day, week after week, semester after semester, year after year. Observe other teachers' classrooms and periodically ask yourself, "If I were that teacher, what could I do to increase these students' arousal upward toward an optimal level?"

Stimulus Change

If an experimenter presents the same stimulus over and over (e.g., the same movie, the same musical melody) to a person, the stimulus will quickly lose its "surprisingness" and the person will quickly ignore it (Berlyne, 1966; Berlyne, Craw, Salapatek, & Lewis, 1963; Reeve, 1993). To revive the person's curiosity, stimulus change must occur in the form of a new or unexpected event. In a classroom setting, a teacher might introduce stimulus change (i.e., variety, novelty, unpredictability) by replacing the daily routine (especially the monotonous parts) with periodic group discussions, films, guest speakers, altered seating arrangements, field trips, question and answer sessions, cooperative learning, role playing, mind-teasers, logic puzzles, the vocabulary word for the day, and so on. One teacher brings in Friday's activity to her elementary-grade class wrapped in a brown grocery bag and places it, covered, in the middle of a table in the center of the room. Her students just about die of curiosity wondering what in the world is in that bag!

Other teachers recommend the use of classroom demonstrations because they argue that students generally remain focused on a lecture for only about the first ten minutes (Bernstein, 1994). Active, participation-generating demonstrations (e.g., a memory strategy to recall a list of ten words) can revive lost curiosity. Social stimulation, as through group work, also sparks lost curiosity, especially among adolescents (Mitchell, 1993). Group work arouses curiosity in two ways, as it requires students to become active communicators instead of passive listeners and because it involves students' social needs and social skills in a way that individual work does not. Of course, it is possible to introduce too much stimulus change into the classroom setting (especially for some students, such as those with attention deficit disorder), so the teacher must struggle to find a balance between the stimulus change that gives life to curiosity and the stimulus predictability that gives the classroom its order and structure. For example, giving pop quizzes and randomly calling on students to answer questions both increase the classroom's arousal potential, but the anxiety that such unpredictability brings to some students overwhelms any curiosity they feel. The teacher must also balance the stimulus change that sparks curiosity and promotes learning against the stimulus change that sparks only distraction and interferes with learning.

Suspense

In the drama of the theater, suspense follows a predictable recipe (Hitchcock, 1959; Zillman, 1980). Suspense occurs when well-liked protagonists struggle to overcome obstacles and cope triumphantly with threats and dangers to their well-being. Such events occasion hopes and fears in the audience—hopes for positive outcomes and fears of negative outcomes to the liked persons (as well as hopes for negative outcomes and fears of positive outcomes to the "bad guys"). Suspense thrives on hope and fears (on the anticipation of positive and negative outcomes). Seeing the hero battle obstacles and overcome crises engages the viewer in an emotional struggle in which the drama's story line and its conclusion events carry an emotional impact that would otherwise be missing. For instance, we feel little curiosity upon watching a Pony Express rider deliver mail at the next outpost, but we feel great curiosity (via suspense) if that same rider is a Western hero who loses his horse to a hostile environment, overcomes rattlesnake bites, outsmarts evil-minded outlaws, and otherwise fights his way triumphantly to the next outpost (after Bryant, 1978).

The dynamics of suspense offer the classroom teacher curiosity-inducing opportunities. In the classroom, attention is not so much on heroes and villains as it is on information and solutions to intellectual problems. Focusing students' attention on competing hypotheses and problems with uncertain conclusions imbeds information in a context of mental struggle, not unlike the Western hero's physical struggle with hostile outlaws. Mental struggle is no great fun in and of itself. Conflicts, uncertainties, and problems are emotionally distressing in and of themselves, but resolutions, discoveries, answers, and solutions are emotionally pleasant (e.g., Mandler, 1982). According to excitation-transfer theory (Zillman, 1978), conflict, uncertainties, and problems create autonomic nervous system arousal (e.g., increased heart rate), which is experienced for the most part as an emotionally negative. The resolutions, discoveries, answers, and solutions that soon follow, however, take place in a context of emotional struggle and high arousal that produces a stronger emotionally positive experience than students would otherwise have felt had they simply been given the resolutions, discoveries, and so on without the earlier emotional struggle.

In practice, students feel a negative emotionality upon hearing (and being stumped by) questions such as, "What caused the Civil War?" "Why are dinosaurs extinct?" or "Why are most major cities located near water?" But these questions can be presented in a context of suspense that relies on inviting students to consider competing hypotheses. Competing hypotheses create in students a mental struggle, which produces an emotional readiness for further information that students believe will be instrumental in reconciling their tentative hypotheses and conclusions. The intellectual struggle and the suspense it engenders create an emotionally arousing context in which answers and conclusions will have some emotional punch to them.

The habit of presenting suspense-rich information to students has positive long-term implications for students' willingness to undertake intellectual challenges. Intellectual growth is an emotional struggle that, in itself, can be somewhat aversive and frustrating. Teachers, however, can give students a problem-solving history that pairs intellectual problems with intellectual triumphs and thus essentially pairs emotionally positive experiences with antecedent aversive experiences. Over time, students learn that intellectual struggle often brings emotional pleasure in the end. Eventually, students willingly tolerate a certain degree of aversion because it is a reliable antecedent of pleasure. Some students even come to find the suspense of intellectual problem solving to be a pleasant, eagerly anticipated experience. When mental struggle brings emotional pleasure, problem solving becomes entertaining.

Guessing and Feedback

Generally speaking, students have major gaps in their knowledge but remain unaware of them and unconcerned about these intellectual deficiencies. Students who are unaware of their knowledge gaps are not likely to be curious and therefore are not likely to engage themselves in the effort necessary to attain the information necessary to close such gaps. On the other hand, it is difficult for a student to ignore or deny a gap in his knowledge once he has guessed an answer to a question and then been told his guess is wrong. (This is the inherent appeal of trivia games: Few people really care which Elvis song sold the most records—until asked and stumped.) Feedback that one has guessed incorrectly (No, it wasn't "Jailhouse Rock") is important because, without it, the guesser can believe that she has guessed correctly when she has not. For instance, as you read this you might not be acutely aware of or concerned about your U.S. geographical knowledge gap, but let us try an exercise. Which of the following is the northernmost state: Colorado, Kansas, or Nebraska? Just guessing at the answer or having the answer told to you ("Nebraska") does not necessarily pique your curiosity. But guessing "Colorado" and being told, "Wrong!" does pique your curiosity (Loewenstein, Adler, Behrens, & Gillis, 1992). Likewise, guessing "California" or "Florida" to the question, "Which of the forty-eight contiguous states has the most miles of shoreline?" and being told that one's guess is wrong does raise your curiosity as to which state must be the correct answer. Curiosity over which state it could be might be high enough to prompt a student to ask a question or look the answer up on a map.

It is easy to generalize guessing and feedback to other knowledge domains. The teacher need only ask herself, "What new (unfamiliar) knowledge or theory am I going to tell students about today, and how can I introduce that information in the form of a question to be guessed at?" A physics teacher might hold a heavy object in one hand and a light object in the other and ask students, "If I drop these two objects simultaneously, which one will hit the floor first?" Most students (even first-year college students) guess incorrectly. The wrong guess, mixed with the answer-revealing demonstration, can set the stage for curiosity that opens the door to questioning and learning.

Playing to Students' Sense of Knowing

At some point as a student learns about a particular subject, he experiences a shift in his orientation away from "what I know" and toward "what I don't know." For instance, the Shakespearean novice attends mostly to what little he or she knows about Shakespeare (lived in England, wrote *Romeo and Juliet*), whereas Shakespearean experts attend mostly to what they do *not* know (what was the inspiration for *Romeo and Juliet*?). For people who attend mostly to what they know about a particular domain of knowledge, curiosity is typically low (while anxiety is high); for people who attend mostly to what they do not know, curiosity is typically high (while anxiety is low). Test yourself on the following question: "Name the eight states that border one of the Great Lakes." Monitor yourself on these variables: How many states can you name? How many are you unable to name? Do you feel a sense of knowing or a sense of not knowing? Does your curiosity outweigh your anxiety, or does your anxiety outweigh your curiosity? How much desire do you feel to pull an atlas off the shelf? If you can name many of the states, your attention will likely go toward the few unnamed states, you will feel mostly a sense of knowing, your curiosity will outweigh your anxiety, and you will desire to some degree to use the atlas. If you can name only three or so of the states, however, your attention will probably go mostly toward the few named states, you will feel mostly a sense of not knowing, your anxiety will outweigh your curiosity, and you will have little or no desire to use the atlas.

The same example can be extended to "whodunit" mysteries (curiosity is lowest with ten suspects, but highest after narrowing the suspects down to two or three) and to learning how-to projects. In learning how to use a computer, a student might believe there are eight essential bits of knowledge necessary to work a computer (e.g., turn on, log on, type document, edit it, save it, print it, log off, and turn off). Gaining each piece of how-to information goes along way in reducing the student's sense of not knowing and increasing her sense of knowing. At some point in her learning, she will cross over from a sense of not knowing about computers that carries with it an anxiety-ridden avoidance motivation to a sense of knowing about computers that carries with it a curiosity-enriched exploration motivation. The ability that a sense of knowing has to promote curiosity leads to a recommendation that teachers might present information in such a way that it adds to students previously learned information (appeals to their sense of knowing) rather than in a way that tells them what they do know (appeals to their sense of not knowing).

Controversy

Controversy occurs in the classroom when one person's ideas, information, conclusions, theories, or opinions are incompatible with those of another and the two attempt to reach an agreement (Johnson & Johnson, 1979). Controversy creates a mental struggle to resolve divergent points of view, and the mental struggle sparks the curiosity that leads interactants to engage in the information seeking necessary to achieve agreement or consensus. Lowry and Johnson

(1981) put this idea to the test by asking fifth- and sixth-grade students to learn some new information in a small-group setting. Some students were to critique, argue, and debate one another (controversy group), while others were to compromise and not to argue (no-controversy group). As each group discussed and learned the information, the researchers unobtrusively recorded a variety of the students' information-seeking behaviors, including each student's use of optional books, use of pictures and filmstrips in the library, use of an in-class folder full of topic-relevant information, and attendance at an optional topic-relevant film shown during recess period. On each of these four measures of exploration, students in the controversy group used them more than students in the no-controversy group. The students in the controversy group also expressed the stronger desire to learn about the topic, and they scored higher on a later achievement test on the information. Overall, encouraging controversy among ideas promotes students' willingness to seek out and attain information and evidence necessary to defend an idea, to resolve differences of opinion, or to reach group consensus.

Contradiction

A contradiction occurs after a student assimilates a succession of facts that lead him to formulate a conclusion, only to be confronted by additional information that opposes—or contradicts—that previously inferred conclusion. Vidler (1974) provides the following three examples of the use of contradiction to create the curiosity that leads to information-seeking and learning:

1. Biology students generally hold the conclusion that human beings sit atop the evolutionary developmental ladder. A contradiction occurs, however, when they hear that insects dominate the world in terms of both number of species and number of individuals (i.e., there are more species of insects than there are of all other animals put together) and that the weight of insects on the earth is greater than the weight of all other animals combined (Vidler, 1974). Given these facts, why do not biologists say insects sit atop the evolutionary ladder?

2. The shell of mollusks (e.g., clams, oysters) seems to be an advantage because it increases safety, allows for considerable size and bulk, and makes muscles efficient (because there is a firm point of attachment for the muscle). The contradiction is that the most successful mollusks (e.g., octopus, squid) abandoned the shell.

3. Sodium (Na+) and chlorine (Cl–) are both human poisons. Combined as NaCl, however, they constitute basic table salt. How can a nutritional staple be composed of a pair of poisons?

To resolve each contradiction, the student requires additional information. In the face of a contradiction, it becomes clear that one's present level of knowledge is inadequate. The perception of inadequate knowledge is the essential cause of curiosity, so contradiction creates curiosity, which in turn energizes and directs the student's search for information.

Interest

In many people's minds, curiosity and interest are the same. Many motivation theorists use the two terms interchangeably (e.g., Renninger, Hidi, & Krapp, 1992). In contrast, I find it helpful to distinguish between curiosity and interest. As I see it, *curiosity* is like an itch for students—they hurriedly do what they can to get rid of it. Satisfying curiosity is an emotional positive, but feeling curious is not. As Loewenstein (1994) pointed out, if people liked feeling curious, they would put down the mystery novel before reading the final chapter, or leave the baseball stadium before the final inning of a close game (so they could continue feeling curious). In contrast, students find the experience of *interest* to be pleasurable in and of itself (Reeve, 1989). Students very much want to continue activities that allow them to feel interested. Another difference is that curiosity is typically a short-lived emotion that disappears quickly upon learning the information that fills a knowledge gap. Interest, on the other hand, endures more steadily (e.g., Hidi & Anderson, 1992). Our interest in literature, science, and the New York Yankees endures.

Understanding how interest develops and endures over time is the focus of the next section: "The Cause of Interest." In the final section, "Individual Interests," I address questions such as, "Why is it that one student picks up an interest in math, a second student picks up an interest in English, while a third student picks up no interest in school at all?"

The Cause of Interest

Interest is an emotion that flows from a person's relationship with a particular activity. Both the person and the activity bring their unique characteristics into this relationship. That is, different people have unique needs, capacities, and skills; different activities present unique opportunities, challenges, and demands. Interest occurs when a person's needs, capacities, and skills are a good match for the opportunities, challenges, and demands offered by a particular activity (Deci, 1992b; Gibson, 1988). That is, the task students find most interesting is the one that provides opportunities to satisfy their needs, challenges the skills they have and care about, and demands they exercise and develop the capacities that are important to them.

Some students need greater affiliation than others; some students have greater capacity to sing well while others have greater capacity to run fast; some have greater skill in reading while others have more skill in interpersonal relationships. Likewise, some activities provide opportunities to be with friends while others offer a more solitary participation; some activities require vocal talents while others demand perceptual-motor coordination; and some activities challenge reading skills while others challenge social skills. As students carry their needs, capacities, and skills into the school setting, they encounter some tasks that match nicely with their constellation of needs and abilities as well as some tasks that do not match at all. The greater the match between a person's needs, capacities, and skills and the activity's opportunities, challenges, and demands, they greater is the probability that the student will show high interest in that particular activity (Deci, 1992b). Consider a student who has a relatively strong need for affiliation and relatedness and, over time, has developed rather sophisticated interpersonal and communicative skills. This student may well be most interested in activities such as hanging out with a group of friends, acting in a school play, and chatting on the telephone, assuming that such activities involve his need to relate to others and challenge his interpersonal skills. I would also imagine that he would have little interest in activities such as playing a musical instrument, fishing alone, or solving crossword puzzles, unless of course these activities addressed other needs, capacities, and skills that were important to him.

The Educational Importance of Interest

How interested a student is in an activity or in a domain of knowledge predicts how much or how little he or she attends to it and how well he or she processes, comprehends, and remembers that information (e.g., Hidi, 1990; Renninger, Hidi, & Krapp, 1992; Renninger & Wozniak, 1985; Schiefele, 1991; Shirey & Reynolds, 1988). Stated in a single sentence, the educational importance of interest is this: "Interest, particularly one's personal investment in the topic or domain, stimulates depth of processing in the content and, thus, enhances subject-matter learning" (Alexander, Kulikowich, & Jetton, 1994, p. 217).

Individual Interests

To study interest, some educators focus mostly on characteristics of the student, as they ask questions such as why a particular student is interested in mathematics, in a foreign language, or in reading, (e.g., Renninger, 1990). Other educators focus mostly on the characteristics of the activity, as they ask questions such as why one particular subject, book, lecture, friend, teacher, or video game comes across to students as more interesting than another does (e.g., Hidi & Baird,

1986). In the terminology of educators who study motivation, the first approach to the study of interest refers to *individual interests,* the second approach to *situational interests.* Individual interests are the interests students bring with themselves into the classroom; situational interests are the interests students experience as they participate in and become acquainted with a particular activity at a particular time. Thus, individual interest researchers study individual differences among students, whereas situational interest researchers study classroom settings and task characteristics (Mitchell, 1993). I will first touch on the topic of situational interests, but mostly this section focuses on individual interests.

Situational Interests: Characteristics of Interesting Activities

Students find some activities more interesting than others. For one reason or another, students generally come to agree that some books, lectures, games, classes, topics of discussion, teachers, friends, activity centers, sports, stores, or days of the week are more interesting than are others. As discussed earlier, when tasks generate positive emotional states (or the anticipation of positive emotional states) such as excitement, enthusiasm, joy, satisfaction, mastery, or pride, students find them to be relatively interesting. Tasks generate such positive emotional states when they allow students to involve and satisfy their needs, optimally challenge their skills, and stretch their capacities (Danner & Lonky, 1981; Malone, 1981). When tasks involve students' needs and provide developmentally appropriate challenges, the interest aroused is termed *situational interest* because the same task may or may not arouse interest the next time the student encounters it. For instance, the first time a student encounters a computer software program, its sensory stimulation and cognitive curiosities might be highly interesting, but once the student learns and masters the skill in question, then these same sensory and cognitive stimulations may not arouse an equal amount of interest on the next encounter. Mitchell (1993) makes the same point by arguing that a wonderful color illustration in a book may *catch* a student's interest, but once the student places the book aside, then the illustration might not be able to *hold* the student's interest.

Individual Interests: Characteristics of Interested Students

All students have individual interests (e.g., Renninger, 1992). For one reason or another, one student picks up an interest in math, while a second student picks up an interest in English. Individual interests arise from two major sources of experience: (1) extensive background knowledge in a particular domain and (2) an internalized valuing of a particular domain (Hidi, 1990; Hidi & Baird, 1986; Kintsch, 1980; Mitchell, 1993; Schank, 1979; Tobias, 1994).

When a student gains extensive background knowledge in a particular domain, he or she has several interest-enhancing advantages over the less knowledgeable. Students with extensive background knowledge are able to formulate numerous knowledge-based expectancies about how tasks and activities in that domain should be. The knowledgeable student recognizes when tasks, activities, and information violate her expectancies and can therefore add to her knowledge. This perception of a gap in her knowledge plays to her sense of knowing, and the curiosity that emanates from a sense of knowing generates an interest in learning further. The unknowledgeable student, on the other hand, finds unfamiliar tasks, activities, and information too unfamiliar and therefore too anxiety-provoking. The knowledgeable student also engages in deeper cognitive processing (while reading), employs more imagery, and accesses a wider, more emotional, and more personal associate network of information about the task (Tobias, 1994). Thus, this first source of individual interest is a knowledge-triggered interest (Renninger, Hidi, & Krapp, 1992; Schiefele, 1991; Tobias, 1994). Domain-relevant knowledge is a particularly important interest activator for older students, because as students advance from one grade to the next their knowledge becomes increasingly specialized and grows in depth (Alexander, Kulikowich, & Jetton, 1994).

The second source of individual interest is a value-triggered interest. When a student attaches a personal significance or meaning to a particular domain, he feels a special interest for tasks and activities within that domain (Schiefele, 1992). The origins of a positive feeling and of a positive valuing of a particular topic or task owe their origins to perceptions that the subject area allows the student (1) to perform meaningful projects that make sense within both a personal and cultural context and (2) to involve the needs and improve the skills students care about or see as important. So the student with an interest in science (or literature, or whatever) is the student whose personal experience in that domain has been one rich in meaningful, life-relevant projects as well as in actualized opportunities for need involvement and skill development.

Social influences—parents, teachers, peers—determine much of the value or personal significance a students learns to associate with a particular activity or a particular academic domain. Parents, teachers, and peers pass on to the student a hierarchial view of the value of tasks (i.e., *X* is most important, *Y* is moderately important, *Z* is not at all important). The communication of the socializing agent's value hierarchies to students translates into how much enthusiasm and interest students show toward each domain of activity (Eccles & Hoffman, 1984; Eccles, 1993; Hess & Holloway, 1984). Parents communicate their value hierarchies directly to their children. They provide opportunities and encouragement for some activities, provide scaffolding or support so their children can develop the competencies necessary for doing those valued tasks, and make direct statements of what is important and meaningful and what is not (Eccles, 1993). For instance, a parent might communicate value for reading by providing the child with books and magazines, by listening to the child read and helping out with the difficult words, and by making direct statements like, "Reading is important." Teachers, however, communicate their value hierarchies more subtly than parents do. Teachers rarely comment on the interest value or importance of a task (Blumenfeld, Hamilton, Bossert, Wessels, & Meece, 1983). They resist such direct commentary because students typically react to such teacher statements with suspicion and assume that if the teacher emphasizes a task as interesting or important, then that task must therefore be an especially difficult one. Instead of making direct statements, teachers show discriminating enthusiasm to subjects and spend varying amounts of time involving students in individual subjects. Students value most those activities for which the teacher shows the highest enthusiasm (Blumenfeld & Pintrich, 1983), and students often say that science and social studies are relatively unimportant because these are subjects that are taught infrequently during the school day (Blumenfeld, Pintrich, Meece, & Wessels, 1982).

Conclusion

The teacher's ability to facilitate curiosity in students has two major benefits. First, curiosity gives information an emotional punch that it might otherwise lack. When teachers teach, they typically pass information on to students in the hope that the students will learn it. One determinant of whether students learn information is how much emotional punch that information has. When curious, students desire to learn the information they hear. Second, arousing students' curiosity is sometimes the most effective instructional strategy to teach a complex idea. To teach a complex idea, a teacher might present the information in a lecture and hope that students comprehend the idea sufficiently to understand it for themselves. Alternatively, a teacher might present the information in a curiosity-provoking way that attempts to increase students' desire to read the textbook, visit the library, ask questions in and out of class, and, basically, learn for themselves (e.g., Bernstein, 1994). Here, the teacher's strategy is not so much to present specific information as it is to create a high motivation to learn. As alluded to earlier, sometimes the best way to teach about "laws of gravity" is not to lecture but, rather, to demonstrate a mystery for students to solve (e.g., why didn't the golf ball hit the ground before the Ping-Pong ball when they were dropped side by side and at the same time?).

Classroom techniques to facilitate curiosity work wonders in stimulating the motivation to learn, but a distinction remains between *catching interest* and *maintaining interest* (Mitchell, 1993). Curiosity-inducing strategies mostly catch interest. Holding students' interests is more of a long-term developmental processes. Interest emanates from students' enduring characteristics. To facilitate students' interests, a teacher would structure her classroom around the goals of (1) inviting students to participate in meaningful projects that make sense both to them and to the culture, (2) communicating her value hierarchy as to which tasks and subjects are most important and meaningful (as through enthusiasm and time devoted to a subject), (3) providing activities that involve students needs and provided them with developmentally appropriate challenges, and (4) increasing students' knowledge in a particular domain. Taken together, the teacher's efforts to facilitate curiosity and interest generate in her students a high motivation to learn. I based the contents of this chapter on the assumption that learners not only need access to information, but they also need the motivation to learn. The combination of information and the motivation to learn empowers the learning processes in such a more powerful way than does just information by itself or just motivation by itself.

Note

1. Individual differences in levels of curiosity and anxiety need also to be considered in interpreting Figure 9-1 because such individual differences effect the asymtope of the two curves shown in Figure 9-1 (Spielberger & Starr, 1994). For instance, in the same moderately arousing classroom, students with relatively high trait curiosity would ask more questions of the teacher (approach behavior, as curiosity overwhelms anxiety), while high trait anxiety students would avoid answering questions asked by the teacher (avoidance behavior, as anxiety overwhelms curiosity) (Peters, 1978).

Recommended Readings

Berlyne, D. E. (1966). Curiosity and exploration. *Science, 153,* 25–33.

Deci, E. L. (1992). The relation of interest to the motivation of behavior: A self-determination theory perspective. In K. A. Renninger, S. Hidi, & A. Krapp (Eds.), *The role of interest in learning and development* (pp. 43–70). Hillsdale, NJ: Lawrence Erlbaum.

Hidi, S. (1990). Interest and its contribution as a mental resource for learning. *Review of Educational Research, 60,* 549–571.

Lepper, M. R. (1988). Motivational considerations in the study of instruction. *Cognition and Instruction, 5,* 333–369.

Loewenstein, G. (1994). The psychology of curiosity: A review and reinterpretation. *Psychological Bulletin, 116,* 75–98.

Lowry, N., & Johnson, D. W. (1981). Effects of controversy on epistemic curiosity, achievement, and attitudes. *Journal of Social Psychology, 115,* 31–43.

Malone, T. W. (1981). Toward a theory of intrinsically motivating instruction. *Cognitive Science, 4,* 333–369.

Mitchell, M. (1993). Situational interest: Its multifaceted structure in the secondary school mathematics classroom. *Journal of Educational Psychology, 85,* 424–436.

Schiefele, U. (1991). Interest, learning, and motivation. *Educational Psychologist, 26,* 229–323.

Tobias, S. (1994). Interest, prior knowledge, and learning. *Review of Educational Research, 64,* 37–54.

Observational Activities

Observational Activity 9.1: Teaching Strategies to Induce Curiosity

The purpose of this observation is to become aware of the curiosity-inducing strategies that classroom teachers use to facilitate students' motivation to learn. Observe two different teachers, and keep separate records of your observations. You will need to gain the permission of each classroom teacher in advance. Once you receive permission, sit unobtrusively at the back of the classroom, and record the number and variety of curiosity-inducing strategies that occur. Define and categorize whatever curiosity-inducing strategies you observe, but I suggest you also look specifically for the following:

1. *Stimulus change—novelty, variety, and surprise:* Breaks classroom monotony by changing the routine or by introducing a task in a new (novel, unexpected, surprising) way.
2. *Suspense:* Gradually gives students the information they needed to formulate a conclusion or answer, but the teacher delays giving the students' the answer or conclusion per se.
3. *Guessing and feedback:* Asks students to guess the answers to questions or to explain how something works. Following the guessing, the teacher gives feedback that effectively shows students that they have gaps in their knowledge (i.e., their initial answer was an incorrect guess).
4. *Plays to students' sense of knowing:* Presents information in a way that informs students of what they do not know about a topic they understand fairly well, rather than telling them what they do know about a topic they understand fairly poorly.
5. *Contradiction:* Presents information as a contradiction or as a paradox (e.g., *X* is true, *Y* is true, but *X* contradicts *Y;* how can this be?).

After your observations, answer the following questions for both teachers:
Briefly describe an illustration of each of the preceding five strategies. Of course, the teacher might use only one or two of these categories (so ignore the missing categories). The teacher might also use strategies not listed here (so add these categories). Describe the emotional climate of the students during the class, especially during the curiosity-inducing strategies. Did the students seem bored? Curious? Stressed? Challenged? When the students were curious, how did they express their curiosity? Through asking questions? By becoming

absorbed in on-task activity? Do you think the teachers used curiosity-inducing strategies too little or too much?

Observational Activity 9.2: Understanding Bookworms and Their Interest in Reading

The purpose of this interview is to understand why some students (bookworms) love reading, why other students sort of like reading, and why others would just as soon not open a book. For this activity, interview three students. The interviews should be done individually and should last about twenty minutes each. *Feel free to change the activity from reading to another task or subject that is more relevant to your own teaching plans.* I will phrase the questions here, however, as if the subject under investigation is reading.

Before you conduct your first interview, draft a number of predetermined questions that you will ask. Among your questions, include the following:

- Do you find books and reading to be interesting or not interesting? Why, or why not?
- How do you feel (emotionally) when you read—interested? Excited? Bored? Frustrated?
- How frequently do you read?
- Would you say that your interest in reading has increased, decreased, or remained steady during the last year to two?
- Do you own any books or subscribe to any magazines? If so, did you pick them out or did someone pick them out for you?
- How much or how little encouragement to read do you get from your parents? Peers? Teacher?
- Compared to activities like sports and hanging out with your friends, how much emphasis do your parents (peers) give to reading?
- How much reading do your parents (peers) do?

After your interviews, complete the following twofold project:

Describe your impression of how interested each of your students found reading to be. Develop your own mini-theory (explanation) as to why some people come to enjoy reading while others do not.

10

The Goal-Setting Process

It's finals week and you have two more exams to go. Both finals count one-third of your course grade, and both are three days away. You enjoy each course, and both are in your major and are equally important to you. The only difference between these two finals is that you need a high score on one but only a passing score on the other. You decide to set a goal of "make an A" for yourself on the first final and a goal of doing your best, or "just pass it," on the second. As the three days of study come and go, you spend most of your time thinking about and preparing for the first exam—you read and reread the textbook, organize your notes, form a study group with your classmates, and drop by the professor's office to ask some questions. On the morning of the exams, you look back at your week to notice that you spent almost all of your time and energy preparing for the first final but relatively little time and energy preparing for the second.

What happened over these three days is a goal-setting phenomenon. The hard goal ("make an A") focused your attention, intensified your effort, and prompted you to formulate creative study strategies; the easy goal ("just pass it") fizzled your preparation enthusiasm and left you uninspired. In this chapter, I ask you to consider a paradoxical truism—*people do not do their best when they try to do their best* (from Locke & Latham, 1984). Instead, students do their best when they pursue a challenging, quantitative goal that requires they get the most out of their knowledge and skills. The goals we set for ourselves (and those others set for us) determine how we allocate our attention and how hard we try to maximize our performance. In the preceding example trying to make an A demands the student use his or her academic skills most fully, trying just to pass simply confirms the truism that we do not do our best when we "just try to do our best."

The Concept of Goal Setting

A goal is whatever a student is striving to accomplish (Locke, Shaw, Saari, & Latham, 1981). Some student-related goals are as follows: Make a 4.0 GPA, read a chapter to its end, solve a particular problem, make an 80 on a test, define ten unfamiliar vocabulary words, memorize a poem, and record perfect attendance for the school year. Goals generate motivation for action by focusing students' attention on the fact that a difference exists between their present level of performance (e.g., "I have a 2.5 GPA") and their desired level of performance (e.g., "I need a 3.0 GPA."), or what researchers call a *goal–performance discrepancy*. When students effortfully attempt to raise their level of actual performance to their level of desired performance (i.e., the goal level), then students engage in goal-directed behavior.

Differences between our goals and performances come in two forms (Bandura, 1990): discrepancy reduction and discrepancy creation. Discrepancy reduction is the type of discrepancy referred to in the preceding paragraph, as it involves performing a task at level X and then deciding to set a performance goal of $>X$. For instance, a student might have a 3.0 GPA but then learn that she needs a 3.5 GPA for a particular scholarship; or a student might be typing at a rate of 20 words per minute (wpm) but then have a teacher tell him that he must type 30 wpm to pass the keyboarding course. The students' 3.0 GPA and 20 wpm reflect current level of performance; the scholarship's 3.5 GPA and the teacher's 30 wpm represent goals to be sought.

The second type of goal–performance discrepancy is *discrepancy creation*. Discrepancy creation involves the intentional and proactive setting of a challenging goal for oneself. For instance, a student might, for whatever reason, have a 3.0 GPA and type 20 wpm and then create for himself the goals of a 3.5 GPA and 30 wpm. During discrepancy creation, the person purposely sets a goal for himself, rather than having some outside force, such as a scholarship or teacher, impose it on him. Thus, all goal-directed behavior stems from goal–performance discrepancies; but some discrepancies already exist and students behave to reduce or eliminate them, while other discrepancies do not yet exist and students choose to create them.

With these two types of goal–performance discrepancies in mind, we need to understand (1) how goals, once set, increase performance and (2) under what conditions students voluntarily set goals for themselves. This first phenomenon is the essence of goal–performance discrepancy reduction and concerns questions such as, "Do goals increase performance?" "How do goals increase performance?" "What are the emotional side effects of imposing goals on others?" and "How can I set effective, performance-enhancing goals for others?" The second phenomenon is the essence of goal–performance discrepancy creation, and concerns questions such as, "Where do personal goals come from?" and "Does it matter whether the idea for the goal originates within the mind of the teacher or within the mind of the student?"

Relationship between Goals and Performance

The relationship between goals and performance is this: As goals increase in specificity and difficulty, performance increases in a positive, linear fashion (Locke & Latham, 1990; Mento, Steel, & Karren, 1987; Tubbs, 1986). *Goal difficulty* refers to how easy versus hard a goal is to accomplish. Goals such as "make a C" and "read this book by the end of the semester" are relatively easy in comparison to goals such as "make an A" and "read this book by the end of the week." Figure 10-1 illustrates the goal difficulty–performance relationship by showing that performance increases linearly as goals increase in difficulty.

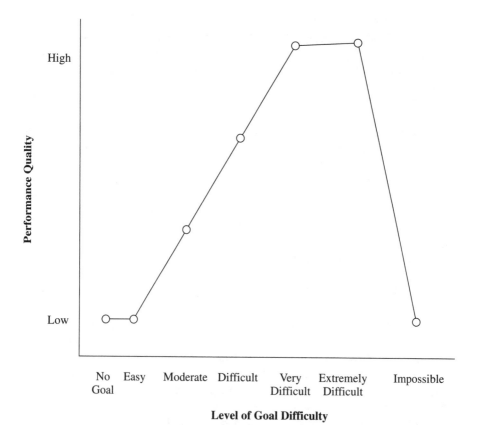

FIGURE 10-1   Relationship between Goal Difficulty and Performance

Imagine a teacher asking a group of students to read a text passage and then take a test. The teacher asks some students to read to answer correctly 18 of 20 questions (difficult goal) and some other students to read to answer correctly 5 of 20 questions (easy goal). In such a study, students who read with the difficult goal in mind outperform students who read with the easy goal in mind when the teacher administers both groups of students a postreading multiple-choice test (56 percent to 36 percent; LaPorte & Nath, 1976). There is a point, however, at which goals become so difficult as to be impossible (and therefore not worth the investment of high effort). At first, this led researchers to recommend that teachers employ "difficult but realistic" goals for their students (Garland, 1983; Locke & Latham, 1985), but subsequent research consistently found that when people accept goals that are beyond their reach, performance stays high and does not decline (Locke, 1982; Weinberg, Bruya, Jackson, & Garland, 1987). Hence, the conclusion that "as goal difficulty increases, performance increases" holds across all levels of goal difficulty except those rare goals that are *unambiguously* impossible.

To enhance performance, a goal needs to be not only difficult but specific as well (Locke, Shaw, Saari, & Latham, 1981). *Goal specificity* refers to how clearly a goal informs the student precisely what he or she is to do. Telling a student to "do your best" sounds like a goal (albeit a vague, easy, and unchallenging one), but in actuality the admonition to do one's best is only an ambiguous statement that tells the person little about what to do. On the other hand, "read the first three chapters in the book and be able to list two emerging themes for tomorrow's discussion" is a precise, specific goal that communicates clearly and unambiguously what the performer is to do. Clarifying goal specificity does not have to be complicated; it can be as simple as restating a goal of "do your best" on the test to a goal of "make a B+." Through its specificity, a goal removes the ambiguity that might otherwise diffuse a performance and, instead, supplies a clear standard to direct the performance. Another way to increase goal specificity is to decrease the range of performance options, such as narrowing the range of the options from "revise your paper multiple times" to "revise your paper twice" (e.g., Klein, Whitener, & Ilgen, 1990).

Difficult, specific goals facilitate performance; yet, no absolute one-to-one correspondence between goals and performance exists because people sometimes lack the ability, training, or resources to accomplish the goals they set (Locke & Latham, 1984; Locke et al., 1981). Put another way, goals supply motivation for performance, but performance also depends on nonmotivational factors such as ability, training, and resources. When difficult goals fail to improve performance, the poor performance might not be a motivational problem but, rather, may result from deficits in task-related skills, absence of knowledge acquirable through training, or exposure to inadequate resources (i.e., the student needs instruction, practice, role models, videotaped performance feedback, or resources such as access to a computer, tutor, books, equipment, or a more generous budget). As you can see from Figure 10-1, when ability, training, and resources are held constant, specific and difficult goals will increase performance.

Why Goals Enhance Performance

Four fundamental reasons explain why goal setting improves performance: effort, persistence, attention, and strategic planning (Earley, Wojnaroski, & Prest, 1987; Locke & Latham, 1990). These reasons constitute *goal mechanisms* because effort, persistence, attention, and planning are the means, or mechanisms, through which a cognitive goal translates itself behaviorally into improved performance.

Fundamental Goal Mechanisms

Expenditure of Effort
One of the sure findings in the goal setting literature is that a performer's effort is directly proportional to the perceived demands of the goal (Bassett, 1979; Locke & Latham, 1990). The more difficult the goal, the greater the amount of effort marshalled towards its realization, as shown in studies measuring physical effort (Bandura & Cervone, 1983, 1986) as well as subjective effort (Earley et al., 1987). For example, students exert greater effort (study time, note taking, class attendance, etc.) during their difficult courses relative to their easy ones.

Duration of Persistence
Goals also increase a performer's persistence. Goals increase persistence because they effectively define that point during task participation at which it is most appropriate to withdraw effort. When a student performs a task without a goal in mind, there is a reasonably high probability that her performance will be distracted, interrupted, or abandoned prematurely. Agents of quitting include distraction, fatigue, boredom, frustration, and the like. With a goal in mind, however, the student has a clearly defined point in the performance that defines when it is time to withdraw effort, namely when the goal is attained (Locke & Latham, 1985). Several studies on the learning of text material show that students given difficult goals spend more time (i.e., persist longer) reading and studying than do students given easy or "do your best" goals (Kaplan & Rothkopf, 1974; LaPorte & Nath, 1976; Reynolds & Anderson, 1982; Reynolds, Standiford, & Anderson, 1979; Rothkopf & Billington, 1979).

Direction of Attention
Goals direct the student's performance toward the task at hand and away from tasks that are incidental. Compared to when they have no goal in mind,

goal-minded performers pay more attention to the task (Kahneman, 1973; Locke & Bryan, 1969). Rothkopf and Billington (1979) assigned students either to a difficult goal or to no goal and monitored each group of students' eye fixations and movements during reading as a dependent measure of attention allocation. Students with the difficult goal spent significantly more time attending to the text than did students with no goal. Specific goals essentially give the performer an explicit instruction of where their attention is to be and what specifically they are to do (Latham, Mitchell, & Dossett, 1978; Locke, Chah, Harrison, & Lustgarten, 1989). For instance, compare the relatively specific goal of "solve math problems 1 through 5 in the next ten minutes" with the relatively vague goal of "improve your math abilities," and it becomes clear that vague (i.e., nonspecific) goals can be accomplished in many different ways, so attention becomes more prone to dispersion (i.e., more amenable to distraction).

Strategic Planning

To accomplish a goal, a person needs to plan an effective course of action (i.e., a strategy; Latham & Baldes, 1975; Terborg, 1976). Goal setting initiates strategic planning because the presence of a goal forces the student to decide how to proceed (Earley & Perry, 1987; Earley, Wojnaroski, & Prest, 1987). Students who set specific goals for themselves, for instance, spend more time while reading a text using comprehension strategies (e.g., note-taking) than do students with no such goals (Terborg, 1976). So goals facilitate preperformance planning, but goals also mix with ongoing performance feedback to prompt students to abandon ineffective strategies in favor of new and improved strategies. The fact that goal setting instigates a strategic planning process shows that students do not simply increase effort (a motivational effect) during goal pursuits but that students also show an improvement in their problem-solving and decision-making processes (a cognitive effect). A final but potentially important practical point is that the *quality* of planning is more important to effective performance than is the *quantity* (amount of time spent) of that planning. Consequently, asking students to spend fifteen minutes of time planning how to accomplish their goal is less important to effective performance than is the two-minute act of coming up with one particularly strategic and viable plan.

It is because goals improve performance by enhancing effort, persistence, attention, and strategic planning that goals need to be both difficult and specific. As goals increase in difficulty, students exert greater effort and greater persistence. As goals increase in specificity, students direct their attention in more focused ways and have more direction for choosing or developing appropriate task strategies (Earley et al., 1987). Thus, goal difficulty relates to effort and persistence, while goal specificity relates to attention and strategy. A teacher, therefore, has a pair of guidelines to follow in diagnosing why a student's performance is poor—is it an effort problem? A persistence problem? An attention problem? A strategy problem? According to goal-setting theory, teachers best address effort and persistence problems by increasing goal difficulty, while teachers best address attention and strategy problems by increasing goal specificity.

Secondary Goal Mechanisms

In addition to the fundamental goal mechanisms of effort, persistence, attention, and planning, two secondary goal mechanisms further explain why goals improve performance. First, goals counteract the apathy and boredom of uninteresting tasks (e.g., subtracting numbers, running laps around a track, driving cross-country) in that goal seeking can provide a task with a sense of challenge and purpose (i.e., accomplishing the goal) that it would otherwise lack (Bandura & Schunk, 1981; Locke & Bryan, 1967). Of course, some tasks are inherently challenging and interesting, but goal setting is best suited for those other tasks that seem otherwise challengeless and purposeless. Second, goals make feedback important. Without goals, performance can be emotionally unimportant and uninvolving ("I performed at level X—so what?"). With a goal, a person experiences emotional satisfaction with goal attainment and emotional dissatisfaction with goal failure (Bandura, 1991). Hence, goal attainment can generate feelings of pride, satisfaction, or competence that the task itself cannot (Bandura & Schunk, 1981). So goals improve performance directly through enhancing effort, persistence, attention, and planning, but goals also improve performance indirectly when they counteract task-associated apathy and add an emotional involvement to purposeless tasks via a sense of challenge and emotion-generating feedback.

The Fundamental Importance of Feedback

Goal mechanisms are the means through which goals translate themselves into effective performance, but there is an additional variable that is crucial to making goal setting effective: feedback. Goals have little influence on performance unless students receive timely feedback that informs them of their progress toward goal attainment (Bandura & Cervone, 1983; Becker, 1978; Erez, 1977; Strang, Lawrence, & Fowler, 1978; Tubbs, 1986). For performance to improve, students need *both* a goal and feedback.

Feedback is merely information ("You scored a 75"), but it gives the performer the means to evaluate his or her performance as being at, above, or below the level of the goal standard. Teachers can deliver such feedback either during the performance or after students have completed a series of performances (e.g., using a feedback chart such as weekly test scores) (Earley, Northcraft, Lee, & Lituchy, 1990). When feedback informs a student that performance is below standard ("My goal was to score an 85"), she recognizes that performance shortcoming, she experiences some level of dissatisfaction, and that felt dissatisfaction (often) prompts improved future performance (Bandura & Cervone, 1983, 1986). When feedback informs a student that performance is at standard or above standard ("My goal was to score a 70"), she experiences satisfaction and a sense of self-efficacy, perhaps enough self-efficacy and enough anticipated self-satisfaction to encourage her to set a higher future goal that breeds ongoing or future goal-directed action (Wood, Bandura, & Bailey, 1990).

According to Bandura (1991), goals do not necessarily motivate behavior; rather, motivation springs from people's responses of satisfaction and dissatisfaction as they react evaluatively to feedback about their goal-striving performances. The role of the goal is to specify for the performer a condition of self-satisfaction (i.e., "I will be satisfied if I make an 80 on this test"), while the role of feedback is to inform the performer of the quality of his or her performance. Together, the goal and feedback constitute the mix of ingredients that generate feelings of satisfaction and dissatisfaction in performers. Self-dissatisfaction and anticipated self-satisfaction, in turn, fundamentally motivate goal-directed behavior (Bandura, 1991).

Goal Processes

So far, we have established that specific and difficult goals increase performance, at least when they occur in the context of feedback; but three additional psychological processes exert important influences on how and whether goals influence performance. Feedback is certainly an important goal process, and it has the benefit of being an external variable directly under the control of the teacher. The three additional goal processes, however, are psychological processes that lie less directly under the teacher's control: goal acceptance, goal choice, and goal proximity.

Goal Acceptance (Commitment)

Goal acceptance exists on a continuum from rejection to acceptance (Erez & Zidon, 1984) and applies to all those instances in which one person attempts to assign a goal to another person (Erez & Kanfer, 1983). For instance, in the process in which a teacher (or parent, coach, peer, etc.) assigns a goal to a student, the student makes a conscious decision whether to accept or reject that goal. Goal acceptance refers to the process involved in the transformation of an other-assigned goal into an internalized goal that has some degree of personal commitment associated with it. With goal rejection, however, the student does not accept the goal, does not internalize it, and will not commit energy to it; that goal therefore will not facilitate performance because, for all practical purposes, it does not exist in the student's mind; the student "blows it off." Goal acceptance/rejection, like feedback, is a necessary condition if a goal is going to translate itself into increased performance (Erez & Kanfer, 1983). Only internalized, personally committed-to goals improve performance (Erez, Earley, & Hulin, 1985).

Four factors affect the goal acceptance/rejection process: student participation, goal difficulty, the credibility of the goal assigner, and extrinsic incentives. As for student participation, all efforts in which one person attempts to persuade another to pursue a goal involve an interpersonal negotiation process. At stake during this negotiation is the student's internalization of the assigned goal versus rebellion against it (i.e., the student's goal commitment). Students reject assigned goals when teachers try to ram these down their throats in a controlling, impersonal way (Latham & Yukl, 1975). In contrast, when teachers support students' autonomy, listen carefully to their points of view, and provide a clear rationale for why they think it is a good idea to assign that particular goal to the student, students frequently internalize the assigned goal and attach a degree of importance to it (Latham, Erez, & Locke, 1988; Latham & Saari, 1979).

Goal difficulty relates inversely to goal acceptance. That is, easy goals bring out the greatest acceptance while difficult goals bring out the least (Erez et al., 1985). The student's cognitive evaluation of goal difficulty explains why some students reject assignments as being "unreasonable" (i.e., too difficult). As for the credibility of the goal assigner, students accept teachers' goals when they perceive that the teacher has high credibility—that he or she is trustworthy, supportive, knowledgeable, and likable, rather than authoritarian, manipulative, and pejorative (Locke & Latham, 1990; Oldham, 1975). Finally, as for extrinsic incentives, it is a general finding that when incentives and rewards are at stake for goal attainment, goal acceptance increases proportionally (Locke & Latham, 1990). That is, students accept goals attached to attractive extrinsic incentives (e.g., a gold star, a scholarship, public recognition) more than they accept goals without such associations of personal benefit.

Goal Choice

Even when students internalize an externally imposed goal, most goals carry with them a range of subgoals (Campbell, 1982). Two subgoals that typically accompany the actual assigned goal are minimal and ideal goals. The *actual goal* is the goal level assigned to the student by some other person. The *minimal (sub)goal* is the level of performance that will satisfy the student, even if performance does not meet the actual goal. The *ideal (sub)goal* is the student's "try for" or "hope for" goal. For instance, a student might enter a class with the explicit, actual goal to "make a B in this course." But the existence of minimal

("I would like a B, but a C will be O.K.") and ideal ("I would like a B, but an A would be wonderful") subgoals adds a layer of complexity to the goal–performance relationship.

In addition to the actual, assigned goal per se (e.g., "Memorize 40 of the 50 state capitals"), four additional variables have independent effects on eventual goal choice: ability, past performance, self-efficacy, and incentives (Locke & Latham, 1990). In general, students who perceive themselves to have high ability, a history of success at the task, high self-efficacy, and an attractive incentive at stake pursue ideal goals (e.g., they memorize 45 capitals); whereas students who perceive themselves to have low ability, a history of failure at the task, low self-efficacy, and no attractive incentive at stake pursue minimal goals (e.g., they memorize only half of the capitals). Thus, when understanding which goal a student chooses to pursue, each of the following three factors must be taken into consideration: the actual goal level assigned to the student, the student's expectation of accomplishing that goal (as determined by ability, past performance, and self-efficacy), and the value or desire the student places on that goal (as determined by incentives for goal attainment).

Goal Proximity

Goal proximity refers to the time frame of the goal and distinguishes between short-term and long-term goals. Students pursue short-term goals (e.g., "Pass this Friday's quiz"), long-term goals (e.g., "Become a teacher"), and short-term goals that relate to long-term goals (e.g., "Pass this Friday's quiz", "Pass this course", "Graduate high school", "Be accepted into a school of education", "Graduate college", "Get hired by the local school district", and "Become a teacher"). Several investigators sought to determine which type of goal is most effective in improving performance—short-term, long-term, or long-term goals with short-term goals mixed in? Results show no significant performance differences among these groups (Hall & Byrne, 1988; Weinberg, Bruya, & Jackson, 1985; Weinberg, Bruya, Longino, & Jackson, 1988), suggesting that the effect of goal proximity on performance is minimal.

Although it does not affect performance, goal proximity does affect a number of important non-performance-based processes—feedback, reinforcement, and intrinsic motivation. As for feedback and reinforcement, long-term goals (e.g., become a teacher) inevitably create a prolonged period of time in which goal-striving efforts produce few opportunities for either feedback or reinforcement. A focus on short-term goals (e.g., learn the principles of discovery learning), in contrast, provides the opportunity for immediate feedback (right and wrong answers) and reinforcement (grades, understanding versus confusion). From this point of view, it appears to be a good idea to work to translate students' long-term goals into a series of interrelated short-term goals.

On the other hand, long-term goals are sometimes preferable because they are less likely to undermine intrinsic motivation (Mossholder, 1980), because short-term goals create a sense of being pressured and controlled that long-term goals do not. Fortunately, the ambiguity surrounding the goal proximity issue can be cleared up with the following conclusion: When the task is uninteresting and unenjoyable (e.g., mathematical problems) short-term goals are preferable over long-term goals—because uninteresting tasks benefit from maximum opportunities for positive feedback and reinforcement; when the task is interesting and enjoyable (e.g., musical instrument, sports) long-term goals are preferable over short-term goals—because feedback and reinforcement are superfluous to maintaining goal commitment and instead interfere with task participation in a controlling way that undermines intrinsic motivation.

How to Set Goals for Others (Observational Activity 10.1)

Effective goal setting is an acquired skill. Mastering the skill of setting goals for others entails discovering and then learning to implement the following seven sequential procedures (based on Locke & Latham, 1984):

1. Identify the objective to be accomplished.
2. Specify how performance will be measured.
3. Define goal difficulty.
4. Clarify goal specificity.
5. Specify the time span until performance assessment.
6. If multiple goals exists, prioritize them by importance.
7. Discuss goal attainment plans and strategies.

Identity the Objective to Be Accomplished

To identify a student objective, a teacher simply asks, "What do you want to accomplish?" Some exemplary educational objectives might be to increase GPA, increase school attendance, increase class participation, increase reading speed, decrease errors on a particular task, remember people's names more frequently, increase reading comprehension, master sonnet writing, graduate from high school, and so on. Sought-after objectives need not be just problems (increase attendance) but can include aspirations as well (get a job as a high school teacher). Neither do they need to be limited to just accomplishments (e.g., make an A on my English term paper); they can include more general strivings as well: Increase school enjoyment, decrease boredom, increase tolerance for student diversity in the classroom, increase group cohesion and solidarity in the classroom, increase parental involvement in students' education, and so on.

Specify How Performance Will Be Measured

Specifying how performance will be measured involves discovering the means to quantify performance—that is, find a way to translate performance into numbers. Academic achievement can be quantified by a test score or GPA, attendance can be quantified by a rate or percentage of days present versus days absent, parental involvement can be quantified by percentage of parents attending teacher–parent meetings, and so on. Clearly, however, some outcomes are harder to quantify (i.e., measure) than are others (e.g., increased tolerance for cultural diversity in the classroom). Likewise, portfolio assessments are more difficult to quantify than are multiple-choice tests. With a combination of personal experience, creativity, and soliciting suggestions from others, *any* objective can be quantified. In fact, performance outcomes typically can be measured in multiple ways. Creative writing, for instance, can be measured by a portfolio featuring short stories, poems, literary critiques, and personal narratives, and perhaps by other ways as well.

Define Goal Difficulty

Defining goal difficulty is a particularly important aspect of the goal-setting process because the harder the goal, the better the performance (see Figure 10-1). The idea behind specifying hard goals for others is that students apply themselves in proportion to the challenge they face. While the goal-setting literature is clear that this hard goal → improved performance relationship is a valid one, the literature is also clear that setting a hard goal for someone else is futile if the other person rejects the goal. The task of setting difficult goals for others carries with it the subtask of attaining goal acceptance and commitment. As discussed earlier, students are most likely to commit to goals when they are invited to participate in the goal-setting process, see the goal as within their capabilities, perceive that the teacher assigning them the goal is credible, and associate goal attainment with a personal benefit. Another consideration in specifying goal difficulty is that the same performance standard may be ill suited for all students because differences in experience and ability exist such that a classwide standard will be easy for some students yet difficult for others. One option in such cases is for the teacher to use each student's previous performance on the task as an individual standard of difficulty (i.e., the student's own past average or best performance). A second option is for the teacher to put forth a variety of goal choices for students—actual goals, ideal goals, and minimal goals. For instance, a geography teacher might want students to learn the 50 state capitals and put forth an actual goal (learn 45), an ideal goal (learn all 50), and a minimal goal (learn 40).

Clarify Goal Specificity (Observational Activity 10.2)

Once the teacher defines goal difficulty, he or she can work toward specifying the goal more clearly. Vague goals—"Learn math," "Run faster," "Make more friends"—can be translated into more precise, specific objectives: "Memorize the multiplication tables through 12×12," "Run a mile in eight minutes or less," "Initiate one conversation with a classmate each day this week." The principle underlying goal specificity is this: Specific goals focus a student's attention more precisely on the goal at hand and tell the student unambiguously what he or she is to do on that particular task. In practice, the art of goal specificity is to focus students' attention precisely toward those actions that can most directly accomplish their goals.

Specify the Time Span until Performance Assessment

Specifying the time span until performance assessment essentially means setting a time frame for reaching the goal. Specifying a goal as specific and difficult (learn 45 of the 50 state capitals) leaves open the question, "O.K., by when?" Most goals need a clear specification of when the performance that determines goal attainment versus failure will occur. The problem is that deadlines can be highly controlling events if put forth in a coercive, inflexible way (see Chapter 2). Thus, in specifying the time span of the performance, the teacher needs to keep in mind the distinction between *controlling limits* and *informational limits* (Koestner et al., 1984). The best way to make a deadline (i.e., time frame) informational is to communicate clearly to students why the time frame exists and what the rationale is for imposing it on students.

If Multiple Goals Exist, Prioritize Them by Importance

In any classroom, multiple goals exist—pass the final exam, write a term paper, participate actively in class discussions, attend class regularly, learn specific skill *A,* learn specific skill *B,* improve communication skills, establish new friendships, maintain existing friendships, discover the practical relevance of the course content, and so on. Yet, students have only so much attention, energy, and time to commit to such classroom objectives. Perhaps all course goals are equally important, but it is more often the case that some goals are more important and more worthy of attention, energy, and time than are others. When goals vary in their importance (either to the teacher or to the students), explicit priorities among the goals help to crystalize students' expenditures of attention, energy, and time. A good example of goal priorities can be found in the syllabi of the courses you are taking in the present semester. That is, look over your course syllabi with an eye to review how much importance each professor assigned to the course's examinations? To papers? To class participation? To personal projects?

Discuss Goal Attainment Strategies

An effective plan is essential to attain the goals we seek. Teachers should explicitly discuss with students possible courses of action to consider in their efforts toward goal attainment. Often, teachers know a number of effective plans and can easily communicate such strategies for students to consider for their own possible adoption. At other times, however, neither the teacher nor the student knows the best way to attain a given goal in advance of the effort to try to attain it. For instance, a teacher might wonder, "What is the best way for students to learn ancient history?" That teacher might develop a strategic plan but also continually reevaluate the effectiveness of the chosen strategy. In both the planning and reevaluation processes, teachers would be well advised to consult with their students because students can be the teacher's richest source of improvement opportunities. For instance, the teacher might overlook students' beliefs that their individual goal attainments hinge on the assistance, cooperation, and social interaction of their classmates (as through modeling, cooperative learning, etc.).

An Example

Consider for a moment how students routinely and habitually approach learning opportunities. Here are three examples involving reading, watching, and listening:

- Read Shakespeare's *Hamlet* and do your best to follow the plot and identify the themes.
- Watch the film on the human nervous system and do your best to understand how the brain works.
- Listen to the lecture on ancient history and learn as much as you can.

Routinely and habitually, a learner's approach toward goal attainment follows this sequential course:

1. As students try to do their best, they actually adopt minimal, easy goals.
2. These vague, easy goals lead learners to establish for themselves an expectation of performance while reading, watching, and listening.

3. This expectation determines the learner's behaviors (effort, persistence, attention, strategic planning) while reading, watching, and listening.
4. Such learning behaviors occur at a minimal, lackluster level.
5. Therefore, students' learning and performance are poor (i.e., minimal and lackluster).

In contrast, learners set high(er) goals for themselves when teachers assign them hard goals (compared to easy or no goals). Following guidelines 1–7 above, the first step—Identify the objective to be accomplished—has been done (i.e., read *Hamlet* and identify its themes). For step 2, the teacher might say, "I will give you a multiple-choice test asking you to identify the main characters and plots in the play, and then an essay test on the themes that run throughout the play. For step 3, "I want everyone to score at least an 80 on the test." For step 4, "The test focuses on the four main characters and on the one major plot in each of the play's five acts." For step 5, "The test will be on Monday, December 2." For step 6, "The open-ended essay questions will count twice as much as will the multiple-choice questions." For step 7, the teacher might suggest that students read one act tonight but no more—to become comfortable with the individual characters before proceeding further.

Dangers and Pitfalls in Goal Setting

Goal setting has its advantages, but it also has many dangers and pitfalls. Locke and Latham (1984) identified a full set of such disadvantages, but three are particularly noteworthy—increased stress, possibility for failure, and undermining intrinsic motivation.

Stress

The high performance standards introduced by goal setting increase students' stress. Goals increase stress partly because harder goals mean greater effort (Locke & Latham, 1984) and partly because difficult goals engender a fear that the challenge one faces will exceed the capacities one possess (Lazarus, 1991). If goal setting works to increase a student's performance demands from under-challenged and lackluster to optimally challenging, then the student experiences a positive, productive, challenge-based stress. If, on the other hand, goal setting works to increase a student's performance demands from optimally challenging to overchallenging and unreasonably difficult, then the student experiences an anxious, unproductive, threat-based stress. So assigning goals that are too difficult creates unnecessary, performance-impairing stress. When students are overchallenged, stress-revealing symptoms surface such as reliance on poor (hasty) strategies, low goal commitment, and negative affect. In the face of such symptomatology, the teacher needs to consider either lowering the goal difficulty or raising the extent to which student receive skill training, task strategies, performance feedback, or supportive resources. Goal overload (from having too many goals to achieve) can also create unnecessary stress, as a student might strive after goals in school, in athletics, in music, and so on to such an extent as to risk burnout.

Failure

The setting of explicit goals, especially difficult ones, opens the door to the possibility of failure. Failure typically brings with it worries about its implications in terms of its aversive tangible (e.g., poor grades), social (e.g., loss of respect of family and friends), and emotional (e.g., feelings of distress, inadequacy) consequences. Teachers can deal with the possibility of failure in two ways. First, teachers can work to minimize the probability that students will fail in the first place by working with students to develop necessary task-related skills that make success a more likely goal outcome. Second, teachers can minimize failure's aversive consequences by taking a nonpunitive attitude toward student failure (i.e., taking an error-tolerant attitude; Clifford, 1984, 1990), by treating poor performance as a problem to be solved rather than a target for criticism (Deci, Connell, & Ryan, 1989), and by giving some credit for partial goal attainment (Locke & Latham, 1984).

Undermining Intrinsic Motivation

Under some conditions, students experience goals as controlling, intrusive, and annoying to such as extent that they undermine intrinsic motivation (Harackiewicz & Manderlink, 1984; Mossholder, 1980; Vallerand, Deci, & Ryan, 1985). That is, teachers sometimes use goals in much the same way that they use extrinsic rewards, namely as means of coercion and control to make students do what they otherwise do not desire to do. When educational tasks are interesting, students experience goals as controlling and they react to such control with lesser intrinsic motivation (Mossholder, 1980; Vallerand et al., 1985). When educational tasks are uninteresting, however, students can show increased intrinsic motivation because goal attainment can generate competence feedback (Bandura & Schunk, 1981; Mossholder, 1980). How this research translates into practical advice is that teachers who assign goals to students on interesting tasks should pay special attention to protect students' internal perceived locus of causality through facilitating the goal acceptance processes (via student participation, rationale for goals, etc.), while teachers who assign goals to students on uninteresting tasks should pay special attention to the competence-affirming cues associated with goal attainment.

Additional Goal-Setting Pitfalls

In addition to potential dangers related to stress, failure, and intrinsic motivation, goal setting can raise three additional concerns. First, an emphasis on setting goals in one area raises the possibility that nongoal areas will be ignored. After all, the purpose of setting a goal is to focus students' attention and action in a certain direction. So, in effect, nongoal areas are intentionally devalued in the sense that if I ask you to read the first three chapters in the book by tomorrow, then I am also in effect asking you not to open your history book and not to spend time talking with your friends on the telephone. Second, an emphasis on setting goals often encourages relatively short-range planning and thinking. That is, by asking students to focus on daily goals, a teacher interferes with students' view of the longer term, higher purposes of education. A parallel might be that by asking you to read this book and pass a test on its content, I am focusing your attention more on the short-range goal of mastering this book than on the long-range goal of becoming an effective classroom teacher. All that a teacher needs to do to overcome shortsighted tendencies cultivated through goal setting, however, is to integrate short-term daily goals with long-range (semester or career) goals. Third, an emphasis on goal attainment might encourage students to cheat. Cheating is made more likely whenever goal setting combines with extrinsic incentives to create performance pressures and a bottom-line classroom mentality in which students value outcomes and results more than learning and development.

Precautions in Implementing Goal Setting in the Classroom

Goal-setting theory originated within the field of business and management—in the world of work and industry—in the name of increasing worker productivity and output. Thus, it is more a theory of performance than it is a theory of motivation. What is increased in goal setting is performance and productivity, rather than some inner motivational resource. This, therefore, is the first precaution: The purpose of goal setting is to enhance performance and boost productivity (Locke, 1968; Locke & Latham, 1990).

The second precaution is that goal setting works best when the tasks are relatively uninteresting and asks for a straightforward procedural involvement (Wood, Mento, & Locke, 1987). For instance, goal setting facilitates performance on the uninteresting, habitual, procedurally based tasks of numerical addition (Bandura & Schunk, 1981), sit-ups (Weinberg, Bruya, & Jackson, 1985), typing (Latham & Yukl, 1976), proofreading (Huber, 1985), and assembling nuts and bolts (Mossholder, 1980). In contrast, goal setting does not facilitate performance on tasks that are relatively interesting and ask for a creative, problem-solving approach (Earley, Connolly, & Ekegren, 1989; Wood & Bandura, 1989). In fact, goal setting even undermines motivation on interesting tasks (Mossholder, 1980; Vallerand, Deci, & Ryan, 1985) and leads to poorer rather than better performance on complex tasks that require creativity and cognitive flexibility (Bandura & Wood, 1989; McGraw, 1978). Another way of looking at this precaution is that performance is sometimes a quantity issue and other times a quality issue. Goal-setting theory concerns itself with maximizing quantity of performance, a performance emphasis in which effort and persistence translate into improved performance on tasks that are uninteresting, habitual, and repetitive. Goal-setting theory is less effective in domains concerned with maximizing quality of performance, that type of performance in which creativity and flexibility translate into improved performance on tasks that are interesting, conceptual, and complex (Deci, 1992a).

Goal Origin and Participative Goal Setting

These two goal-setting precautions are strong reasons to raise the red flag of caution to any teacher interested in implementing goal setting in the classroom. These limitations and precautions against goal-setting theory can be overcome, in part, by the concepts of *goal origin* (Hollenbeck & Brief, 1987) and *participative goal setting* (Latham & Yukl, 1976). A goal is simply an idea, so the issue of goal origin revolves around the questions, "Where do personal goals come from?" and "Whose idea is it for me to pursue a particular goal—mine or someone else's?" The issue of participative goal setting revolves around the question, "How much say do I have in determining the goal level that others set for me—minimal influence or maximal influence?"

In the practice of education, when goals are assigned to students, the ideas that guide action will come from teachers, parents, coaches, and the like. Alternatively, goals can be self-set, and the ideas that guide action will come from the students themselves. When goals originate from other people, such as teachers, they may take on a controlling nature and become just another means for educators to make students do what the educators want them to do. The result might well be enhanced performance, but it is just as likely to lead to pawnlike compliance (deCharms, 1968) and student alienation (Deci, 1992a). With externally imposed goals, the process of nurturing inner motivational resources is not involved. In contrast, teachers can ask students to participate in the goal-setting process such that the goal level assigned is a negotiated one in which the student benefits from a maximal say in whether or not she will pursue the goal and, if so, how difficult that goal will be. When goals originate from within the student, goals can be the cognitive means (i.e., ideas) students use to satisfy their needs, build personal competencies, and pursue their personal strivings (Emmons, 1986, 1989).

Role of Self-Efficacy in Goal Origin

The interrelationships among assigned goals, self-efficacy, and self-set personal goals combine to establish a means of gradually transferring the goal-setting process away from a teacher-directed exercise and toward a student-directed one. The following four empirical findings from goal-setting theory define this sequential process:

1. Difficult (compared to easy) goals increase task performance.
2. Improved performance increases the student's chance for success and decreases his or her chance for failure.
3. An increased ratio of task successes over failures in a student's performance history increases perceived self-efficacy.
4. High self-efficacy students spontaneously set more difficult goals than do low self-efficacy students.

When teachers assign students difficult (rather than easy or no) goals, students' task performances are likely to increase (through the goal mechanisms of increased effort, persistence, attention, and planning; Locke et al., 1981). Improved performance, in turn, alters the feedback experienced in that success will be a more probable outcome. A history of increasing successes in personal accomplishments is the most potent source of strong self-efficacy beliefs (Bandura, 1986; see Chapter 5). Finally, students with high self-efficacy set more difficult goals for themselves than do lows (Garland, 1985; Wood & Locke, 1987; Wood et al., 1990). Thus, increases in self-efficacy produce an increased tendency to set relatively more difficult goals for oneself. Such a cyclical sequence of events relates to goal origin in that self-efficacy is perhaps the most robust predictor of how difficult a goal a student will spontaneously set for himself or herself, even without another person's prompting or requesting that he or she do so (Meyer, Schact-Cole, & Gellatly, 1988; Schunk, 1985). Students with high self-efficacy set high and challenging goals for themselves, whereas students with relatively low self-efficacy do not (Zimmerman & Bandura, 1994).

The Goal-Setting Process as an Inner Motivational Resource

As discussed in the section, "How to Set Goals for Others," goal setting is an acquired skill. The goal-setting process can serve as a valuable means for students to translate their needs, interests, and aspirations into the life objectives they seek. In terms of facilitating inner motivational resources in students, attention is less on any particular goals the student seeks than on the goal-setting process itself. The ultimate benefit of the goal-setting process is not in the accomplishment of making a B on a test but, rather, in the accomplishment of acquiring the skill to set goals for oneself. When teachers encourage students to conceptualize the goal-setting process as an inner motivational resource, goal setting loses some of its stigma as a recipe for manipulating students into doing whatever the teacher wants students to do. In contrast, the goal-setting process gains some potential to show students how to organize their own behavior to accomplish personal aspirations. At its best, goal setting is an internal, rather than an external, process.

Conclusion

The central problem that inspired so much of the research on goal-setting theory was the paradoxical truism that students do not do their best when they *try* to do their best. Instead of doing their best, students generally pursue vague or minimal goals that lead them to poor and lackluster performances. When students pursue difficult goals that challenge their capabilities, they are most likely to put forth high effort and enduring persistence. When students pursue specific goals that tell them precisely what they are to do, they are most likely to direct their attention toward the task at hand and engage in elaborate planning and strategy development.

    As I think more and more about it, I conclude that one of the strongest appeals of goal-setting theory is its conceptual simplicity. It all seems so straightforward: Assign a goal, performance goes up. In one sense, goal setting is as straightforward as it seems, and I hope the seven guidelines put forth in the section "How to Set Goals for Others" testify to that effect. In another sense, however, goal setting is not so straightforward, as several qualifications exist to confound and moderate the goal–performance relationship. Goals do not always enhance performance. Even specific, difficult goals will not enhance performance unless the performer receives timely and frequent performance feedback informing her that her performance is below goal, at goal, or above goal. In addition, goals must be accepted and internalized by the performer if the assigned goal is to enhance performance. On top of these qualifying conditions, the practice of goal setting is not without its dangers and pitfalls—increased stress, possibilities for failure, and undermined intrinsic motivation. All this is to say that although goal setting is conceptually simple, the art of setting goals for others demands that teachers devote considerable attention to satisfying the limiting conditions of effective goal setting—feedback, goal acceptance, goal choice, goal proximity—and monitoring (and overcoming) its potential pitfalls.

There is a second major appeal of goal-setting theory. Goal theory works to increase motivation on the most uninteresting of tasks and for the least motivated of students. As mentioned, goal-setting theory originated in the business world and was introduced by researchers working with people who had very little motivation to excel at the simple, uninteresting, and largely manual activities they faced. The parallel to schooling is that teachers too often ask students to engage in tasks that have little intrinsic appeal such as subtracting numbers, reading books, or running laps. Yet, teachers desire more than mere compliance; they also want to see students excel and achieve in these tasks. Goal theory is popular because it speaks to the issue of creating motivation where little exist. This is the second appeal of the goal-setting process: It speaks successfully to the otherwise exasperating task of creating high motivation in students who begin activities in a way that can only be described as motivationally empty.

Recommended Readings

Bandura, A., & Schunk, D. H. (1981). Cultivating competence, self-efficacy, and intrinsic interest through proximal self-motivation. *Journal of Personality and Social Psychology, 41*, 586–598.

Earley, P. C., Wojnaroski, P., & Prest, W. (1987). Task planning and energy expended: Exploration of how goals influence performance. *Journal of Applied Psychology, 72*, 107–113.

Erez, M., Earley, P. C., & Hulin, C. L. (1985). The impact of participation on goal acceptance and performance: A two-step model. *Academy of Management Journal, 28*, 50–66.

Hollenbeck, J. R., & Klein, H. J. (1987). Goal commitment and the goal-setting process: Problems, prospects, and proposals for future research. *Journal of Applied Psychology, 72*, 212–220.

LaPorte, R. E., & Nath, R. (1976). Role of performance goals in prose learning. *Journal of Educational Psychology, 68*, 260–264.

Locke, E. A., & Bryan, J. F. (1968). Grade goals as determinants of academic achievement. *Journal of General Psychology, 79*, 217–228.

Locke, E. A. Shaw, K. N. Saari, L. M., & Latham, G. P. (1981). Goal setting and task performance: 1969–1980. *Psychological Bulletin, 90*, 125–152.

Rothkopf, E. Z., & Billington, M. J. (1979). Goal-guided learning from text: Inferring a descriptive processing model from inspection times and eye movements. *Journal of Educational Psychology, 71*, 310–327.

Tubbs, M. E. (1986). Goal setting: A meta-analytic examination of the empirical evidence. *Journal of Applied Psychology, 71*, 474–483.

Wood, R. E., & Locke, E. A. (1987). The relation of self-efficacy and grade goals to academic performance. *Educational and Psychological Measurement, 47*, 1013–1024.

Observational Activities

Observational Activity 10.1: Setting a Goal for Another Person

The purpose of this interview is to gain experience with the procedural steps involved in the attempt to facilitate the goal-setting process in others. For this activity, you will need to solicit the cooperation of one student volunteer. The interview will last about forty-five minutes.

Begin your interview by introducing the general idea of goal setting. Ask your student to think of an academic goal that has particular personal significance. Keep brainstorming about possible goals until you feel assured that this is a goal that the person feels is important (for whatever reason). The goal could be improving a skill (e.g., writing poems, public speaking) or it could be attaining some specific outcome (e.g., making a B in English). Tell the student that you would like to work with them to establish an effective goal-setting program. Go through steps 1–7, discussed in the section, "How to Set Goals for Others":

1. Identify the objective to be accomplished.
2. Specify how performance will be measured.
3. Define goal difficulty.
4. Clarify goal specificity.
5. Specify the time span until performance assessment.
6. If multiple goals exists, prioritize each by importance.
7. Discuss goal attainment plans and strategies.

As you proceed through steps 1–7 encourage your student to participate actively and to take the lead in the discussion by generating ideas and possible means to accomplish each objective inherent in each of the seven steps. Your main functions are to guide the student through the steps in sequence, to suggest improvements (e.g., "Can you define that goal in more specific terms?"), and to take notes.

After the interview, answer the following set of questions: In trying to encourage the student toward a difficult and specific goal, did you feel any resistance against either goal difficulty or goal specificity? Do you have a sense of his or her ideal and minimal subgoals? If so, what are they? Rate your impressions of the student's sense of goal acceptance versus goal rejection. What factors lead you to sense acceptance or rejection? Would you consider the goal one goal or many subgoals? Would you consider the goal to be short-term, long-term, or a combination of the two? Was there any conflict or difficulty in prioritizing the subgoals (in step 6)? How important or necessary do you expect extrinsic incentives to be for this person to attain his or her goal?

Observational Activity 10.2: Clarifying Goal Specificity

The purpose of this interview is to develop the skill of clarifying goal specificity for others. Goal specificity directs students' attention precisely toward those actions that can most directly accomplish their goals. Solicit the cooperation of two students. Each interview will last twenty to thirty minutes, and each interview should be done individually.

Begin each interview by asking the student about his or her life goals in general. You may need to define the term *goal* and be ready to give some examples. Once he or she understands the concept of *goal,* invite the student to brainstorm any three goals for himself or herself. One is to be an educational goal, one is to be a social goal, and one is to be an athletic or physical goal. Let the student define a goal in each area, although you might want to offer examples if the student seems stuck, as if asking, "What do you mean by a *social* goal?"

During your interview, work collaboratively with each student to refine each goal continually until each goal has a specific, quantifiable, verifiable outcome stated within a specific time frame. For instance, a student might begin with an academic goal: "I would like to learn to speak Spanish." Your task is to work with the student until that vague, general goal becomes a specific, quantifiable, and verifiable goal. Try to make the goal specificity discussion as much a two-way negotiation process as possible. Your objective is to work the goal toward maximum specificity while keeping in mind the other person's objective of feeling comfortable with the goals that are set.

After your interviews, answer the following set of questions:

How quantitative versus qualitative was the final, most specific set of goals? At what point did you see the first signs of resistance from the other person? Can you identify any stumbling blocks that surfaced during the negotiation of taking a vague, general, easy goal and translating it into one that was more specific (and perhaps more difficult as well)? Were some goal areas—educational, social, or athletic—more difficult to specify than were others? If so, why do you think this was the case? Was one student better able to specify the goals than was the other? If so, why do you think this was the case?

11

Engaging Classroom Climates

A good idea just popped to mind. For the last couple of days, you have been thinking about developing your teaching skills, and today it dawned on you that you need to know what specific skills need developing. This thought came: What if you spent the day at the local school and, in the morning, observed one teacher everyone agreed was excellent, in the afternoon observed one teacher everyone agreed was terrible, and in the evening sat down to figure out the difference between the two?

You follow your plan, but by the end of the day you realize that comparing the two styles will be more difficult than you first suspected. The two teachers had different students; they taught different content; and one teacher had a smaller, more comfortable room than the other did. Still, a comparison is possible. As you expected, the students of the first teacher participated actively and enjoyed their class time, whereas the students of the second teacher were passive and vacillated between being bored and being anxious. The first teacher was friendlier than the second; she was warm and showed a special care for her students by spending extra time interacting with them. She was also clear in her instructions as she explained precisely what the students were to do and how they were to do it. The first teacher answered questions in a way that made it clear that she knew what she was talking about, and she showed a special spark of enthusiasm and support for her students. The second teacher was vague about the what and the how, and she came across as dry and directive.

By the end of the day, what did you learn? If you were actually to pursue a day such as this, I imagine you would learn three principal lessons:

1. Teaching style does make a difference in how motivated and responsive students are.
2. Styles differ from one teacher to the next.
3. Some teaching styles are better than others.

Educational researchers, too, spend many of their days like the one outlined here (although they use more formal procedures; see Murray, 1983). Over the years, researchers have learned these same three lessons. Before diving into the specifics of engaging teaching styles, however, I first want to introduce what an academically motivated student looks like so he or she will be easier to recognize.

Student Engagement

Student engagement exists along a continuum ranging from engagement to disengagement (Skinner & Belmont, 1993). In general, the engagement continuum captures the intensity and emotional quality of a student's involvement in initiating and carrying out learning activities in the school setting (Connell & Wellborn, 1991; Skinner, 1991). When highly engaged, students behave actively and express positive emotion; when disengaged, students behave passively and express negative emotion (Patrick, Skinner, & Connell, 1993).

Engagement manifests itself as students show sustained behavioral involvement and positive emotion during learning activities. When given the opportunity, engaged students initiate learning, show high concentration, select optimal challenges, and exert intense and persistent effort. More concretely, educators identify student engagement by extent of class participation, attention, on-task behavior, effort and persistence, and extracurricular academics (Connell & Wellborn, 1991; Patrick et al., 1993). Further, during such action, engaged students express excitement, interest, curiosity, and enjoyment (Connell, 1990). Disengagement manifests itself as students show passivity, do not try hard, and give up easily in the face of challenge or difficulty. When given the opportunity, disengaged students retreat from learning opportunities and withdraw from school activities in general (e.g., "When I'm in class, I usually think about other things"; Skinner & Belmont, 1993). During school, disengaged students express boredom, discouragement, anxiety, or even anger (Connell, 1990).

Student engagement is a continuous variable, but some researchers find it helpful to specify six distinct gradients within this continuum. Going from most disengaged to most engaged, the six gradients are as follows: withdrawn, ritualistic, rebellious, conformist, innovative, and enmeshed (Connell, 1990; Connell & Wellborn, 1991). Withdrawn students have abandoned the school process and lack commitment to school. Ritualistic students go through the motions of schooling but find no value in learning. Rebellious students take little responsibility for their own learning and are often angry and disruptive. Conformist students are the prototypically good students who do everything the teacher asks. Innovative students value school but show inconsistency in engagement across school subjects because they attend to activities based primarily on personal interests. Enmeshed students value school, participate seriously in school-related activities, and have a high commitment to school (from Connell & Wellborn, 1991). These six gradients sound stereotypical, but they should help you develop a more concrete understanding of the concept of the disengagement-to-engagement continuum.

Engagement also manifests itself over time. Dropping out of school (the ultimate act of disengagement) is less a single event than a culmination of a continual process of failure in school that begins early in a student's academic career. Early signs of disengagement include low educational aspirations, underachievement (low GPA), poor attendance, negative attitudes toward school-work, and negative attitudes toward going to college (Astone & McLanahan, 1991). Partly, such disengagement outcomes stem from sociocultural influences such as poverty, home insecurity, few adults in the household, and a lack of parental encouragement or assistance for educational aspirations (Astone & McLanahan, 1991). Teachers, too, exert a significant and determinative sociocultural influence on students' engagement in school. Csikszentmihalyi and McCormack (1986) present a convincing argument that the single most important opportunity young people have to internalize educational aspirations, positive attitudes toward school, and the like comes from time spent with teachers (rather than with parents or other adults).

Elements of an Engaging Teaching Style

Some specific teacher behaviors promote students' classroom engagement—guidance, modeling, enthusiasm, provision of choice, curiosity induction, and sincere praise (Brophy, 1983, 1986). Similarly, some teaching styles promote engagement more than do others—warmth (Fraser & Fisher, 1982), understanding (Murray, 1983), a focus of learning goals (Ames & Archer, 1988), organization and clarity (Hines, Cruickshank, & Kennedy, 1985), respect for all students' performance initiatives (Ryan & Stiller, 1991), and support for students' autonomous behavior (Deci, Vallerand, Pelletier, & Ryan, 1991). Some of these teaching styles overlap with one another (e.g., warmth and understanding), but other styles represent independent elements, or dimensions. Educators ask: "What are the essential dimensions of teaching style that promote student engagement?" Connell and Skinner (Connell, 1990; Connell & Wellborn, 1991; Skinner & Belmont, 1993) developed a theoretical model to integrate the aspects of engaging teaching; they propose the following three essential dimensions: involvement, structure, and autonomy support.

Connell and Skinner's model is specifically a motivational model, a claim I make for two reasons. First, each of these three aspects of teaching style exerts an independent and positive influence on student engagement. That is, the reason they selected these dimensions rather than others is that these are the ones that relate specifically to students' motivation. Second, each aspect relates directly to a particular need that regulates student motivation. According to self-determination theory (Deci & Ryan, 1985, 1991), the theory of motivation on which Connell and Skinner based their model, the needs for relatedness, competence, and self-determination (or autonomy) energize and direct students' behaviors in the classroom. Connell and Skinner related their model to self-determination theory by arguing that (1) involvement increases student engagement because it works to involve and satisfy a student's need for relatedness, (2) structure increases student engagement because it works to involve and satisfy a student's need for competence, and (3) autonomy support increases student engagement because it works to involve and satisfy a student's need for self-determination. Figure 11-1 shows Connell and Skinner's model of the three elements of an engaging teaching style.

Involvement

Involvement refers to the quality of the interpersonal relationship between a teacher and her students as well as the teacher's willingness to dedicate psychological resources (e.g., time, interest) to students. The opposite of involvement

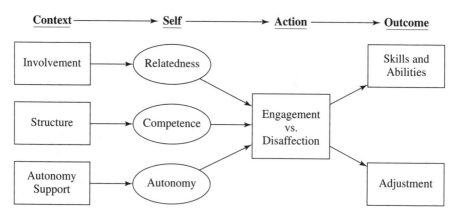

FIGURE 11-1   Three Aspects of an Engaging Teaching Style and Their Links to Students' Needs

Source: Adapted with permission from Connell J. P., & Wellborn, J. G. (1991). Competence, autonomy, and relatedness: A motivational analysis of self-system processes. In M. R. Gunnar & L. A. Sroufe (Eds.), *Self-processes in development Minnesota symposium on child psychology* (Vol. 23, pp. 167–216). Hillsdale, NJ: Lawrence Erlbaum.

is rejection, or neglect. Teacher involvement expresses itself when teachers take time for students' concerns, express affection, enjoy interactions with students, pay attention to students' needs and emotions, and dedicate resources to students. In empirical studies, involvement is operationally defined by the extent to which the teacher shows affection (liking, appreciation, and enjoyment of the student), care ("My teacher cares about how I do"; Connell, 1990), attunement (understanding, sympathy), dependability (availability in cases of need), interest in and detailed knowledge about the student ("My teacher knows a lot about what happens to me in school"; Connell & Wellborn, 1991), and dedication of resources (e.g., time, interest, aid, energy, emotional support) (Connell, 1990; Connell & Wellborn, 1991; Grolnick & Ryan, 1989; Grolnick, Ryan, & Deci, 1991; Skinner & Belmont, 1993). Lack of involvement, on the other hand, emanates from a teacher who treats students in a way that makes them feel isolated, neglected, or ignored (Connell, 1990).

Involvement is a powerful motivator for students because students have a need for relatedness or belongingness. Involvement motivates students mostly in the areas of socialization (Ainsworth, 1989), positive emotion (Skinner & Belmont, 1993), and commitment to the school's goals (Csikszentmihalyi & McCormack, 1986). When a teacher assigns students to perform a task but then ignores their efforts, students quickly lose interest in engaging the activity and instead become concerned with pulling for the teacher's involvement (Anderson, Manoogian, & Reznick, 1976). Students find permissive, nonresponsive classrooms amotivational (e.g., "The teacher doesn't care, so why should I?"). In contrast, when they perceive teachers to be high in involvement, students experience greater emotional security (Connell & Wellborn, 1991), enjoy class time, and show more enthusiasm (Skinner & Belmont, 1993).

Structure

Structure refers to the amount and clarity of information the teacher provides to students about how to achieve desired academic and behavioral outcomes. The opposite of structure is chaos, or confusion. Teachers provide high structure by clearly communicating their expectations for students' work on assignments, academic performance, and adherence to rules ("My teacher tells us what will happen when we break the rules"; Connell, 1990), by administering consequences in a consistent, predictable, and contingent way ("My teacher does what she says she is going to do"), by offering instrumental help (when requested to do so), and by providing students with optimal challenges ("My teacher doesn't expect me to do things I can't do"). In empirical studies, structure is operationally defined by clarity of expectations (e.g., "I know what my teacher expects of me in class"; Skinner & Belmont, 1993), predictability and consistency of rules and regulations, contingency of responses (e.g., praise, reinforcements, performance feedback), instrumental help, and adjustment of teaching strategies to fit student capabilities (Connell, 1990; Connell & Wellborn, 1991; Skinner & Belmont, 1993). Lack of structure, on the other hand, emanates from a teacher who provides inconsistency, noncontingency, and overly easy or difficult requirements (Connell, 1990).

Structure is a powerful motivator for students because students have a need for competence, or effectance (e.g., Chapter 4). Students who experience their teachers as providing clear expectations, contingent responses, and timely feedback have the advantage of learning within a clear and predictable framework that allows them to test their skills and develop their competencies. A student in a structured classroom knows what it takes to do well in school (how much effort, ability, luck, and assistance from powerful others; Skinner, Chapman, & Baltes, 1988; Skinner, Wellborn, & Connell, 1990). It is classroom structure that allows the student to understand what it takes to do well in school and to assess to what extent he or she possesses those qualities that collectively nurture a sense of competence.

Autonomy Support

Autonomy support refers to the amount of freedom a teacher gives to a student so the student can connect his or her behavior to personal goals, interests, and values. The opposite of autonomy support is coercion, or being controlled. Teacher autonomy support expresses itself when teachers allow students choices, respect their agendas, and provide learning activities that are relevant to personal goals and interests. The telltale sign of low autonomy support (i.e., high control) is a classroom rich in external rewards, pressures, and controls. In empirical studies, autonomy support is operationally defined by the extent to which the teacher provides choices ("I let this student do classwork at his or her own pace"; Skinner & Belmont, 1993) and options ("My teacher lets me make a lot of my own decisions when it comes to schoolwork"; Connell & Wellborn, 1991), shows respect for students (by acknowledging the importance of their opinions and feelings), gives rationale for learning activities, resists using coercive behavior (control or force through authority, as in "My teacher tries to control everything I do"; Skinner & Belmont, 1993), and supports students' initiatives ("Your teacher tells students to interrupt him/her whenever they have a question"; Karabenick & Sharma, 1994) (Connell, 1990; Connell & Wellborn, 1991; Grolnick & Ryan, 1989; Grolnick, Ryan, & Deci, 1991; Karabenick & Sharma, 1994; Skinner & Belmont, 1993). Lack of autonomy support, on the other hand, emanates from a teacher pressuring students toward teacher-directed goals and behaviors (Connell, 1990).

Autonomy support is a powerful motivator for students because students have a need for autonomy, or self-determination (e.g., Chapter 2). Autonomy support motivates students in the initiation and persistence of academic activity.

At one extreme, a student's academic behavior can be fully teacher-regulated, through the teacher's directions on what to do, how long to do it, and when to switch to a new activity. At the other extreme, a student's academic behavior can be fully self-regulated, through the choice to begin a task, the choice to continue or cease doing the activity, and the choice of which activity to attend. Ryan and Connell (1989) discussed such self-regulatory styles on a continuum of self-determination as externally-regulated (no self-determination), intro-jected-regulated, identified-regulated, and intrinsically-regulated (full self-de-termination). The more self-determining students are, the more active their behavior in the classroom and the more positive their emotion (Patrick, Skinner, & Connell, 1993; Ryan & Connell, 1989).

Involvement, Structure, and Autonomy Support in the Typical Classroom (Observational Activity 11.1)

It is difficult to find a "typical" classroom, but it is nevertheless an interesting question to ask how students rate classrooms in terms of involvement, struc-ture, and autonomy-support. Skinner and Belmont (1993) asked 144 elemen-tary-grade (grades 3, 4, and 5) children and their 14 female teachers to rate their classrooms on these three categories. On a four-point scale (from 1 = not at all true, to 4 = very true), teacher ratings were structure = 3.56, involvement = 3.37, and autonomy support = 3.04, while student ratings were structure = 3.11, involvement = 2.98, and autonomy support = 2.79. That is, for both teachers and students, teachers offered classrooms that were very high in structure, high in involvement, and moderate (but still somewhat high) in autonomy support.

In making their ratings of how involved, how structured, and how suppor-tive their teachers were, students mostly used the involvement dimension such that students who perceived the teacher as highly involved also rated that teacher as high in structure and autonomy support. For elementary-grade students, then, it seems that teacher warmth and affection are particularly important teacher dimensions (Soar & Soar, 1979). Teacher-provided structure and autonomy support become increasingly discriminative for older students (Murray, 1983).

Determinants of Involvement, Structure, and Autonomy Support

Educational programs do an excellent job in showing teachers how to provide structure in the classroom. That is, teachers are well trained in the art of limit setting, the principles of behavior modification, the giving of contingent praise, the importance of increasing children's success experiences, the importance of timely feedback, and so on. Teacher certification programs also emphasize involvement, but in some sense involvement is discretionary—nice but not required. As to autonomy support, Skinner and Belmont (1993, following deCharms, 1976) argue that supporting students' autonomous behavior is basically a foreign concept to many teachers. (This book should offset some of that unfamiliarity.)

In addition to teacher-training programs, there are other determinants of how much teachers show involvement, structure, and autonomy support. One large determinant of teacher involvement, structure, and support is the extent of student engagement in the classroom. Students who show relatively strong engagement in the classroom receive relatively greater involvement, structure, and autonomy support from teachers, whereas students who show relatively strong disengagement receive relatively more neglect, chaos, and coercion from teachers (Skinner & Belmont, 1993). Such a finding takes us full circle and leads to the conclusion that teacher behaviors in the classroom enhance student motivation *and* that students' engagements enhance teacher behavior in the classroom (a reciprocal causation effect).

A third determinant of teacher involvement, structure, and autonomy support is institutional support from the school system at large (e.g., school administrators, parents, colleagues, school board members, unions, state legislators). As students receive involvement, structure, and autonomy support from teachers, so teachers themselves are embedded in a school system that can facilitate or hinder their own needs for relatedness, competence, and self-determination (Connell & Wellborn, 1991; Maehr & Midgley, 1991). When schools involve and satisfy teachers' needs for relatedness, competence, and self-determination, teachers show greater classroom engagement and adopt teaching styles relatively rich in involvement, structure, and autonomy support.

Putting Motivational Classroom Climates into Practice

Creating a classroom climate rich in involvement, structure, and autonomy support is a difficult task. There are certainly easier ways to manage a classroom. A teacher might, for instance, just tell students what to do and then provide potent enough extrinsic incentives and consequences to guarantee students' compliance. Or a teacher might just permit students to do whatever they wish and then hope some learning takes place. While both of these teaching approaches—control and neglect—have short-term benefits for the teacher (teaching is easier), they entail long-term costs for the students' learning and development (Connell & Ryan, 1984). Many teachers recognize that their efforts to create a climate rich in involvement, structure, and autonomy support are well worth the while; but, at the same time, learning about and becoming enthusiastic over the possibilities of creating motivational classrooms do not necessarily translate into day-to-day practice. Why not?

The problem is not in the attempt to understand, accept, or master principles such as involvement, structure, and autonomy support. Rather, teachers report they experience a literal bombardment of demands and imperatives from a culture obsessed with achievement and performance (Connell & Ryan, 1984) and from a school system obsessed with ability assessments (Maehr & Anderman, 1993). In a very real sense, the larger social context of administrators, parents, teacher unions, school boards, and public opinion provide a school climate for the teacher that is more controlling and more pressuring than the controlling classroom climates students sometimes face. In the classroom, teachers speak of being "guided by the curriculum" and of having their lesson plans "mandated" to them. Teachers tell me that they face "teacher-proof" lesson plans that tell them what should be done on a particular day. They feel pressure to teach for high standardized test scores and to meet the unrealistic expectations placed on them and their students by principals, parents, and others. As a result of responding to the week-in, week-out drenching of being controlled themselves, teachers find little room in the curriculum and little time in the classroom schedule for the luxuries of involvement, structure, and autonomy support. In their place, teachers are asked (told?) to raise achievement scores, keep the principal and parents happy, finish the required lessons, and just get through the day (Connell & Ryan, 1984).

The attempt to put motivational classroom climates into practice is not an easy one: Change is needed in the culture of schools and in the culture of teacher education programs (e.g., Maehr & Midgley, 1991). The change needed is to move toward greater ongoing participation of teachers in their own professional development as well as toward a more differentiated set of criteria for objectives of a quality education (Connell & Ryan, 1984). For such changes to occur, teachers must instigate and build a convincing, persuasive case for such change to school officials, parents, members of the community, and federal policymakers. This book, for instance, argues that the purposes of education must be more far-reaching that student achievement per se. Schooling must also embrace as its goals the aims to develop lifelong learners, to facilitate optimal development, and to empower students to make successful transitions into society. But promoting opportunities for lifelong learning, optimal development, and successful adaptation into society is not just for students, but for teachers as well. Before we can expect, or even ask, teachers to embrace the idea of a classroom rich in involvement, structure, and autonomy support, we have to address the way administrators and the public show involvement, structure, and autonomy support (especially involvement and autonomy support) to teachers (Maehr & Fyans, 1989; Maehr & Midgley, 1991).

Teachers and Students: Different Goals, Different Purposes

Sometimes what teachers want students to do clashes with what students want students to do. In an achievement situation, teachers value and promote high effort from students. Teachers verbally and nonverbally reward students who show high effort and verbally and nonverbally punish students who show low effort. Students, on the other hand, value and promote ability. In contrast to teachers, older students devalue effort, because students see high effort as a telltale sign of low ability (i.e., students who try hard must lack the ability to do something). Teachers and students work at cross purposes when students think of school as a place to learn while students think of school as a place to be sorted according to their ability (Covington & Omelich, 1979). Whether school is a place to learn or a place to be sorted according to one's ability is a classroom climate issue.

Classroom climates communicate to students what the purpose of doing an academic project or assignment is. Although a number of different purposes exist, people who study motivation focus their attention on two types of goals—mastery versus performance (or learning versus ability) goals (see Ames & Archer, 1988; Anderman & Maehr, 1994; Dweck & Leggett, 1988; Meece, Blumenfeld, & Hoyle, 1988; Nolen, 1988). When teachers, or classroom climates in general, emphasize mastery goals (task involvement, mastery and improvement, learning, and an intrinsic motivational orientation), then students' attention moves toward thinking about improvement, learning, putting forth effort, engaging challenges, learning from errors, gaining knowledge, and making progress over yesterday (Ames & Archer, 1988). When teachers, or classroom climates in general, emphasize performance goals (ego involvements, successful performance outcomes, ability demonstrations, and an extrinsic motivational orientation), then students' attention moves toward thinking about making high grades, proving their high ability, outperforming others, and avoiding anxiety-provoking (i.e., ability-threatening) situations (Ames & Archer, 1988).

Whether the classroom climate works to orient students toward mastery or performance goals has significant implications on students' willingness to exert high effort and embrace an interest in learning for its own sake (Ames & Archer, 1988). Prescriptions for changing the classroom climate from relatively performance-oriented to relatively mastery-oriented usually involve advice to deemphasize social and normative comparisons (Rosenholtz & Simpson, 1984) and competitive reward structures (Anderman & Maehr, 1994). Deemphasizing performance goals is half of the battle, but the other half of the battle is even more crucial—emphasizing mastery goals. If a teacher wishes to emphasize mastery goals within his or her classroom climate, the teacher must state this explicitly. In addition, to diagnose students' perceptions of the classroom goal orientations, teachers can ask students to agree or disagree with questions such as, "The teacher pays attention to whether I am improving"; "Students are given the chance to correct their mistakes"; "The teacher wants us to try new things"; and "Making mistakes is part of learning" (from Ames & Archer, 1988, p. 262).

Sometimes what teachers see as the purposes of school clashes with what students see as the purposes of school. For instance, Bacon (1993) followed a group of sixth- and seventh-grade adolescents around for a semester to interview them on what they believed was their responsibility for leaning while in school. Bacon interviewed the students at lunch or after their classes and asked them questions such as, "Do you see school as a place for learning?" and "What understanding of responsibility for learning do you have?" While teachers might see school as a place for students to learn and develop life skills, the students in Bacon's study saw school as a place to hang out with their friends. The academic work they did, the students said, merely satisfied the demands of their teachers. As to having a responsibility for learning, the students said their responsibility was to (1) do the work assigned, (2) obey the rules, (3) pay attention, (4) study, and (5) make an effort. Other researchers show that many students' main purpose in education is to "avoid work" (Nicholls, Patashnick, & Nolen, 1985). Findings such as these affirm that the purpose teachers have in mind during school frequently clashes with the purpose at least some students have in mind during school. Teachers must justify their goals and purposes for school, and they do so not only through their words but through their teaching styles as well—by showing enthusiasm, by supporting students' learning initiatives, by showing concern for students, by talking with students after class—by manifesting high involvement, structure, and autonomy support.

Positive Affect

Boiled down to its essentials, student engagement means active, enthusiastic students (and disengagement means passive, bored students). These two aspects of engagement—activity and emotion—interrelate with each other. Activity and emotion correlate positively with each other (e.g., Patrick et al., 1993), and positive emotion (i.e., positive affect) causes engaged activity (e.g., Isen, 1987).

The Nature of Positive Affect

Positive affect refers to the subtle, low-level, mild, everyday, general state of feeling good (Isen, 1987). It is the mild happy feeling that often accompanies pleasant everyday experiences such as listening to music, finding a $1 bill, walking into unexpectedly sunny weather, hearing praise or a sincere compliment, or receiving an unexpected letter or flowers from a friend. Such pleasant surprises bring to life a mild good feeling that we typically are unaware of at the conscious level. We may smile more, whistle while we walk, daydream happy memories, or talk more excitedly, but the change in mood from neutral to positive occurs outside our conscious attention. In fact, if someone brings the mood change to our attention ("My, aren't we in a good mood today!"), then the act of having the good mood brought to our attention paradoxically means the end of it. This is in contrast to the more intense, attention-grabbing positive emotions, such as joy and love. Emotions, in contrast to the type of feelings or mood being discussed here, capture attention and interrupt and direct our ongoing behavior. Positive affect is more subtle.

Once instigated by an eliciting event (e.g., an amusing film), the warm glow of positive affect continues for up to twenty minutes (Isen, Clark, & Schwartz, 1976). Because we enjoy feeling good, happy people act in ways that maintain their good mood (Forest, Clark, Mills, & Isen, 1979; Isen, Shalker, Clark, & Karp, 1978). More often than not, however, some rival event or life task distracts our attention away from the positive-affect-inducing event. That is, we lose our positive mood by attending to or engaging in a neutral or aversive event (e.g., boring work, criticism, congested traffic, bad news, coffee spills, a risk gone bad, malfunctioning Coke machine, pouring rain, and so on).

Where Does Positive Affect Come From?

Mild positive affect states come from life's small successes, gains, amusements, and pleasures. For example, people feel good (i.e., experience positive affect) after finding money in the coin return of a public telephone (Isen & Levin, 1972), receiving a small gift of a bag of candy (Isen & Geva, 1987; Isen, Niedenthal, & Cantor, 1992), receiving a small product sample (worth about a quarter; Isen, Clark, & Schwartz, 1976), receiving a candy bar (Isen, Johnson, Mertz, & Robinson, 1985; Isen, Daubman, & Nowicki, 1987), learning that one's task performance was successful (Isen, 1970), receiving a cookie (Isen & Levin, 1972), receiving refreshments such as orange juice (Isen et al., 1985), receiving positive feedback (Isen, Rosenzweig, & Young, 1991), thinking about positive events (Isen et al., 1985), experiencing sunny weather (Kraut & Johnston, 1979), watching an amusing film (Isen & Nowicki, 1981), or rating funny cartoons (Carnevale & Isen, 1986).

In all of these studies, researchers manipulate positive affect with one task and then invite research participants to engage themselves in a second task (to assess the study's dependent variable). This distinction between one task that is used to manipulate affect and a second task that is used to assess its effect on students' engagement carries important practical implications for teachers. That is, the art of manipulating affect in students involves nonchalantly inducing positive affect in students, and then engaging students in the activity on which they can show engagement.

Effects of Positive Affect on Student Engagement

Compared to people in a neutral mood, people exposed to conditions that allow them to feel good are more likely to help others (Isen & Levin, 1972), act sociably (i.e., initiate conversations; Batson, Coke, Chard, Smith, & Taliaferro, 1979), express greater liking for others (Veitch & Griffitt, 1976), be more generous to others (Isen, 1970) and to themselves (Mischel, Coates, & Raskoff, 1968), take greater risk (Isen & Patrick, 1983), and act more cooperatively and less aggressively (Carnevale & Isen, 1986). Beyond these mostly social aspects of engagement, people who feel good also solve problems more creatively, persist in the face of failure feedback, make decisions more efficiently, and show greater intrinsic motivation toward relatively interesting activities (as discussed in the following paragraphs).

The explanation for *how* and *why* positive affect facilitates active engagement is not as simple as you might first suspect. Positive affect enhances engagement through its effects on students' cognitive processes, such as memories, judgements, and problem-solving strategies (Isen, 1984, 1987). Isen argues that positive affect influences the contents of working memory by biasing what the individual thinks about and what memories and expectations come to mind. In brief, she argues that positive affect serves as a retrieval cue for positive material stored in memory (Isen, Shalker, Clark, & Karp, 1978; Laird, Wagener, Halal, Szegda, 1982; Nasby & Yando, 1982; Teasdale & Fogarty, 1979). As a result, people who feel good have greater access to happy thoughts and positive memories than do people who feel neutral.

As an analogy, consider how revisiting your hometown or hearing a particular song on the radio can act as a retrieval cue to all sorts of unexpected memories. Just as the sight of your childhood home or the sound of a favorite melody affect the contents of short-term memory, positive affect, too, functions as a retrieval cue to happy memories and optimistic thoughts. Now, consider what runs through the mind of a student who confronts an educational task. From her past experiences with that particular activity, she possesses memories of triumph and failure, interest and boredom, challenge and threat. The contribution of positive affect is to bias the student's access to positive task-related (and task-unrelated) material in memory, thereby biasing his or her task involvement toward engagement.

Creativity (Observational Activity 11.2)
Positive affect facilitates cognitive flexibility (Isen, Niedenthal, & Cantor, 1992) and creative problem solving (Isen, Daubman, & Nowicki, 1987). Creativity is

essentially the organization of a student's thoughts into an approach to a problem that is useful or productive (e.g., Mednick, 1962). Isen and colleagues (1987) induced positive or neutral affect into groups of college students and then asked them to try to solve one of two creative problem-solving tasks—the candle task (Dunker, 1945) or the Remote Associates Test (RAT; Mednick, Mednick, & Mednick, 1964). In the candle task, the participant receives a pile of tacks, a candle, and a box of matches. The instruction is to attach the candle to the wall (a corkboard) so it can burn without dripping any wax on the table or floor. In the RAT, the participant sees three words *(soul, busy, guard)* and is to generate a fourth that relates to the other three *(body)*. Positive affect participants solved the candle task and gave creative (i.e., unusual or "remote") associates to the RAT (Isen et al., 1987). In contrast, the candle task stumped the neutral affect participants, who gave routine, stereotypical responses to the RAT.

Persistence in the Face of Failure
Positive affect serves as a buffer against failure such that it encourages students' persistence in the face of failure (Chen & Isen, 1992). Chen and Isen (1992) induced positive or neutral affect in college students; had them experience either success, failure, or an ambiguous outcome; and then gave them an opportunity to persist or not at the task. Only those participants who received a small bag of candy (to induce positive affect) retried the problem after failure or after an ambiguous outcome. Happy and neutral-feeling participants persisted equally after success. Thus, *either* past success or a good mood is sufficient to encourage persistence in the face of failure. The practical classroom applications of this finding are yet to be explored, but it seems that students can buffer themselves against quitting by succeeding at tasks, while teachers can buffer students against quitting by inducing positive mood states.

Decision-Making Efficiency
Positive affect enhances students' efficiency and thoroughness in decision-making (Carnevale & Isen, 1986; Isen & Means, 1983; Isen, Rosenzweig, & Young, 1991). Feeling good biases people toward faster, more efficient, and less effortful decision-making performances. On tasks that are more structured and need to be double-checked for accuracy (e.g., geometry proofs; second drafts of a manuscript), however, positive-affect students do not outperform their neutral-affect counterparts (because their fast, efficient, effortless decision-making style makes them increasingly susceptible to making errors).

Intrinsic Motivation
Positive affect enhances intrinsic motivation on interesting activities (Isen & Reeve, 1994). Isen and Reeve induced either positive or neutral affect in participants and introduced them to two experimental tasks, one that was

interesting (a puzzle) and one that was not (a clerical task). No one felt intrinsically motivated toward the uninteresting task, but the positive-affect participants felt more intrinsically motivated toward the interesting task. Notice that positive affect does not increase intrinsic motivation toward *all* tasks; rather, positive affect increases intrinsic motivation only toward relatively interesting tasks. Thus, there seems to be little profit in inducing positive affect in the classroom in the hopes of making tasks such as subtraction, cleaning up, and looking words up in the dictionary more fun and entertaining. Rather, the conclusion to take to the classroom is that positive affect can enhance intrinsic motivation toward curiosity-provoking, optimally challenging, fantasy-enriching, personally meaningful, and otherwise potentially enjoyable activities.

Conclusion

Classrooms have climates. In some classrooms, students are alert, interested, and actively involved in the classroom's goals; in others, students are bored or stressed and only passively involved. The goal of this chapter was to pinpoint the chief dimensions of classroom climates that significantly affect students' disengagement/engagement. *Involvement* refers to the quality of the interpersonal relationship established between the teacher and her students; *structure* refers to the amount and clarity of information and contingencies the teacher provides to her students in terms of how to achieve the outcomes they desire; and *autonomy support* refers to the amount of freedom the teacher allows her students in their efforts to connect their personal goals, interests, and values to their classroom behaviors. Involvement, structure, and autonomy support not only define the engaging teaching style; they also define the engaging parenting style (Grolnick & Ryan, 1989; Grolnick, Ryan, & Deci, 1991), a finding of some importance because it confirms the generalizability of these three dimensions in specifying aspects of interpersonal climates that motivate others.

Involvement, structure, and autonomy support are not inner motivational resources in and of themselves; instead, they provide the climate to involve and satisfy students' needs for relatedness, competence, and autonomy (or self-determination). When classrooms involve and satisfy these inner motivational resources, student engagement flourishes.

Positive affect is an inner motivational resource, but it is one of a different sort. Each of the previous inner resources discussed throughout this book is either a natural (e.g., need) or an acquired (e.g., cognition) capacity, or resource. Positive affect, on the other hand, is an ephemeral, fragile good feeling that lasts only up to twenty minutes or until interrupted by a neutral or aversive event.

Yet, when present within students, positive affect exerts a subtle but pervasive effect on engagement. Given its beneficial effects on sociability, creativity, persistence in the face of failure, decision-making efficiency, and intrinsic motivation, a practical question becomes, "How can a teacher enhance positive affect in students?" In most studies, researchers induce positive affect via a task-irrelevant means, such as a small gift, an amusing film, or juice and cookies as refreshments. In addition to task-irrelevant sources of positive affect, however, participation in the task itself can generate positive feelings. That is, perceptions of competence, mastery, and self-efficacy that emanate from effective task performances also generate positive moods in students (e.g., Carver & Scheier, 1990). Chapter 4 discussed task-related positive affect (under the term *enjoyment*), and it is every bit as important to student motivation and engagement as is the task-irrelevant positive affect discussed in this chapter. The great advantage teachers gain by learning about task-irrelevant sources of positive affect, however, is that such sources of students' good moods reside under the influence of the teacher.

Recommended Readings

Brophy, J. (1986). Teacher influences on student achievement. *American Psychologist, 41,* 1069–1077.

Connell, J. P. (1990). Context, self, and action: A motivational analysis of self-system processes across the life-span. In D. Cicchetti (Ed.), *The self in transition: From infancy to childhood* (pp. 61–97). Chicago: University of Chicago Press.

Connell, J. P., & Ryan, R. M. (1984). A developmental theory of motivation in the classroom. *Teacher Education Quarterly, 11,* 64–77.

Grolnick, W. S., & Ryan, R. M. (1989). Parent styles associated with children's self-regulation and competence in school. *Journal of Educational Psychology, 81,* 143–154.

Isen, A. M. (1987). Positive affect, cognitive processes, and social behavior. In. L. Berkowitz (Ed.), *Advances in experimental social psychology* (Vol. 20, pp. 203–253). New York: Academic Press.

Isen, A. M., Daubman, K. A., & Nowicki, G. P. (1987). Positive affect facilitates creative problem-solving. *Journal of Personality and Social Psychology, 51,* 1122–1131.

Isen, A. M., & Levin, P. F. (1972). Effects of feeling good on helping: Cookies and kindness. *Journal of Personality and Social Psychology, 21,* 384–388.

Karabenick, S. A., & Sharma, R. (1994). Perceived teacher support of student questioning in the college classroom: Its relation to student characteristics and role in the classroom questioning process. *Journal of Educational Psychology, 86,* 90–103.

Murray, H. G. (1983). Low-inference classroom teaching behaviors and student ratings of college teaching effectiveness. *Journal of Educational Psychology, 75,* 138–149.

Skinner, E. A., & Belmont, M. J. (1993). Motivation in the classroom: Reciprocal effects of teacher behavior and student engagement across the school year. *Journal of Educational Psychology, 85,* 571–581.

Observational Activities

Observational Activity 11.1: Rating Teachers on Involvement, Structure, and Autonomy Support

The purpose of this observation is to become aware of how teachers express themselves in terms of involvement, structure, and autonomy support. During this observation, you will observe two different teachers. Be sure to gain the permission of each teacher in advance. If possible, observe one teacher who students say is an effective teacher and one teacher who students say is ineffective.

To record the three categories of teaching style, you will first need to construct your own rating scale in which you list each of the following individual items on a 1–5 scale (1 = never, 2 = rarely, 3 = sometimes, 4 = often, 5 = always). You can use some or all of my suggestions, you can get additional suggestions from Murray (1983), or you can generate your own indices of involvement, structure, and autonomy support. Also, construct a measure (with 1–5 scales) to assess students' engagement in terms of their behavior (active/engaged versus passive/disengaged) and emotionality (positive versus negative).

1. *Involvement:* The teacher . . . cares about how students do on their projects, addresses students by name, enjoys spending time with the students, talks with students before or after class, offers help with problems.
2. *Structure:* The teacher . . . gives clear directions, gives preliminary overview of a forthcoming lecture or task, communicates his or her expectations for students' learning or performance, communicates a standard of excellence, administers consequences in a consistent and contingent fashion, provides feedback.
3. *Autonomy support:* The teacher . . . gives students a choice of what to do, gives rationale for learning activities, resists using coercive and controlling language, encourages questions and comments, asks students for suggestions.

With your observations complete, answer the following questions: Were the teachers mostly similar to one another or mostly dissimilar? On which dimensions did teachers rate highest and lowest? Was the ordering as in the text (structure > involvement > autonomy support) or was it different? If different, why? What sort of information did you use to make your teacher ratings?— What the teacher said? What the teacher did? How the student–teacher interactions went? The way the classroom was set up (e.g., seating arrangements)? How the students treated the teacher? Did you notice any sort of pattern between teacher involvement, structure, and autonomy support and the students' behavioral engagement and/or emotional engagement. Was it your impression that the teacher's behavior caused the differences in student engagement, or did the level of student engagement cause differences in teacher behavior?

Observational Activity 11.2: Effect of Students' Moods on Their Creativity

The purpose of this interview is to assess the effect that students' moods have on their creativity. This activity is a different sort of interview, as you will be using a questionnaire rather than face-to-face interactions. You will need access to a classroom of students, and you will need twelve to fifteen minutes of the students' time to complete your data collection. The students need to be at fifth-grade level or higher, because you will be asking them to compose a short poem. Before you begin, gain the permission of *both* the teacher *and* the students in advance. Make it clear (by announcing it to the class) that any student who does not want to participate does not have to.

Construct a simple two-page questionnaire/handout for each student. On the first page, type only one question: "At the present moment—that is, right now—how do you feel?" Then, under this question offer the following three options for the student to complete in a multiple choice format (i.e., pick one): (a) positive, good; (b) neutral, neither good nor bad; or (c) negative, bad. This is your measure of affect. On the second page, write the title "SNOW" at the top, and then type the numbers 1 through 5 vertically down the left side of the page, leaving room to the right of the numbers to write in some words. Ask the students to write a poem, using these instructions (from Amabile, 1985, p. 396): "Write five-lines of unrhymed poetry. Line 1 is a single noun; line 2 has two adjectives that describe the noun; line 3 has three verbs that relate to the noun; line 4 contains a phrase or sentence that relates to the noun; and line 5 repeats the noun in line 1."

Hand out the two-page questionnaire simultaneously to all students. Ask them *not* to put their name on it. Instruct them to complete the first page, and then use the instructions above to guide them through the second page. Allow students five to ten minutes to write their poems. Once you have collected all the questionnaires, fold each in a way that page 2 is visible and page 1 is behind it (and not visible). Then, use your own subjective criteria to rate each poem on a 1–10 scale of how creative it is. As you read and rate each poem for creativity, do *not* look at the first page to see what the student's mood was. When your creativity ratings are done, then group the questionnaires into three piles based on students' responses to the question on the first page—positive, neutral, and negative affect groups—and calculate the mean creativity scores for each group.

Once you have a mean creativity score for each of your three groups, answer these two questions: Was there any relationship between students' self-reported mood and the extent of their creativity expressed on the poem? Can you explain why, or why not, mood predicted creativity? Keep in mind that trying to explain why the two variables did not correlate can be just as informative as trying to explain why they did.

12

Conclusions

I want to begin this final chapter by relating two recent experiences. The first happened just minutes ago, as I sat at the computer readying myself to work. Grinning ironically, my spouse showed me the morning's newspaper headline, "Teachers Say Discipline Is Top Priority" (from the Baton Rouge *Advocate*). I knew what the article was going to say, and I knew what tone it would take, but I began to read anyway. The first sentence quoted a local principal who stressed "keeping students in line." The next paragraph explained the state's plan to institute "boot camps" for students so they "can be taught respect and discipline." The article then blasted parents and quoted a teacher who wanted a new law "aimed at getting parents more involved." I am not making this up; these are actual quotations from the mouths of public school teachers and administrators. My reaction is simply to ask, "Is this what we in education have come to—boot camps for students and laws against their parents? Must we adopt such a defensive, controlling, totalitarian approach 'to keep students in line'?" Yet, what can a teacher do when students lack inner motivational resources? What can a teacher do when students also lack outer motivational resources (e.g., parental involvement, structure in the home)? Should discipline be our top priority, at least in situations such as this?

In response, I can see how hard discipline might help out a teacher, but I wonder what good it does students. Is our objective in education to keep students from "getting into trouble with the law," as the article argues? It is a telltale sign, I believe, that education has lost its vision when school is for teachers rather than for students.

The second experience occurred last week as I read an article in the journal *Teaching of Psychology* entitled, "Motivating Students to Read Journal Articles" (Carkenord, 1994). A college professor describe his technique of motivating students to read a dozen journal articles they otherwise had little interest in reading. For each article read, the student was to write a summary on an index card and hand it in for extra credit. The professor would hand the cards back just before the exams so students could use them to answer questions about the articles. Sure enough, students read the journal articles, and many students read them all. This article upset me because the professor, who had the power of grades over students, used that power to manipulate students to do what he wanted them to do. The students compliantly read the articles, but the only thing I know they got out of their efforts were better grades. I wondered why the article was not entitled "Coercing Students to Read Journal Articles."

As you can probably tell from my sarcasm, strategies in which one person tries to trick, force, make, coerce, pressure, or otherwise manipulate others into doing what they would otherwise have no interest in doing has little to do with motivation. Motivating others is not about control, manipulation, or putting students "on the right track." This journal article, like the newspaper article in the first paragraph, had the theme of trying "to keep students in line," even if it means forcing them to do something "for their own good."

These are hard words. My hope in using them is that they will challenge you to ask yourself just what the nature of motivation is and just what a teacher can do to facilitate it in students. How can a teacher motivate students in a way that excites them and contributes positively to their development, rather than in a way that alienates them and contributes to their levels of resentment and anger over being manipulated like a child, like a pawn. From my point of view, motivating students creates opportunities in their lives to pursue their own self-development; it is an opportunity to empower students with enthusiasm and energy to seek and accomplish the strivings and goals that are important to them. I simply do not hear such a perspective in the newspaper interviews or in the journal article.

Inner and Outer Motivational Resources

Every teacher I have ever talked to agrees that we need to find ways to increase students' motivation to learn. In practice, a teacher can increase student motivation through either outer or inner motivational resources. A reliance on the use of outer motivational resources in effects bypasses students' needs, cognitions, and emotions, and instead regulates their behavior through the strategic introduction and removal of important environmental consequences. Think for a moment of all the energetic and directed behavior you see in your own experiences, both as a student and as a teacher. I am sure you see students exerting high effort in their pursuits of grades, scholarships, extra credit opportunities, and rewards in general as well as in the name of keeping to a schedule or to a promise made to another person. I am sure you also see students put forth high effort to conform to rules and deadlines and to avoid being yelled at, put into a time out, rejected interpersonally, or suspended from school. Take another moment and think about your own daily life and how you rely on outer motivational resources to energize and direct your behavior—alarm clocks, appointment books, yellow Post-It notes, and all those commands we put on ourselves ("Now, remember, you have to pass this test—so study, study, study!"). It is only a mild overstatement to say that when outer motivational resources are salient and strong enough, then even the motivationally emptiest among us will show energetic and directed behavior. Like it or not, we *have to* show energetic and directed behavior if we desire the incentive or fear the punishment enough.

In thinking about the usefulness of outer motivational resources, I have to ask two questions. First, how much does all this energetic and directed behavior have to do with motivation? Motivation is not about the principles of operant conditioning and behavioral management; rather, motivation is about how students' inner resources (rather than other people and environmental contingencies) energize and direct behavior. That is, the subject matter in the study of motivation includes the *internal* forces that give behavior its energy and direction—needs, cognitions, and emotions. Second, I have to ask what benefits students get out of being pushed and pulled about by outer motivational resources? The big payoff is, of course, that we see students engage in behavior we deem to be of value—they read books, write papers, study for hours—and we see increases in their academic achievements. So if students are showing high effort and achievement, then you might ask, "Hey, what's the big deal; as long as students are doing what they are supposed to be doing why get so uptight about whether such behavior is guided by outer or by inner motivational resources?"

The big deal is that the logic that one or the other (inner or outer) ways of motivating student will do equally well is erroneous. Maladaptive motivation can cover up and even replace adaptive motivation. All this is to suggest that we might be well advised to consider that there are types of motivation, and some of these produce more adaptive behavioral patterns than others do (i.e., compare external regulation, introjected regulation, identified regulation and intrinsic motivation; compare learning versus performance goals; compare the tendency to approach success versus the tendency to avoid failure). A reliance on outer motivational resources to accomplish the goals of education is to put at risk students' later ability to generate their own motivation to accomplish the strivings they have for themselves. That is, it puts students at risk of becoming increasingly motivationally empty and increasingly unable to show self-direction, self-regulation, and self-motivation in the absence of outer motivational resources. A reliance on inner motivational resources, on the other hand, allows us the possibility of accomplishing more of the goals of education than just behavioral compliance and extrinsically motivated achievement. When teachers work to facilitate students' inner motivational resources (involve and satisfy students' needs, build optimistic beliefs systems, and arouse positive emotions), then education opens the door to additional positive outcomes—a positive attitude toward learning, healthy personal development, and a competent and meaningful adjustment into society (see Table 1-1).

A Misunderstanding

One theme that runs throughout both this book and any discussion of pitting inner versus outer motivational resources is that autonomy-supportive, student-centered approaches to teaching promote higher and qualitatively more healthy motivation, learning, and development than do controlling, teacher-centered approaches. The apparent appeal of the controlling, teacher-centered approach is that it pushes students to achieve and it challenges them to excel. Such a teaching style is rooted in the belief that if students are left to "do their own thing," there is little or no reason to expect that students will spontaneously motivate themselves to become competent readers, writers, and the like. Such a belief is well founded. *Laissez-faire* ("hands off") classrooms that allow students to do whatever they want to do indeed prove themselves to be ineffective and ill advised. Laissez-faire classrooms provide a poor and ineffective model for teachers to emulate. Even the renowned humanist Abraham Maslow could not successfully conduct a college class using a laissez-faire approach (see Maslow, 1979, and the follow-up responses). But to equate laissez-faire with autonomy support is a misrepresentation; indeed, it is a misunderstanding.

The opposite of "pressuring students to learn" is *not* "leaving students to their own devices." Rather, autonomy support involves an effortful attempt to support students' autonomous behavior—that is, to nurture students' inner motivational resources. The opposite of support is actually neglect, or laissez-faire permissiveness. Like control, autonomy support sometimes manifests itself in directed instruction (as through "freedom within limits"; see Chapter 2). Autonomy support differs from a controlling approach in that it is student-centered rather than teacher-centered.

Some Things I Have Learned

One thing I have learned as I visit schools and talk to teachers is that most teachers prefer to use outer motivational resources. Many teachers hold pessimistic attitudes about the utility or even the wisdom of motivating students via inner motivational resources. There is something there that teachers simply do not trust.

Behind this mistrust, I hear three reasons. First, some teachers actually do not want a theory of motivation; rather, they want a theory of performance. If what you want to accomplish in the classroom is to attain a prescribed degree of performance or achievement, then I can see how motivating students with outer resources can be just as appealing, if not more so, than motivating students with inner resources. Second, many teachers prefer to take a short-term, moment-to-moment approach to motivation instead of a longer term developmental approach. Teachers come to rely on outer resources because inducements like tomorrow's test or today's consequence can snap students into a quick display of on-task behavior more easily and more reliably than through the more laborious attempt first to try to interest students in the day's lesson or point out its relevance for their lives. In contrast, in every chapter I tried to point out not only the long-term, developmental benefits of supporting students' inner motivational resources but the short-term, immediate benefits as well. Third, teachers find motivation via inner motivational resources to be suspicious because it does not correspond to how others motivate them. What I hear is, "Yeah, yeah, yeah; all your talk about autonomy and self-determination is fine and dandy. But it just seems to make sense that if you want Johnny to study, then you make him study and get it over with—just make him do it! That's the way I learned, and I turned out just fine, didn't I?" To this appeal from the Vince Lombardi school of teaching, I simply offer the reader the suggestion that just because you might have experienced a controlling motivational climate in your own education, that does not mean that such a procedure is therefore automatically the best way to motivate the students who will come into your class tomorrow. Such a position ignores the now vast empirical literature available to educators as to which teaching strategies work best.

The Art of Motivating Others

Here is another thing I have learned: Any attempt to improve student motivation begins with the development of effective teaching. Effective teaching, I think, involves rethinking the roles of teachers, students, activities, and classroom climates. Specifically, in effective teaching (1) the teacher's role is not just to present information but also to tap into and support students' inner motivational resources; (2) the student's role is not just passively to copy information but actively to makes sense of problems and to construct meaning; (3) the role of the classroom activities and assignments is not just memorizing and reproducing but also problem solving and information gathering; and (4) the role of the classroom climate is to promote a social environment that uses conversation and experimentation to build a community of cooperative learners (e.g., Brophy, 1989; McCombs & Pope, 1994; Slavin, 1984, 1995). In some classrooms, the teacher already defines the roles of the teacher, students, activities, and classroom climate in this fashion. In other classrooms, however, a need exists to rethink radically how teachers conduct lessons, at least if student motivation is a priority. The idea that mathematics, history, or a foreign language can be *told* to students is a deeply ingrained orientation in the minds of some teachers and in the minds of many students and their parents. I hope that the ideas expressed throughout the book form some of the foundations for all persons participating in the educational process to rethink the idea that students are passive absorbers of knowledge, and to consider the merits of the idea that students are active learners. Active learners are motivated learners, and motivated learners need not only expert instructors but also supportive facilitators.

In closing, I face a paradox. In a book entitled *Motivating Others,* some final words of advice on *precisely* how to motivate others would seem to be appropriate. Yet, any specific advice to "do this" or "do that," I think, misses the point. Any advice about learning the art of motivating others needs to be flexible, because a student-centered approach to motivating others must logically vary with each student. I offer this final thought. I find value in responding to students' questions about motivating others by asking, simply, "Well, what do you think?" It is the questioner who faces the problem, and it is the questioner who knows the history of the individual and situations involved. Invariably, the questioner also has some tentative solution in mind. Instead of prescribing a solution to fix the motivational problem, I find it more helpful to work cooperatively with the questioner toward a solution. I am certainly open to giving my opinions and perspective, but the questioner almost always walks away from the conversation knowing that he or she (rather than I) solved the problem. And, of course, the questioner did. Thus, I find the challenge of motivating others to be the same as the challenge in teaching others—namely, both involve a scaffolding process in which others solve the problems they face by using and by trusting both the support of experts *and* the inner resources they possess.

References

Abramson, L. Y., Seligman, M. E. P., & Teasdale, J. D. (1978). Learned helplessness in humans: Critique and reformulation. *Journal of Abnormal Psychology, 87,* 49–74.

Ainsworth, M. D. S. (1989). Attachments beyond infancy. *American Psychologist, 44,* 709–716.

Alexander, P. A., Kulikowich, J. M., & Jetton, T. L. (1994). The role of subject-matter knowledge and interest in the processing of linear and nonlinear text. *Review of Educational Research, 64,* 201–252.

Altmaier, E. M., & Happ, D. A. (1985). Coping skills training's immunization effects against learned helplessness. *Journal of Social and Clinical Psychology, 3,* 181–189.

Amabile, T. M. (1979). Effects of external evaluations on artistic creativity. *Journal of Personality and Social Psychology, 37,* 221–233.

Amabile, T. M. (1983). *The social psychology of creativity.* New York: Springer-Verlag.

Amabile, T. M. (1985). Motivation and creativity: Effect of motivational orientation on creative writers. *Journal of Personality and Social Psychology, 48,* 393–399.

Amabile, T. M., & Hennessey, B. A. (1992). The motivation for creativity in children. In A. K. Boggiano & T. S. Pittman (Eds.), *Achievement and motivation: A social developmental perspective* (pp. 54–76). New York: Cambridge University Press.

Amabile, T. M., Hennessey, B. A., & Grossman, B. S. (1986). Social influences on creativity: The effects of contracted-for reward. *Journal of Personality and Social Psychology, 50,* 14–23.

Ames, C., & Ames, R. (1984). Goal structures and motivation. *The Elementary School Journal, 85,* 39–53.

Ames, C., & Archer, J. (1988). Achievement goals in the classroom: Student learning strategies and motivational processes. *Journal of Educational Psychology, 80,* 260–267.

Anderman, E. M., & Maehr, M. L. (1994). Motivation and schooling in the middle grades. *Review of Educational Research, 64,* 287–309.

Anderson, D. C., & Jennings, D. L. (1980). When experiences of failure promote expectations of success: The impact of attributing failure to ineffective strategies. *Journal of Personality, 48,* 393–407.

Anderson, R., Manoogian, S. T., & Reznick, J. S. (1976). The undermining and enhancing of intrinsic motivation in preschool children. *Journal of Personality and Social Psychology, 34,* 915–922.

Andrews, G. R., & Debus, R. L. (1978). Persistence and the causal perception of failure: Modifying cognitive attributions. *Journal of Educational Psychology, 70,* 154–166.

Anthony, H., & Anderson, L. (1987, April). *The nature of writing instruction in regular and special education classrooms.* Paper presented at the annual meeting of the American Educational Research Association, Chicago.

Arkin, R. M., & Baumgardner, A. H. (1985). Self-handicapping. In J. H. Harvey & G. Weary (Eds.), *Basic issues in attribution theory and research* (pp. 169–202). New York: Academic Press.

Ashton, P. T. (1984). Teacher efficacy: A motivational paradigm for effective teacher education. *Journal of Teacher Education, 35,* 28–32.

Ashton, P. T. (1985). Motivation and the teacher's sense of efficacy. In C. Ames & R. Ames (Eds.), *Research on motivation in education: The classroom meliu* (Vol. 2, pp. 141–174). Orlando, FL: Academic Press.

Ashton, P. T., & Webb, R. B. (1986). *Making a difference: Teacher's sense of efficacy and student achievement.* New York: Longman.

Astone, N. M., & McLanahan, S. S. (1991). Family structure, parental practices, and high school completion. *American Sociological Review, 56,* 309–320.

Atkinson, J. W. (1964). A theory of achievement motivation. In *An introduction to motivation* (pp. 240–268). New York: Van Nostrand.

Azar, B. (1994, October). Seligman recommends a depression 'vaccine.' *APA Monitor, 27,* 4.

Bacon, C. S. (1993). Student responsibility for learning. *Adolescence, 28,* 199–212.

Bandura, A. (1977). Self-efficacy: Toward a unifying theory of behavioral change. *Psychological Review, 84,* 191–215.

Bandura, A. (1982). Self-efficacy mechanisms in human agency. *American Psychologist, 37,* 122–147.

Bandura, A. (1983). Self-efficacy mechanisms of anticipated fears and calamaties. *Journal of Personality and Social Psychology, 45,* 464–469.

Bandura, A. (1986). Self-efficacy. In *Social foundations of thought and action: A social cognitive theory* (pp. 390–453). Englewood Cliffs, NJ: Prentice-Hall.

Bandura, A. (1988). Self-efficacy conception of anxiety. *Anxiety Research, 1,* 77–98.

Bandura, A. (1989). Human agency in social cognitive theory. *American Psychologist, 44,* 1175–1184.

Bandura, A. (1990). Reflections on nonability determinants of competence. In J. Kolligan & R. Sternberg (Eds.), *Competence considered* (pp. 315–362). New Haven: Yale University Press.

Bandura, A. (1991). Self-regulation of motivation through anticipatory and self-regulatory mechanisms. In R. A. Dienstbier (Ed.), *Nebraska symposium on motivation: Perspectives on motivation* (Vol. 38, pp. 69–164). Lincoln: University of Nebraska Press.

Bandura, A. (1993). Perceived self-efficacy in cognitive development and functioning. *Educational Psychologist, 28,* 117–148.

Bandura, A., & Adams, N. E. (1977). Analysis of self-efficacy theory of behavioral change. *Cognitive Therapy and Research, 1,* 287–308.

Bandura, A., Adams, N. E., Hardy, A. B., & Howells, G. N. (1980). Tests of the generality of self-efficacy theory. *Cognitive Therapy and Research, 4,* 39–66.

Bandura, A., & Cervone, D. (1983). Self-evaluative and self-efficacy mechanisms governing the motivational effects of goal systems. *Journal of Personality and Social Psychology, 45,* 1017–1028.

Bandura, A., & Cervone, D. (1986). Differential engagement of self-reactive influences in cognitive motivation. *Organizational Behavior and Human Decision Processes, 38,* 92–113.

Bandura, A., Cioffi, D., Taylor, C. B., & Brouillard, M. E. (1988). Perceived self-efficacy in coping with cognitive stressors and opioid activation. *Journal of Personality and Social Psychology, 55,* 479–488.

Bandura, A., & Jourden, F. J. (1991). Self-regulatory mechanisms governing the impact of social comparison on complex decision making. *Journal of Personality and Social Psychology, 60,* 941–951.

Bandura, A., Reese, L., & Adams, N. E. (1982). Microanalysis of action and fear arousal as a function of differential levels of perceived self-efficacy. *Journal of Personality and Social Psychology, 43,* 5–21.

Bandura, A., & Schunk, D. H. (1981). Cultivating competence, self-efficacy, and intrinsic interest through proximal self-motivation. *Journal of Personality and Social Psychology, 41,* 586–598.

Bandura, A., Taylor, C. B., Williams, S. L., Mefford, I. N., & Barchas, J. D. (1985). Catecholamine secretion as a function of perceived coping self-efficacy. *Journal of Consulting and Clinical Psychology, 53,* 406–414.

Bandura, A., & Wood, R. E. (1989). Effect of perceived controllability and performance standards on self-regulation of complex decision making. *Journal of Personality and Social Psychology, 56,* 805–814.

Barker, G., & Graham, S. (1987). A developmental study of praise and blame as attributional cues. *Journal of Educational Psychology, 79,* 62–66.

Barrett, M., & Boggiano, A. K. (1988). Fostering extrinsic orientations: Use of reward strategies to motivate children. *Journal of Social and Clinical Psychology, 6,* 293–309.

Barrios, B. A. (1983). The role of cognitive mediators in heterosexual anxiety: A test of self-efficacy theory. *Cognitive Therapy and Research, 7,* 543–554.

Bassett, G. A. (1979). A study of the effects of task goal and schedule choice on work performance. *Organizational Behavior and Human Performance, 24,* 202–227.

Batson, C. D., Coke, J. S., Chard, F., Smith, D., & Taliaferro, A. (1979). Generality of the "Glow of goodwill": Effects of mood on helping and information acquisition. *Social Psychology Quarterly, 42,* 176–179.

Baumeister, R. F. (1982). A self-presentational view of social phenomena. *Psychological Bulletin, 91,* 3–26.

Baumeister, R. F. (1986). *Identity: Cultural change and the struggle for self.* New York: Oxford University Press.

Baumeister, R. F. (1987). How the self became a problem: A psychological review of historical research. *Journal of Personality and Social Psychology, 52,* 163–176.

Baumeister, R. F. (1989). The optimal margin of illusion. *Journal of Social and Clinical Psychology, 8,* 176–189.

Baumgardner, A. H., Lake, E. A., & Arkin, R. M. (1985). Claiming mood as a self-handicap: The influence of spoiled and unspoiled public identities. *Personality and Social Psychology Bulletin, 11,* 349–357.

Beane, J. A. (1991). Sorting out the self-esteem controversy. *Educational Leadership, 49,* 25–30.

Beck, N. E., & Hackett, G. (1986). Applications of self-efficacy theory to understanding career choice behavior. *Journal of Social and Clinical Psychology, 4,* 279–289.

Becker, L. J. (1978). Joint effect of feedback and goal setting on performance: A field study of residential energy conservation. *Journal of Applied Psychology, 63,* 428–433.

Benware, C., & Deci, E. L. (1984). The quality of learning with an active versus passive motivational set. *American Educational Research Journal, 21,* 755–765.

Berglas, S., & Jones, E. E. (1978). Drug choice as a self-handicapping strategy in response to noncontingent success. *Journal of Personality and Social Psychology, 36,* 405–417.

Berlyne, D. E. (1960). *Conflict, arousal, and curiosity.* New York: McGraw-Hill.

Berlyne, D. E. (1966). Curiosity and exploration. *Science, 153,* 25–33.

Berlyne, D. E. (1967). Arousal and reinforcement. In D. Levine (Ed.), *Nebraska symposium on motivation* (Vol. 15, pp. 1–110). Lincoln: University of Nebraska Press.

Berlyne, D. E. (1978). Curiosity and exploration. *Motivation and Emotion, 2,* 97–175.

Berlyne, D. E., Craw, M. A., Salapatek, P. H., & Lewis, J. L. (1963). Novelty, complexity, incongruity, extrinsic motivation and the GSR. *Journal of Experimental Psychology, 66,* 560–567.

Bernstein, D. A. (1994). Tell and show: The merits of classroom demonstrations. *APS Observer, 7,* 24–25, 37.

Bertenthal, B., & Fisher, K. (1978). Development of self-recognition in the infant. *Developmental Psychology, 14,* 44–50.

Betz, N. E., & Hackett, G. (1986). Applications of self-efficacy theory to understanding career choice behavior. *Journal of Social and Clinical Psychology, 4,* 279–289.

Birney, R. C., Burdick, H., & Teevan, R. C. (1969). *Fear of failure.* New York: Van Nostrand.

Blank, P. D., Reis, H. T., & Jackson, L. (1984). The effects of verbal reinforcements on intrinsic motivation for sex-linked tasks. *Sex Roles, 10,* 369–387.

Blankenship, V. (1992). Individual differences in resultant achievment motivation and latency to and persistence at an achievement task. *Motivation and Emotion, 16,* 35–63.

Bloom, B. (1981). *All our children learning.* New York: McGraw-Hill.

Blumenfeld, P., Hamilton, V. L., Bossert, S., Wessels, K., & Meece, C. (1983). Teacher talk and student thought: Socialization into the student role. In J. Levine & U. Wang (Eds.), *Teacher and student perceptions: Implications for learning.* Hillsdale, NJ: Lawrence Erlbaum.

Blumenfeld, P., & Pintrich, P. (1983, April). *The relation of student characteristics and children's perception of teachers and peers in varying classroom environments.* Paper presented at the annual meeting of the American Educational Research Association, Montreal.

Blumenfeld, P., Pintrich, P., Meece, J., & Wessels, K. (1982). The formation and role of self perceptions of abililty in elementary school classrooms. *Elementary School Journal, 82,* 401–420.

Boggiano, A. K., Barrett, M., Silvern, L., & Gallo, S. (1991). Predicting emotional concomitants of learned helplessness: The role of motivational orientation. *Sex Roles, 25,* 577–592.

Boggiano, A. K., Barrett, M., Weiher, A. W., McClelland, G. H., & Lusk, C. M. (1987). Use of the maximal-operant principle to motivate children's intrinsic interest. *Journal of Personality and Social Psychology, 53,* 866–879.

Boggiano, A. K., Flink, C., Shields, A., Seelbach, A., & Barrett, M. (1993). Use of techniques promoting students' self-determination: Effects on students' analytic problem-solving skills. *Motivation and Emotion, 17,* 319–336.

Boggiano, A. K., Main, D. S., & Katz, P. A. (1988). Children's preference for challenge: The role of perceived competence and control. *Journal of Personality and Social Psychology, 54,* 134–151.

Boggiano, A. K., Pittman, T. S., & Ruble, D. N. (1982). The mastery hypothesis and the overjustification effect. *Social Cognition, 1,* 38–49.

Boggiano, A. K., & Ruble, D. N. (1979). Competence and the overjustification effect: A developmental study. *Journal of Personality and Social Psychology, 37,* 1462–1468.

Boggiano, A. K., & Ruble, D. N. (1986). Children's responses to evaluative feedback. In R. Schwarzer (Ed.), *Self-related cognitions in anxiety and motivation.* Hillsdale, NJ: Lawrence Erlbaum.

Borman, K. (1978). Social control and schooling: Power and process in two kindergarten settings. *Anthropology and Education Quarterly, 9,* 138–153.

Brophy, J. (1983). Fostering student learning and motivation in the elementary school classroom. In S. Paris, G. Olson, & H. Stevenson (Eds.), *Learning and motivation in the classroom* (pp. 283–305). Hillsdale, NJ: Lawrence Erlbaum.

Brophy, J. (1986). Teacher influences on student achievement. *American Psychologist, 41,* 1069–1077.

Brophy, J. (1989). Conclusion: Toward a theory of teaching. In *Advances in Research on Teaching* (Vol. 1, pp. 345–355). Greenwich, CT: JAI Press.

Brophy, J., & Good, T. (1974). *Teacher-student relationships: Causes and consequences.* New York: Holt, Rinehart & Winston.

Brown, I., Jr., & Inouye, D. K. (1978). Learned helplessness through modeling: The role of perceived similarity in competence. *Journal of Personality and Social Psychology, 36,* 900–908.

Bruner, J. S. (1962). *On knowing: Essays for the left-hand.* Cambridge, MA: Harvard University Press.

Bryant, J. (1978). *The effect of different levels of suspense and of the resolution of suspense on the appreciation of dramatic presentations.* Unpublished manuscript, University of Massachusetts.

Bugental, J. F. T., & Zelen, S. L. (1950). Investigations into the "self-concept." 1. The W-A-Y technique. *Journal of Personality, 18,* 483–498.

Butkowsky, I. S., & Willows, D. M. (1980). Cognitive-motivational characteristics of children varying in reading ability: Evidence for learned helplessness in readers. *Journal of Educational Psychology, 72,* 408–422.

Byrne, B. M. (1984). The general/academic self-concept nomological network: A reivew of construct validation research. *Review of Educational Research, 54,* 427–456.

Cameron, J., & Pierce, W. D. (1994). Reinforcement, reward, and intrinsic motivation: A meta-analysis. *Review of Educational Research, 64,* 363–423.

Campbell, D. J. (1982). Determinants of choice of goal difficulty level: A review of situational and personality influences. *Journal of Occupational Psychology, 55,* 79–95.

Cantor, N., Markus, H., Niedenthal, P., & Nurius, P. (1986). On motivation and the self-concept. In R. M. Sorrentino & E. T. Higgins (Eds.), *Handbook of motivation and cognition* (Vol. 1, pp. 96–121). New York: Guilford Press.

Carkenord, D. M. (1994). Motivating students to read journal articles. *Teaching of Psychology, 21,* 162–164.

Carnevale, P. J. D., & Isen, A. M. (1986). The influence of positive affect and visual access on the discovery of integrative solutions in bilateral negotiation. *Organizational Behavior and Human Decision Processes, 37,* 1–13.

Carver, C. S., & Scheier, M. F. (1981). *Attention and self-regulation: A control theory approach to human behavior.* New York: Springer-Verlag.

Carver, C. S., & Scheier, M. F. (1990). Origins and functions of positive and negative affect: A control-process view. *Psychological Review, 97,* 19–35.

Chen, M., & Isen, A. M. (1992). *The influence of positive affect and success on persistence on a failed task.* Unpublished manuscript, Cornell University.

Clifford, M. M. (1984). Thoughts on a theory of constructive failure. *Educational Psychologist, 19,* 108–120.

Clifford, M. M. (1988). Failure tolerance and academic risk-taking in ten- to twelve-year old students. *British Journal of Educational Psychology 58,* 15–27.

Clifford, M. M. (1990). Students need challenge, not easy success. *Educational Leadership, 48,* 22–26.

Clifford, M. M. (1991). Risk taking: Theoretical, empirical, and educational considerations. *Educational Psychologist, 26,* 263–297.

Clifford, M. M., & Chou, F. C. (1991). Children's risk taking as a function of type of payoffs, task context, and tolerance for failure. *Journal of Educational Psychology, 83,* 499–507.

Collins, J. L. (1982, April). *Self-efficacy and ability in achievement behavior.* Paper presented at the annual meeting of the American Educational Research Association, New York, New York.

Condry, J. (1977). Enemies of exploration: Self-initiated versus other-initiated learning. *Journal of Personality and Social Psychology, 35,* 459–475.

Condry, J., & Stokker, L. G. (1992). Overview of special issue on intrinsic motivation. *Motivation and Emotion, 16,* 157–164.

Connell, J. P. (1990). Context, self, and action: A motivational analysis of self-system processes across the life-span. In D. Cicchetti (Ed.), *The self in transition: From infancy to childhood* (pp. 61–97). Chicago: University of Chicago Press.

Connell, J. P., & Ryan, R. M. (1984). A developmental theory of motivation in the classroom. *Teacher Education Quarterly, 11,* 64–77.

Connell, J. P., & Wellborn, J. G. (1991). Competence, autonomy, and relatedness: A motivational analysis of self-system processes. In M. R. Gunnar & L. A. Sroufe (Eds.), *Self processes in development: Minnesota symposium on child psychology* (Vol. 23, pp. 167–216). Hillsdale, NJ: Lawrence Erlbaum.

Corno, L. (1992). Encouraging students to take responsibility for learning and performance. *The Elementary School Journal, 93,* 69–83.

Cota, A. A., & Dion, K. L. (1986). Salience of gender and sex composition of ad hoc groups: An experimental test of distinctiveness theory. *Journal of Personality and Social Psychology, 50,* 770–776.

Covington, M. (1984a). The self-worth theory of achievement motivation: Findings and implications. *The Elementary School Journal, 85,* 5–20.

Covington, M. (1984b). Motivation for self-worth. In R Ames & C. Ames (Eds.), *Research on motivation in education* (Vol. 1, pp. 77–113). New York: Academic Press.

Covington, M., & Omelich, C. L. (1979). Effort: The double-edged sword in school achievement. *Journal of Educational Psychology, 71,* 169–182.

Craske, M. L. (1988). Learned helplessness, self-worth motivation, and attribution retraining for primary school children. *Bristish Journal of Educational Psychology, 58,* 152–164.

Crocker, J. (1994, October). *Who cares what they think?! Relected and deflected apprais-als.* Paper presented at the annual meeting of the Society for Experimental Social Psychologists, Lake Tahoe, Nevada.

Crocker, J., Luhtanen, R., Blaine, B., & Broadnax, S. (1994). Collective self-esteem and psychological well-being among white, black, and Asian college students. *Person-ality and Social Psychology Bulletin, 20,* 503–513.

Cross, S. E., & Markus, H. R. (1994). Self-schemas, possible selves, and competent performance. *Journal of Educational Psychology, 86,* 423–438.

Csikszentmihalyi, M. (1975). *Beyond boredom and anxiety: The experience of play in work and games.* San Francisco: Jossey-Bass.

Csikszentmihalyi, M. (1982). Toward a psychology of optimal experience. *Review of Personality and Social Psychology, 3,* 13–36.

Csikszentmihalyi, M. (1985). Relections on enjoyment. *Perspectives in Biology and Medicine, 28,* 469–497.

Csikszentmihalyi, M. (1990). *Flow: The psychology of optimal experience.* New York: Harper & Row.

Csikszentmihalyi, M., & Csikszentmihalyi, I. (Eds.). (1988). *Optimal experiences: Psy-chological studies of flow in consciousness.* New York: Cambridge University Press.

Csikszentmihalyi, M., & Larsen, R. (1984). *Being adolescent.* New York: Basic Books.

Csikszentmihalyi, M., & McCormack, J. (1986, February). The influence of teachers. *Phi Delta Kappan, 67,* 415–419.

Csikszentmihalyi, M., & Nakamura, J. (1989). The dynamics of intrinsic motivation: A study of adolescents. In C. Ames & R. Ames (Eds.), *Research on motivation in education* (Vol. 3, pp. 45–71). San Diego: Academic Press.

Csikszentmihalyi, M., & Rathunde, K. (1993). The measurement of flow in everyday life: Toward a theory of emergent motivation. In J. E. Jacobs (Ed.), *Nebraska sympo-sium on motivation: Developmental perspectives on motivation* (Vol. 40, pp. 57–97). Lincoln: University of Nebraska Press.

Csikszentmihalyi, M., Rathunde, K., & Whalen, S. (1993). *Talented teenagers: The roots of success and failure.* New York: Cambridge University Press.

Danner, F. W., & Lonky, E. (1981). A cognitive-developmental approach to the effects of rewards on intrinsic motivation. *Child Development, 52,* 1043–1052.

Day, H. I. (1982). Curiosity and the interested explorer. *Performance and Instruction, 21,* 19–22.

Day, J. D., Borkowski, J. G., Punzo, D., & Howsepian, B. (1994). Enhancing possible selves in Mexican American students. *Motivation and Emotion, 18,* 79–103.

deCharms, R. (1968). *Personal causation: The internal affective determinants of behavior.* New York: Academic Press.

deCharms, R. (1976). *Enhancing motivation: Change in the classroom.* New York: Irvington.

deCharms, R. (1984). Motivation enhancement in educational settings. In R. E. Ames & C. Ames (Eds.), *Research on motivation in education: Student motivation* (Vol. 1, pp. 275–310). New York: Academic Press.

Deci, E. L. (1971). Effects of externally mediated rewards on intrinsic motivation. *Journal of Personality and Social Psychology, 18,* 105–115.

Deci, E. L. (1980). *The psychology of self-determination.* Lexington, MA: Lexington.

Deci, E. L. (1992a). On the nature and function of motivation theories. *Psychological Science, 3,* 167–171.

Deci, E. L. (1992b). The relation of interest to the motivation of behavior: A self-determination theory perspective. In K. A. Renninger, S. Hidi, & A. Krapp (Eds.), *The role of interest in learning and development* (pp. 43–70). Hillsdale, NJ: Lawrence Erlbaum.

Deci, E. L., Connell, J. P., Ryan, R. M. (1989). Self-determination in a work organization. *Journal of Applied Psychology, 74,* 580–590.

Deci, E. L., Driver, R. E., Hotchkiss, L., Robbins, R. J., & Wilson, I. M. (1993). The relation of mother's controlling vocalizations to children's intrinsic motivation. *Journal of Experimental Child Psychology, 55,* 151–162.

Deci, E. L., Eghrari, H., Patrick, B. C., & Leone, D. R. (1994). Facilitating internalization: The self-determination theory perspective. *Journal of Personality, 62,* 119–142.

Deci, E. L., Nezlek, J., & Sheinman, L. (1981). Characteristics of the rewarder and intrinsic motivation of the rewardee. *Journal of Personality and Social Psychology, 40,* 1–10.

Deci, E. L., & Ryan, R. M. (1980). The empirical exploration of intrinsic motivational proccess. In L. Berkowitz (Ed.), *Advances in experimental social psychology* (Vol. 13, pp. 39–80). New York: Academic Press.

Deci, E. L., & Ryan, R. M. (1985). *Intrinsic motivation and self-determination in human behavior.* New York: Plenum Press.

Deci, E. L., & Ryan, R. M. (1987). The support of autonomy and the control of behavior. *Journal of Personality and Social Psychology, 53,* 1024–1037.

Deci, E. L., & Ryan, R. M. (1991). A motivational approach to self: Integration in personality. In R. Dienstbier (Ed.), *Nebraska symposium on motivation: Perspectives on motivation* (Vol. 38, pp. 237–288). Lincoln: University of Nebraska Press.

Deci, E. L., Schwartz, A., Scheinman, L., & Ryan, R. M. (1981). An instrument to assess adults' orientations toward control versus autonomy in children: Reflections on intrinsic motivation and perceived competence. *Journal of Educational Psychology, 73,* 642–650.

Deci, E. L., Spiegel, N. H., Ryan, R. M., Koestner, R., & Kauffman, M. (1982). Effects of performance standards on teaching styles: Behavior of controlling teachers. *Journal of Educational Psychology, 74,* 852–859.

Deci, E. L., Vallerand, R. J., Pelletier, L. G., & Ryan, R. M. (1991). Motivation in education: The self-determination perspective. *Educational Psychologist, 26,* 325–346.

Detterman, D. K. (1993). The case for the prosecution: Transfer as an epiphenomenon. In D. K. Detterman & R. J. Sternberg (Eds.), *Transfer on trial: Intelligence, cognition, and instruction* (pp. 1–24). Norwood, NJ: Ablex.

Diener, C. I., & Dweck, C. S. (1978). An analysis of learned helplessness: Continuous chances in performance, strategy, and achievement cognitions following failure. *Journal of Personality and Social Psychology, 36,* 451–462.

Dollinger, S. J., & Thelen, M. H. (1978). Overjustification and children's intrinsic motivation: Comparative effects of four rewards. *Journal of Personality and Social Psychology, 36,* 1259–1269.

Dunker, K. (1945). On problem-solving. *Psychological Monographs, 58,* Whole No. 5.

Dusek, J. (1980). The development of test anxiety in children. In I. Sarason (Ed.), *Test anxiety: Theory, research, and applications* (pp. 87–110). Hillsdale, NJ: Lawrence Erlbaum.

Dusek, J. (Ed.). (1985). *Teacher expectancies.* Hillsdale, NJ: Lawrence Erlbaum.

Dusek, J., Kermis, M., & Mergler, N. (1975). Information processing in low- and high-test-anxious children as a function of grade level and verbal labeling. *Developmental Psychology, 11,* 651–652.

Dusek, J., Mergler, N., & Kermis, M. (1976). Attention, encoding, and information processing in low- and high-test-anxious children. *Child Development, 47,* 201–207.

Dweck, C. S. (1975). The role of expectancies and attributions in the alleviation of learned helplessness. *Journal of Personality and Social Psychology, 31,* 674–685.

Dweck, C. S. (1986). Motivational processes affecting learning. *American Psychologist, 41,* 1040–1048.

Dweck, C. S., & Leggett, E. (1988). A social-cognitive approach to motivation and personality. *Psychological Review, 95,* 256–273.

Dweck, C. S., & Repucci, N. D. (1973). Learned helplessness and reinforcement responsibility in children. *Journal of Personality and Social Psychology, 25,* 109–116.

Dyck, D. G., & Breen, L. J. (1978). Learned helplessness, immunization, and importance of task in humans. *Psychological Reports, 43,* 315–321.

Earley, P. C., Connolly, T., & Ekegren, G. (1989). Goals, strategy development and task performance: Some limits on the efficacy of goal setting. *Journal of Applied Psychology, 74,* 24–33.

Earley, P. C., Northcraft, G. B., Lee, C., & Lituchy, T. R. (1990). Impact of processes and outcome feedback on the relation of goal setting to task performance. *Academy of Management Journal, 33,* 87–105.

Earley, P. C., & Perry, B. C. (1987). Work plan availability and performance: An assessment of task strategy priming on subsequent task completion. *Organizational Behavior and Human Decision Processes, 39,* 279–302.

Earley, P. C., Wojnaroski, P., & Prest, W. (1987). Task planning and energy expended: Exploration of how goals influence performance. *Journal of Applied Psychology, 72,* 107–113.

Eccles, J. S. (1984a). Sex differences in achievement patterns. In T. Sonderegger (Ed.), *Nebraska symposium on motivation: Psychology and gender* (Vol. 32, pp. 97–132). Lincoln: University of Nebraska Press.

Eccles, J. S. (1984b). Sex differences in mathematics participation. In M. Steinkamp &

M. L. Maehr (Eds.), *Advances in motivation and achievement* (Vol. 2, pp. 93–137). Lincoln: University of Nebraska Press.

Eccles, J. S. (1993). School and family effects on the ontogeny of children's interests, self-perceptions, and activity choices. In J. E. Jacobs (Ed.), *Nebraska symposium on motivation: Developmental perspectives on motivation* (Vol. 40, pp. 145–208). Lincoln: University of Nebraska Press.

Eccles, J. S., & Hoffman, L. W. (1984). Socialization and the maintenance of a sex-segregated labor market. In H. W. Stevenson & A. E. Siegel (Eds.), *Research in child development and social policy* (Vol. 1, pp. 367–420). Chicago: University of Chicago Press.

Eccles, J. S., & Midgley, C. (1989). Stage/environment fit: Developmentally appropriate classrooms for early adolescents. In R. E. Ames & C. Ames (Eds.), *Research on motivation in education* (Vol. 3, pp. 139–186). New York: Academic Press.

Eccles, J. S., Midgley, C., & Adler, T. (1984). Grade-level changes in the school environment: Effects on achievement motivation. In J. G. Nicholls (Eds.), *The development of achievement motivation* (pp. 283–331). Greenwich, CT: JAI Press.

Eccles-Parsons, J., Adler, T. F., Futterman, R., Goff, S. B., Kaczala, C. M., Meece, J. L., & Midgley, C. (1983). Expectancies, values, and academic behaviors. In J. T. Spence (Ed.), *Achievement and achievement motivation.* San Francisco: W. H. Freeman.

Eccles-Parsons, J. E., Adler, T. F., & Kaczala, C. M. (1982). Socialization of achievement attitudes and beliefs: Parental influences. *Child Development, 53,* 310–321.

Eckelman, J. D., & Dyck, D. G. (1979). Task- and setting-related cues in immunization against learned helplessness. *American Journal of Psychology, 92,* 653–667.

Elliot, E., & Dweck, C. (1988). Goals: An approach to motivation and achievement. *Journal of Personality and Social Psychology, 54,* 5–12.

Emmons, R. A. (1986). Personal strivings: An approach to personality and subjective well-being. *Journal of Personality and Social Psychology, 51,* 1058–1068.

Emmons, R. A. (1989). The personal striving approach to personality. In L. A. Pervin (Ed.), *Goal concepts in personality and social psychology* (pp. 87–126). Hillsdale, NJ: Lawrence Erlbaum.

Entin, E. E., & Raynor, J. O. (1973). Effects of contingent future orientation and achievement motivation on performance in two kinds of tasks. *Journal of Experimental Research in Personality, 6,* 314–320.

Erez, M. (1977). Feedback: A necessary condition for the goal setting-performance relationship. *Journal of Applied Psychology, 62,* 624–627.

Erez, M., Earley, P. C., & Hulin, C. L. (1985). The impact of participation on goal acceptance and performance: A two-step model. *Academy of Management Journal, 28,* 50–66.

Erez, M., & Kanfer, F. H. (1983). The role of goal acceptance in goal setting and task performance. *Academy of Management Review, 8,* 454–463.

Erez, M., & Zidon, I. (1984). Effects of goal acceptance on the relationship to goal difficulty and performance. *Journal of Applied Psychology, 60,* 69–78.

Ericsson, K. A., Krampe, R. T., & Tesch-Romer, C. (1993). The role of deliberate practice in the acquisition of expert performance. *Psychological Review, 100,* 363–406.

Erikson, E. (1959). Identity and the life cycle. *Psychological Issues, 1,* 18–164.

Erikson, E. (1963). *Childhood and society* (2nd ed.). New York: Norton.

Erikson, E. (1964). *Insight and responsibility.* New York: Norton.

Erikson, E. (1968). *Identity, youth, and crisis.* New York: Norton.

Ethington, C. A. (1991). A test of a model of achievement behaviors. *American Educational Research Journal, 28,* 155–172.

Felson, R. B. (1984). The effect of self-appraisals of ability on academic performance. *Journal of Personality and Social Psychology, 47,* 944–952.

Flink, C., Boggiano, A. K., & Barrett, M. (1990). Controlling teaching strategies: Undermining children's self-determination and performance. *Journal of Personality and Social Psychology, 59,* 916–924.

Flink, C., Boggiano, A. K., Main, D. S., Barrett, M., & Katz, P. A. (1992). Children's achievement-related behaviors: The role of extrinsic and intrinsic motivational orientations. In A. K. Boggiano & T. S. Pittman (Eds.), *Achievement and motivation: A social-developmental perspective* (pp. 189–214). New York: Cambridge University Press.

Folkman, S., & Lazarus, R. S. (1985). If it changes it must be a process: Study of emotion and coping during three stages of a college examination. *Journal of Personality and Social Psychology, 48,* 150–170.

Forest, D., Clark, M. S., Mills, J., & Isen, A. M. (1979). Helping as a function of feeling state and nature of the helping behavior. *Motivation and Emotion, 3,* 161–169.

Forsterling, F. (1985). Attribution retraining: A review. *Psychological Bulletin, 98,* 495–512.

Frankel, A., & Snyder, M. L. (1978). Poor performance following unsolvable problems: Learned helplessness or egoism? *Journal of Personality and Social Psychology, 36,* 1415–1423.

Fraser, B. J., & Fisher, D. L. (1982). Predicting students' outcomes from the perceptions of classroom psychosocial environment. *American Educational Research Journal, 19,* 498–518.

Fromm, E. (1941). *Escape from freedom.* New York: Rinehart.

Garland, H. (1983). Influence of ability, assigned goals, and normative information on personal goals and performance: A challenge to the goal attainability assumption. *Journal of Applied Psychology, 68,* 20–30.

Garland, H. (1985). A cognitive mediation theory of task goals and human performance. *Motivation and Emotion, 9,* 345–367.

Gecas, V., & Burke, P. J. (1995). Self and identity. In K. S. Cook, G. A. Fine, & J. S. House (Eds.), *Sociological perspectives on social psychology* (pp. 41–67). Boston: Allyn and Bacon.

Gerrity, M. S. (1994). Medical education and theory-driven research. *Journal of General Internal Medicine, 9,* 354–355.

Getty, C. F., Pliske, R. M., Manning, C., & Casey, J. T. (1987). An evaluation of human act generation performance. *Organizational Behavior and Human Decision Processes, 39,* 23–51.

Gibbons, F. X., Benbow, C. P., & Gerrard, M. (1994). From top dog to bottom half: Social comparison strategies in response to poor performance. *Journal of Personality and Social Psychology, 67,* 638–652.

Gibson, E. J. (1988). Exploratory behavior in the development of perceiving, acting, and the acquiring of knowledge. *Annual Review of Psychology, 39,* 1–41.

Gibson, S., & Dembo, M. (1984). Teacher efficacy: A construct validation. *Journal of Educational Psychology, 76,* 569–582.

Glasser, W. L. (1969). *Schools without failure.* New York: Harper & Row.

Good, T. L. (1981). Teacher expectations and student perceptions: A decade of research. *Educational Leadership, 38,* 415–422.

Goodenow, C. (1993). The role of belongingness in adolescents' academic motivation. *Journal of Early Adolescence, 13,* 21–43.

Gormly, A., & Brodzinsky, D. (1993). *Lifespan human development.* Fort Worth, TX: Harcourt Brace Jovanovich.

Gottfried, A. (1985). Academic intrinsic motivation in elementary and junior high school students. *Journal of Educational Psychology, 77,* 631–645.

Graham, S. (1984). Communicating sympathy and anger to black and white students: The cognitive (attributional) antecedents of affective cues. *Journal of Personality and Social Psychology, 47,* 40–54.

Graham, S. (1990). The role of production factors in learning disabled students' compositions. *Journal of Educational Psychology, 82,* 781–791.

Graham, S. (1994). Classroom motivation from an attributional perspective. In H. F. O'Neil, Jr., & M. Drillings (Eds.), *Motivation: Theory and research* (pp. 31–48). Hillsdale, NJ: Lawrence Erlbaum.

Graham, S., & Barker, G. (1990). An attributional-developmental analysis of help-giving as a low-ability cue. *Journal of Educational Psychology, 82,* 7–14.

Graham, S., & Harris, K. R (1994). The role and development of self-regulation in the writing process. In D. H. Schunk & B. J. Zimmerman (Eds.), *Self-regulation of learning and performance: Issues and educational applications* (pp. 203–228). Hillsdale, NJ: Lawrence Erlbaum.

Graham, S., & MacArthur, C. (1988). Improving learning disabled students' skills at revising essays produced on a word processor: Self-instructional strategy training. *Journal of Special Education, 22,* 133–152.

Graham, S., MacArthur, C., Schwartz, S., & Voth, T. (1992). Improving the compositions of students with learning disabilities using a strategy involving product and process goal-setting. *Exceptional Children, 58,* 322–334.

Gray, W. M., & Hudson, L. M. (1984). Formal operations and the imaginary audience. *Developmental Psychology, 20,* 619–627.

Grolnick, W. S., Frodi, A., & Bridges, L. (1984). Maternal control styles and the mastery motivation of one-year-olds. *Infant Mental Health Journal, 5,* 72–82.

Grolnick, W. S., & Ryan, R. M. (1987). Autonomy in children's learning: An experimental and individual difference investigation. *Journal of Personality and Social Psychology, 52,* 890–898.

Grolnick, W. S., & Ryan, R. M. (1989). Parent styles associated with children's self-regulation and competence in school. *Journal of Educational Psychology, 81,* 143–154.

Grolnick, W. S., Ryan, R. M., & Deci, E. L. (1991). Inner resources for school achievement: Motivational mediators of children's perceptions of their parents. *Journal of Educational Psychology, 83,* 508–517.

Gross, N., Mason, W. S., & McEachern, A. W. (1958). *Explorations in role analysis: Studies of the school superintendency role.* New York: Wiley.

Guskey, T. R., & Passaro, P. D. (1994). Teacher efficacy: A study of construct dimensions. *American Educational Research Journal, 31,* 627–643.

Hackett, G. (1985). The role of mathematics self-efficacy in the choice of math-related majors of college women and men: A path analysis. *Journal of Counseling Psychology, 32,* 47–56.

Hall, H. K., & Byrne, A. T. J. (1988). Goal setting in sport: Clarifying recent anomalies. *Journal of Sport and Exercise Psychology, 10,* 184–198.

Hansford, B. C., & Hattie, J. A. (1982). The relationship between self and achievement/performance measures. *Review of Educational Research, 52,* 123–142.

Harackiewicz, J. M., & Manderlink, G. (1984). A process analysis of the effects of performance-contingent rewards on intrinsic motivation. *Journal of Experimental Social Psychology, 20,* 531–551.

Harris, R. N., & Snyder, C. R. (1986). The role of uncertain self-esteem in self-handicapping. *Journal of Personality and Social Psychology, 51,* 451–458.

Harter, S. (1974). Pleasure derived by children from cognitive challenge and mastery. *Child Development, 45,* 661–669.

Harter, S. (1978a). Effectance motivation reconsidered: Toward a developmental model. *Human Development, 21,* 34–64.

Harter, S. (1978b). Pleasure derived from optimal challenge and the effects of extrinsic rewards on children's difficulty level choices. *Child Development, 49,* 788–799.

Harter, S. (1981). A model of intrinsic mastery motivation in children: Individual differences and developmental change. In A. Collins (Ed.), *A social developmental perspective* (Vol. 14). Hillsdale, NJ: Lawrence Erlbaum.

Harter, S. (1982). The Perceived Competence Scale for Children. *Child Development, 53,* 87–97.

Harter, S. (1983). Developmental perspectives on the self-system. In P. H. Mussen (Ed.), *Handbook of child psychology* (Vol. 4, pp. 275–386). New York: Wiley.

Harter, S. (1986). Processes underlying the construction, maintenance, and enhancement of the self-concept in children. In J. Suls & A.C. Greenwald (Eds.), *Psychological perspectives on the self* (Vol. 3, pp. 137–181). Hillsdale, NJ: Lawrence Erlbaum.

Harter, S. (1990). Processes underlying adolescent self-concept formation. In R. Montemayor, G. R. Adams, & T. P. Gulliton (Eds.), *From childhood to adolescence: A transitional period?* (pp. 205–239). Newbury Park, CA: Sage.

Harter, S. (1992). The relationship between perceived competence, affect, and motivational orientation within the classroom: Processes and patterns of change. In A. K. Boggiano & T. S. Pittman (Eds.), *Achievement and motivation: A social-developmental perspective* (pp. 77–114). New York: Cambridge University Press.

Heckhausen, H. (1967). *The anatomy of achievement motivation.* New York: Academic Press.

Heckhausen, H. (1982). The development of achievement motivation. In W. W. Harup (Ed.), *Review of child development research* (Vol. 6, pp. 600–668). Chicago: University of Chicago Press.

Heider, F. (1958). *The psychology of interpersonal relations.* New York: Wiley.

Heise, D. R. (1979). *Understanding events: Affect and the construction of social action.* New York: Cambridge University Press.

Heise, D. R. (1985). Affect control theory: Respecification, estimation, and tests of the formal model. *Journal of Mathematical Sociology, 1,* 191–222.

Heise, D. R. (1991). *INTERACT 2: A computer program for studying cultural meanings and social interaction.* Department of Sociology, University of Indiana.

Heller, K. A., & Parsons, J. E. (1981). Teacher influences on students' expectancies for success in mathematics. *Child Development 52*, 1015–1019.

Henderson, R. W., & Cunningham, L. (1994). Creating interactive sociocultural environments for self-regulated learning. In D. H. Schunk & B. J. Zimmerman (Eds.), *Self-regulation of learning and performance: Issues and educational applications* (pp. 255–281). Hillsdale, NJ: Lawrence Erlbaum.

Heron, W. (1957). The pathology of boredom. *Scientific American, 196*, 52–56.

Hess, R. D., & Holloway, S. D. (1984). Family and school as educational institutions. In R. D. Parke (Ed.), *Review of child development and research: The family* (Vol. 7, pp. 179–222). Chicago: University of Chicago Press.

Hidi, S. (1990). Interest and its contribution as a mental resource for learning. *Review of Educational Research, 60*, 549–571.

Hidi, S., & Anderson, V. (1992). Situational interest and its impact on reading and expository writing. In Renninger, K. A., Hidi, S., & Krapp, A. (Eds.), *The role of interest in learning and development* (pp. 215–238). Hillsdale, NJ: Lawrence Erlbaum.

Hidi, S., & Baird, W. (1986). Interestingness—A neglected variable in discourse processing. *Cognitive Science, 10*, 179–194.

Higgins, E. T., & Parsons, J. E. (1983). Social cognition and the social life of the child: Stages as subcultures. In E. T. Higgins, D. N. Ruble, & W. W. Hartup (Eds.), *Social cognition and social development* (pp. 15–62). New York: Cambridge University Press.

Hill, K. T. (1980). Motivation, evaluation, and educational testing policy. In L. J. Fyans (Ed.), *Achievement motivation: Recent trends in theory and research* (pp. 34–95). New York: Plenum Press.

Hill, K. T. (1984). Debilitating motivation and testing: A major educational problem, possible solutions, and policy applications. In R. Ames & C. Ames (Eds.), *Research on motivation in education: Student motivation* (Vol. 1). New York: Academic Press.

Hill, K. T., & Sarason, S. (1966). The relation of test anxiety and defensiveness to test and school performance over the elementary-school years: A further longitudinal study. *Monographs of the society for research in child development, 104*, 31 (Whole No. 2).

Hill, K. T., & Wigfield, A. (1984). Test anxiety: A major educational problem and what can be done about it. *The Elementary School Journal, 85*, 105–126.

Hill, K. T. , Wigfield, A., & Plass, J. A. (1980). *Effects of different kinds of optimizing instructions on seventh- and eighth-grade children's achievement test performance.* Paper presented at the annual meeting of the American Educational Research Association, Boston.

Hines, C. V., Cruickshank, D. R., & Kennedy, J. J. (1985). Teacher clarity and its relation to student achievement and satisfaction. *American Educational Research Journal, 22*, 87–99.

Hirt, M., & Genshaft, J. L. (1981). Immunization and reversibility of cognitive deficits due to learned helplessness. *Personality and Individual Differences, 2*, 191–196.

Hitchcock, A. (1959, July 13). Interview by H. Brean. *Life*, 72.

Holahan, C. K., & Holahan, C. J. (1987). Self-efficacy, social support, and depression in aging: A longitudinal analysis. *Journal of Gerontology, 42*, 65–68.

Hollenbeck, J. R., & Brief, A. P. (1987). The effects of individual differences and goal origin on goal setting and performance. *Organizational Behavior and Human Decision Processes, 40,* 392–414.

Hom, Jr., H. L. (1994). Can you predict the overjustification effect? *Teaching of Psychology, 21,* 36–37.

Huber, V. L. (1985). Effects of task difficulty, goal setting, and strategy on performance of a heuristic task. *Journal of Applied Psychology, 70,* 492–504.

Hudley, C., & Graham, S. (1993). An attributional intervention to reduce peer-directed aggression among African-American boys. *Child Development, 64,* 124–138.

Hunsley, J. (1985). Test anxiety, academic performance, and cognitive appraisals. *Journal of Educational Psychology, 77,* 678–682.

Hunt, J. M. (1965). Intrinsic motivation and its role in psychological development. In D. Levine (Ed.), *Nebraska symposium on motivation* (Vol. 13, pp. 189–282). Lincoln: University of Nebraska Press.

Illardi, B. C., Reeve, J., & Nix, G. (1994). *Discrepant self-ratings of competence in high school students and subsequent test performance.* Unpublished manuscript, University of Rochester.

Isen, A. M. (1970). Success, failure, attention and reactions to others. The warm glow of success. *Journal of Personaltiy and Social Psychology, 15,* 294–301.

Isen, A. M. (1984). Toward understanding the role of affect in cognition. In R. Wyer & T. Srull (Eds.), *Handbook of social cognition* (pp. 179–236). Hillsdale, NJ: Lawrence Erlbaum.

Isen, A. M. (1987). Positive affect, cognitive processes, and social behavior. In. L. Berkowitz (Ed.), *Advances in experimental social psychology* (Vol. 20, pp. 203–253). New York: Academic Press.

Isen, A. M., Clark, M. S., & Schwartz, M. F. (1976). Duration of the effects of good mood on helping: "Footprints in the sands of time." *Journal of Personality and Social Psychology, 34,* 385–393.

Isen, A. M., Daubman, K. A., & Nowicki, G. P. (1987). Positive affect facilitates creative problem-solving. *Journal of Personality and Social Psychology, 51,* 1122–1131.

Isen, A. M., & Geva, N. (1987). The influence of positive affect on acceptable level of risk: The person with a large canoe has a large worry. *Organizational Behavior and Human Decision Processes, 39,* 145–154.

Isen, A. M., Johnson, M. M. S., Mertz, E., & Robinson, G. F. (1985). The influence of positive affect on the unusualness of word associations. *Journal of Personality and Social Psychology, 48,* 1413–1426.

Isen, A. M., & Levin, P. F. (1972). Effects of feeling good on helping: Cookies and kindness. *Journal of Personality and Social Psychology, 21,* 384–388.

Isen, A. M., & Means, B. (1983). The influence of positive affect on decision-making strategy. *Social Cognition, 2,* 18–31.

Isen, A. M., Niedenthal, P., & Cantor, N. (1992). An influence of positive affect on social categorization. *Motivation and Emotion, 16,* 65–78.

Isen, A. M., & Nowicki, G. P. (1981). *Positive affect and creative problem solving.* Paper presented at the annual meeting of the Cognitive Science Society, Berkeley, California.

Isen, A. M., & Patrick, R. (1983). The effect of positive feelings on risk-taking: When the chips are down. *Organizational Behavior and Human Performance, 31,* 194–202.

Isen, A. M., & Reeve, J. (1994). *The influence of positive affect on intrinsic motivation.* Unpublished manuscript, Cornell University.

Isen, A. M., Rosenzweig, A. S., & Young, M. J. (1991). The influence of positive affect on clinical problem solving. *Medical Decision Making, 11,* 221–227.

Isen, A. M., Shalker, T., Clark, M., & Karp, L. (1978). Affect, accessibility of material in memory, and behavior: A cognitive loop? *Journal of Personality and Social Psychology, 36,* 1–12.

Izard, C. E. (1977). *Human emotions.* New York: Plenum Press.

Janis, I. L. (1982). Decision-making under stress. In G. Goldberger & S. Breznitz (Eds.), *Handbook of stress: Theoretical and clincial aspects* (pp. 69–80). New York: The Free Press.

Johnson, D. W., & Johnson, R. T. (1979). Conflict in the classroom: Controversy and learning. *Review of Educational Research, 49,* 51–69.

Johnson, D. W., & Johnson, R. T. (1985). Motivational processes in cooperative, competitive, and individualistic learning situations. In C. Ames & R. Ames (Eds.), *Research on motivation in education: The classroom milieu* (Vol. 2, pp. 249–286). Orlando, FL: Academic Press.

Jones, E. E., & Berglas, S. (1978). Control of attributions about the self through self-handicapping strategies: The appeal of alcohol and the role of underachievement. *Personality and Social Psychology Bulletin, 4,* 200–206.

Jones, M. R. (1955). Introduction. In M. R. Jones (Ed.), *Nebraska symposium on motivation* (Vol. 3, pp. vii–x). Lincoln: University of Nebraska Press.

Jones, S. L., Nation, J. R., & Massad, P. (1977). Immunization against learned helplessness in man. *Journal of Abnormal Psychology, 86,* 75–83.

Jussim, L. (1986). Self-fulfilling prophesies: A theoretical and integrative review. *Psychological Review, 93,* 429–445.

Kagan, J. (1972). Motives and development. *Journal of Personality and Social Psychology, 22,* 51–66.

Kahneman, D. (1973). *Attention and effort.* Englewood Cliffs, NJ: Prentice-Hall.

Kaplan, R., & Rothkopf, E. Z. (1974). Instructional objectives as directions to learners: Effect of passage length and amount of object-relevant content. *Journal of Educational Psychology, 66,* 448–456.

Karabenick, S. A., & Sharma, R. (1994). Perceived teacher support of student questioning in the college classroom: Its relation to student characteristics and role in the classroom questioning process. *Journal of Educational Psychology, 86,* 90–103.

Keinan, G. (1987). Decision-making under stress: Scanning of alternatives under controllable and uncontrollable threats. *Journal of Personality and Social Psychology, 52,* 639–644.

Kelley, H., & Michela, J. (1980). Attribution theory and research. In M. Rosenweig & L. Porter (Eds.), *Annual review of psychology* (Vol. 31, pp. 457–501). Palo Alto, CA: Annual Reviews.

Kintsch, W. (1980). Learning from text, levels of comprehension, or: Why anyone would read a story anyway. *Poetics, 9,* 87–98.

Klein, D. C., & Seligman, M. E. P. (1976). Reversal of performance deficits in learned helplessness and depression. *Journal of Abnormal Psychology, 85,* 11–26.

Klein, H. J., Whitener, E. M., & Ilgen, D. R. (1990). The role of goal specificity in the goal-setting process. *Motivation and Emotion, 14,* 179–193.

Kline, M. (1977). *Why the professor can't teach.* New York: St. Martin's Press.

Koestner, R., Ryan, R. M., Bernieri, F., & Holt, K. (1984). Setting limits on children's behavior: The differential effects of controlling versus informational styles on intrinsic motivation and creativity. *Journal of Personality, 52,* 233–248.

Koestner, R., Zuckerman, M., & Koestner, J. (1987). Praise, involvement, and intrinsic motivation. *Journal of Personality and Social Psychology, 53,* 383–390.

Kraut, R. E., & Johnston, R. E. (1979). Social and emotional messages of smiling: An ethological approach. *Journal of Personality and Social Psychology, 37,* 1539–1553.

Kuhn, M. H., & McPartland, T. S. (1954). An empirical investigation of self-attitudes. *American Sociological Review, 19,* 68–76.

Laird, J. D., Wagener, J. J., Halal, M., & Szegda, M. (1982). Remembering what you feel: The effects of emotion on memory. *Journal of Personality and Social Psychology, 42,* 646–657.

LaPorte, R. E., & Nath, R. (1976). Role of performance goals in prose learning. *Journal of Educational Psychology, 68,* 260–264.

Latham, G. P., & Baldes, J. J. (1975). The "practical significance" of Locke's theory of goal setting. *Journal of Applied Psychology, 60,* 122–124.

Latham, G. P., Erez, M., & Locke, E. A. (1988). Resolving scientific disputes by the joint design of crucial experiments by the antagonists: Application to the Erez–Latham dispute regarding participation in goal setting. *Journal of Applied Psychology, 73,* 753–772.

Latham, G. P., Mitchell, T. R., & Dossett, D. L. (1978). Importance of participative goal setting and anticipated rewards on goal difficulty and job performance. *Journal of Applied Psychology, 63,* 163–171.

Latham, G. P., & Saari, L. M. (1979). Importance of supportive relationships in goal setting. *Journal of Applied Psychology, 64,* 151–156.

Latham, G. P., & Yukl, G. A. (1975). Assigned versus participative goal setting with educated and uneducated woods workers. *Journal of Applied Psychology, 60,* 299–302.

Latham, G. P., & Yukl, G. A. (1976). Effects of assigned and participative goal setting on performance and job satisfaction. *Journal of Applied Psychology, 61,* 166–171.

Lazarus, R. S. (1983). The costs and benefits of denial. In S. Bresnitz (Ed.), *The denial of stress* (pp. 1–32). New York: International Universities Press.

Lazarus, R. S. (1991). *Emotion and adaptation.* New York: Oxford University Press.

Lazarus, R. S., & Folkman, S. (1984). *Stress, appraisal, and coping.* New York: Springer-Verlag.

Lepper, M. R. (1983). Social-control processes and the internalization of social values: An attributional perspective. In E. T. Higgins, D. N. Ruble, & W. W. Hartup (Eds.), *Social cognition and social development.* New York: Cambridge University Press.

Lepper, M. R., & Greene, D. (1975). Turning play into work: Effects of adult surveillance and extrinsic rewards on children's intrinsic motivation. *Journal of Personality and Social Psychology, 31,* 479–486.

Lepper, M. R., & Greene, D. (1978). *The hidden costs of reward.* Hillsdale, NJ: Lawrence Erlbaum.

Lepper, M. R., Greene, D., & Nisbett, R. E. (1973). Undermining children's intrinsic interest with extrinsic rewards: A test of the "overjustification" hypothesis. *Journal of Personality and Social Psychology, 28,* 129–137.

Levin, J. R., & Marshall, H. H. (1993). Editorial. *Journal of Educational Psychology, 85,* 3–6.

Lewis, M. (1987). Social development in infancy and childhood. In J. D. Osofshy (Ed.), *Handbook of infant development,* 2nd ed. New York: Wiley.

Locke, E. A. (1968). Toward a theory of task motivation and incentives. *Organizational Behavior and Human Performance, 3,* 157–189.

Locke, E. A. (1982). Relation of goal level to performance with a short work period and multiple goal levels. *Journal of Applied Psychology, 67,* 512–514.

Locke, E. A., & Bryan, J. F. (1967). Performance goals as determinants of level of performance and boredom. *Journal of Applied Psychology, 51,* 120–130.

Locke, E. A., & Bryan, J. F. (1969). The directing function of goals in task performance. *Organizational Behavior and Human Performance, 4,* 35–42.

Locke, E. A., Chah, D. O., Harrison, S., & Lustgarten, N. (1989). Separating the effects of goal specificity from goal level. *Organizational Behavior and Human Decision Processes, 43,* 270–287.

Locke, E. A., & Latham, G. P. (1984). *Goal-setting: A motivational technique that works!* Englewood Cliffs, NJ: Prentice-Hall.

Locke, E. A., & Latham, G. P. (1985). The application of goal-setting to sports. *Journal of Sport Psychology, 7,* 205–222.

Locke, E. A., & Latham, G. P. (1990). *A theory of goal setting and task performance.* Englewood Cliffs, NJ: Prentice-Hall.

Locke, E. A. Shaw, K. N. Saari, L. M., & Latham, G. P. (1981). Goal-setting and task performance: 1969–1980. *Psychological Bulletin, 90,* 125–152.

Loevinger, J. (1976). Stages of ego development. In J. Loevinger's *Ego development* (pp. 13–28). San Francisco: Jossey-Bass.

Loewenstein, G. (1994). The psychology of curiosity: A review and reinterpretation. *Psychological Bullein, 116,* 75–98.

Loewenstein, G., Adler, D., Behrens, D., & Gillis, J. (1992). *Why Pandora opened the box: Curiosity as a desire for missing information.* Unpublished manuscript, Department of Social and Decision Science, Carnegie Mellon University, Pittsburgh.

Lowry, N., & Johnson, D. W. (1981). Effects of controversy on epistemic curiosity, achievement, and attitudes. *Journal of Social Psychology, 115,* 31–43.

MacArthur, C., Schwartz, S., & Graham, S. (1991). Effects of a reciprocal peer revision strategy in special education classrooms. *Learning Disabilities Research and Practice, 6,* 201–210.

MacKinnon, N. J. (1994). *Symbolic interactionism as affect control.* Albany, NY: SUNY Press.

Maehr, M. L., & Anderman, E. M. (1993). Reinventing schools for early adolescents: Emphasizing task goals. *Elementary School Journal, 93,* 593–610.

Maehr, M. L., & Fyans, L. J., Jr. (1989). School culture, motivation, and achievement. In M. L. Maehr & C. Ames (Eds.), *Advances in motivation and achievement: Motivation enhancing environments* (Vol. 6, pp. 215–247). Greenwich, CT: JAI.

Maehr, M. L., & Midgley, C. (1991). Enhancing student motivation: A schoolwide approach. *Educational Psychologist, 26,* 399–427.

Malone, T. W. (1981). Toward a theory of intrinsically motiving instruction. *Cognitive Science, 4,* 333–369.

Mandler, G. (1982). The structure of value: Accounting for taste. In M. S. Clark & S. T. Fiske (Eds.), *Affect and cognition* (pp. 3–36). Hillsdale, NJ: Lawrence Erlbaum.

Marcia, J. E. (1966). Development and validation of ego identity status. *Journal of Personality and Social Psychology, 3,* 551–558.

Marcia, J. E. (1980). Identity in adolescence. In J. Adelson (Ed.), *Handbook of adolescent psychology.* New York: Wiley.

Markus, H. (1977). Self-schemata and processing information about the self. *Journal of Personality and Social Psychology, 35,* 63–78.

Markus, H., & Nurius, P. (1986). Possible selves. *American Psychologist, 41,* 954–969.

Markus, H., & Wurf, E. (1987). The dynamic self-concept: A social psychological perspective. *Annual Review of Psychology, 38,* 299–337.

Marsh, H. W. (1989). Age and sex effects in multiple dimensions of self-concept: Preadolescence to early childhood. *Journal of Educational Psychology, 81,* 417–430.

Marsh, H. W. (1990). Causal ordering of academic self-concept and academic achievement: A multivariate, longitudinal panel analysis. *Journal of Educational Psychology, 82,* 646–656.

Marsh, H. W., Barnes, J., Cairns, L., & Tidman, M. (1984). Self-Description Questionnaire: Age and sex effects in the structure and level of self-concept for preadolescent children. *Journal of Educational Psychology, 76,* 940–956.

Marsh, H. W., & O'Neill, R. (1984). Self-description questionnaire III: The construct validity of multidimensional self-concept ratings by late adolescents. *Journal of Educational Measurement, 21,* 153–174.

Marsh, H. W., Parker, J., & Barnes, J. (1985). Multidimensional adolescent self-concepts: Their relationship to age, sex, and academic measures. *American Educational Research Journal, 22,* 422–444.

Marsh, H. W., & Shavelson, R. (1985). Self-concept: Its multifaceted hierarchical structure. *Educational Psychologist, 20,* 107–123

Marsh, H. W., Smith, I. D., & Barnes, J. (1983). Multitrait-multimethod analyses of the Self-Description Questionnaire: Student-teacher agreement on multidimensional ratings of student self-concept. *American Educational Research Journal, 20,* 333–357.

Marshall, H. (1987). Motivational strategies of three fifth-grade teachers. *Elementary School Journal, 88,* 135–150.

Maslow, A. H. (1979). Humanistic education. *Journal of Humanistic Psychology, 19,* 13–26.

Maslow, A. H. (1987). *Motivation and personality,* 3rd ed. New York: Harper & Row.

McAuley, E. (1985). Success and causality in sport: The influence of perception. *Journal of Sport Psychology, 7,* 13–22.

McClelland, D. C. (1985). *Human motivation.* San Francisco: Scott, Foresman.

McClelland, D. C., Atkinson, J. W., Clark, R. A., & Lowell, E. L. (1953). *The achievement motive.* New York: Appleton-Century-Crofts.

McCombs, B. L. (1986). The role of the self-system in self-regulated learning. *Contemporary Educational Psychology, 11,* 314–332.

McCombs, B. L., & Pope, J. E. (1994). *Motivating hard to reach students.* Washington, DC: American Psychological Association.

McGraw, K. O. (1978). The detrimental effects of reward on performance: A literature review and a prediction model. In M. R. Lepper & D. Greene (Eds.), *The hidden costs of reward* (pp. 33–60). New York: Wiley.

McGraw, K. O., & McCullers, J. C. (1979). Evidence of a detrimental effects of extrinsic incentives on breaking a mental set. *Journal of Experimental Social Psychology, 15,* 285–294.

McGuire, W. J. (1984). Search for the self: Going beyond self-esteem and the reactive self. In R. A. Zucker, J. Aronoff, & A. I. Rabin (Eds.), *Personality and the prediction of behavior* (pp. 73–120). New York: Academic Press.

McGuire, W. J., McGuire, C. V., Child, P., & Fujioka, T. (1978). Salience of ethnicity in the spontaneous self-concept as a function of one's ethnic distinctiveness in the social environment. *Journal of Personality and Social Psychology, 36,* 511–520.

McGuire, W. J., McGuire, C. V., & Winton, W. (1979). Effects of household sex composition on the salience of one's gender in the spontaneous self-concept. *Journal of Experimental Social Psychology, 15,* 77–90.

Mednick, M. T., Mednick, S. A., & Mednick, E. V. (1964). Incubation of creative performance and specific associative priming. *Journal of Abnormal and Social Psychology, 69,* 84–88.

Mednick, S. A. (1962). The associative basis of the creative process. *Psychological Review, 69,* 220–232.

Meece, J. L., Blumenfeld, P. C., & Hoyle, R. H. (1988). Students' goal orientations and cognitive engagement in classroom activities. *Journal of Educational Psychology, 80,* 514–523.

Meilman, P. W. (1979). Cross-sectional age changes in ego identity status during adolescence. *Developmental Psychology, 15,* 230–231.

Mento, A. J., Steel, R. P., & Karren, R. J. (1987). A meta-analytic study of the effects of goal setting on task performance: 1966–1984. *Organizational Behavior and Human Decision Processes, 39,* 52–83.

Meyer, J. P., Schacht-Cole, B., & Gellatly, I. R. (1988). An examination of the cognitive mechanisms by which assigned goals affect task performance and reactions to performance. *Journal of Applied Social Psychology, 18,* 390–408.

Midgley, C., Feldlaufer, H., & Eccles, J. S. (1989). Change in teacher efficacy and student self- and task-related beliefs during the transition to junior high school. *Journal of Educational Psychology, 81,* 247–258.

Mikulincer, M. (1988). The relationship of probability of success and performance following failure: Reactance and helplessness effects. *Motivation and Emotion, 12,* 139–152.

Miller, D. T., & Ross, M. (1975). Self-serving bias in the attribution of causality: Fact or fiction? *Psychological Bulletin, 82,* 213–215.

Miller, I. W., & Norman, W. H. (1981). Effects of attributions for success on the alleviation of learned helplessness and depression. *Journal of Abnormal Psychology, 90,* 113–124.

Mischel, W., Coates, B., & Raskoff, A. (1968). Effects of success and failure on self-gratification. *Journal of Personality and Social Psychology, 10,* 381–390.

Mitchell, M. (1993). Situational interest: Its multifacted structure in the secondary school mathematics classroom. *Journal of Educational Psychology, 85,* 424–436.

Montemayor, R., & Eisen, M. (1977). The development of self-conceptions from childhood to adolescence. *Developmental Psychology, 13,* 314–319.

Mossholder, K. W. (1980). Effects of externally mediated goal setting on intrinsic motivation: A laboratory experiment. *Journal of Applied Psychology, 65,* 202–210.

Murray, H. G. (1983). Low inference classroom teaching behavior and student ratings of college teaching effectiveness. *Journal of Educational Psychology, 75,* 138–149.

Nasby, W., & Yando, R. (1982). Selective encoding and retrieval of affectively valent information. *Journal of Personality and Social Psychology, 43,* 1244–1255.

Newby, T. J. (1991). Classroom motivation: Strategies of first-year teachers. *Journal of Educational Psychology, 83,* 195–200.

Nicholls, J. G. (1978). The development of the concepts of effort and ability, perceptions of academic achievement, and the understanding that difficult tasks require more ability. *Child Development, 49,* 800–814.

Nicholls, J. G. (1979). Development of perception of own attainment and causal attributions for success and failure in reading. *Journal of Educational Psychology, 71,* 94–99.

Nicholls, J. G. (1984). Achievement motivation: Conceptions of ability, subjective experience, task choice, and performance. *Psychological Review, 91,* 328–346.

Nicholls, J. G., Patashnick, M., & Nolen, S. B. (1985). Adolescents' theories of education. *Journal of Educational Psychology, 77,* 683–692.

Nolen, S. B. (1988). Reasons for studying: Motivational orientations and study strategies. *Cognition and Instruction, 5,* 269–287.

Nurius, P. (1991). Possible selves and social support: Social cognitive resources for coping and striving. In J. A. Howard & P. L. Callero (Eds.), *The self-society interface: Cognition, emotion, and action* (pp. 239–258). New York: Cambridge University Press.

O'Donnell, A. M., Dansereau, D. F., Hythecker, V. I., Hall, R. M., Skaggs, L. P., Lambiotte, J. G., & Young, M. D. (1988). Cooperative procedural learning: The effects of prompting and pre- vs. distributed planning activities. *Journal of Educational Psychology, 80,* 167–171.

O'Donnell, A. M., Dansereau, D. F., Hythecker, V. I., Larson, C. O., Rocklin, T. R., Lambiotte, J. G., & Young, (1986). Effects of monitoring on cooperative learning. *Journal of Experimental Education, 54,* 169–173.

Oldham, G. R. (1975). The impact of supervisory characteristics on goal acceptance. *Academy of Management Journal, 18,* 461–475.

Orbach, I., & Hadas, Z. (1982). The elimination of learned helplessness deficits as a function of induced self-esteem. *Journal of Research in Personality, 16,* 511–523.

Osgood, C. E., May, W. H., & Miron, M. S. (1975). *Cross-cultural universals of affective meaning.* Urbana: University of Illinois Press.

Osgood, C. E., Suci, G. C., & Tannenbaum, P. H. (1957). *The measurement of meaning.* Urbana: University of Illinois Press.

Oyserman, D., & Markus, H. (1990). Possible selves and delinquency. *Journal of Personality and Social Psychology, 59,* 112–125.

Ozer, E. M., & Bandura, A. (1990). Mechanisms governing empowerment effects: A self-efficacy analysis. *Journal of Personality and Social Psychology, 58,* 472–486.

Parsons, J. E., Kaczala, C. M., & Meece, J. L. (1982). Socialization of achievement attitudes and beliefs: Classroom influences. *Child Development, 53,* 322–339.

Parsons, J. E., & Ruble, D. N. (1977). The development of achievement-related expectancies. *Child Development, 48,* 1975–1979.

Patrick, B. C., Skinner, E. A., & Connell, J. P. (1993). What motivates children's behavior and emotion? Joint effects of perceived control and autonomy in the academic domain. *Journal of Personality and Social Psychology, 65,* 781–791.

Peters, R. A. (1978). Effects of anxiety, curiosity, and perceived-instructor threat on student verbal behavior in the college classroom. *Journal of Educational Psychology, 70,* 388–395.

Peterson, C., & Barrett, L. C. (1987). Explanatory style and academic achievement among university freshmen. *Journal of Personality and Social Psychology, 53,* 603–607.

Peterson, C., Maier, S. F., & Seligman, M. E. P. (1993). *Learned helplessness: A theory for the age of personal control.* New York: Oxford University Press.

Peterson, C., & Seligman, M. E. P. (1984). Causal explanations as a risk factor for depression: Theory and evidence. *Psychological Review, 91,* 347–374.

Phillips, D. (1984). The illusion of incompetence among academically competent children. *Child Development, 55,* 2000–2016.

Piaget, J. (1952). *The origins of intelligence in children.* New York: International Universities Press.

Piaget, J. (1963). *The origins of intelligence in children.* New York: Norton.

Piaget, J. (1969). *Psychology of intelligence.* New York: Littlefield, Adams.

Pintrich, P. R., & DeGroot, E. V. (1990). Motivational and self-regulated learning components of classroom academic performance. *Journal of Educational Psychology, 82,* 33–40.

Pittman, T. S., Emery, J., & Boggiano, A. K. (1982). Intrinsic and extrinsic motivational orientations: Reward induced changes in preference for complexity. *Journal of Personality and Social Psychology, 42,* 789–797.

Pokay, P., & Blumenfeld, P. C. (1990). Predicting achievement early and late in the semester: The role of motivation and use of learning strategies. *Journal of Educational Psychology, 82,* 41–50.

Pyszczynski, T., & Greenberg, J. (1983). Determinants of reduction in intended effort as a strategy for coping with anticipated failure. *Journal of Research in Personality, 17,* 412–422.

Pyszczynski, T., Greenberg, J., & LaPrelle, J. (1985). Social comparison after success and failure: Biased search for information consistent with a self-serving conclusion. *Journal of Experimental Social Psychology, 21,* 195–211.

Reeve, J. (1989). The interest-enjoyment distinction in intrinsic motivation. *Motivation and Emotion, 13,* 83–103.

Reeve, J. (1993). The face of interest. *Motivation and Emotion, 17,* 353–375.

Renninger, K. A. (1990). Children's play interests, representation, and activity. In R. Fivush & J. Hudson (Eds.), *Knowing and remembering in young children* (pp. 127–165). Cambridge, MA: Cambridge University Press.

Renninger, K. A. (1992). Individual interest and development. Implications for theory and practice. In Renninger, K. A., Hidi, S., & Krapp, A. (Eds.), *The role of interest in learning and development* (pp. 361–395). Hillsdale, NJ: Lawrence Erlbaum.

Renninger, K. A., Hidi, S., & Krapp, A. (Eds.) (1992). *The role of interest in learning and development.* Hillsdale, NJ: Lawrence Erlbaum.

Renninger, K. A., & Wozniak, R. H. (1985). Effect of interest on attentional shift, recognition, and recall in young children. *Developmental Psychology, 21,* 624–632.

Reynolds, R. E., & Anderson, R. C. (1982). Influence of questions on the allocation of attention during reading. *Journal of Educational Psychology, 74,* 623–632.

Reynolds, R. E., Standiford, S. N., & Anderson, R. C. (1979). Distribution of reading time when questions are asked about a restricted category of text information. *Journal of Educational Psychology, 71,* 183–190.

Rigby, C. S., Deci, E. L., Patrick, B.P., & Ryan, R. M. (1992). Beyond the intrinsic-extrinsic dichotomy: Self-determination in motivation and learning. *Motivation and Emotion, 16,* 165–185.

Riggs, J. M. (1992). Self-handicapping and achievement. In A. K. Boggiano & T. S. Pittman (Eds.), *Achievement and motivation: A social-developmental perspective* (pp. 244–267). New York: Cambridge University Press.

Riley, T., Adams, G. R., & Nielsen, E. (1984). Adolescent egocentrism: The association among imaginary audience behavior, cognitive development, and parental support and rejection. *Journal of Youth and Adolescence, 13,* 401–417.

Robinson, D. T., & Smith-Lovin, L. (1992). Selective interaction as a strategy for identity maintenance: An affect control model. *Social Psychology Quarterly, 55,* 12–28.

Robinson, D. T., Smith-Lovin, L., & Tsoudis, O. (1994). Heinous crime or unfortunate accident? The effects of remorse on responses to mock criminal confessions. *Social Forces, 73,* 175–190.

Rogers, C. R. (1969). *Freedom to learn.* Columbus, OH: Merrill.

Rogoff, B. (1990). *Apprenticeship in thinking.* New York: Oxford University Press.

Rosenberg, M. (1986). Self-concept from middle childhood through adolescence. In J. Suls & A. G. Greenwald (Eds.), *Psychological perspectives on the self* (Vol. 3, 107–136). Hillsdale, NJ: Lawrence Erlbaum.

Rosenholtz, S. J., & Rosenholtz, S. H. (1981). Classroom organization and the perception of ability. *Sociology of Education, 54,* 132–140.

Rosenholtz, S. J., & Simpson, C. (1984). The formation of ability conceptions: Developmental trend or social construction? *Review of Educational Research, 54,* 301–325.

Rothkopf, E. Z., & Billington, M. J. (1979). Goal-guided learning from text: Inferring a descriptive processing model from inspection times and eye movements. *Journal of Educational Psychology, 71,* 310–327.

Ruble, D. (1983). The development of social comparison processes and their role in achievement-related self-socialization. In E. T. Higgins, D. N. Ruble, & W. W. Hartup (Eds.), *Social cognition and social development: A sociocultural perspective* (pp. 134–157). New York: Cambridge University Press.

Ruble, D. N., Crosovsky, E. H., Frey, K. S., & Cohen, R. (1992). Developmental changes in competence assessment. In A. Boggiano & T. S. Pittman (Eds.), *Motivation and achievement: A social-developmental perspective* (pp. 138–166). New York: Cambridge University Press.

Ruble, D. N., & Frey, K. S. (1991). Changing patterns of comparative behavior as skills are acquired: A function model of self-evaluation. In J. Suls & T. A. Wills (Eds.), *Social comparison: Contemporary theory and research* (pp. 79–107). Hillsdale, NJ: Lawrence Erlbaum.

Ruble, D., Parsons, J., & Ross, J. (1976). Self-evaluative responses of children in an achievement setting. *Child Development, 47,* 990–997.

Ryan, R. M. (1982). Control and information in the intrapersonal sphere: An extension of cognitive evaluation theory. *Journal of Personality and Social Psychology, 43,* 450–461.

Ryan, R. M. (1991). The nature of the self in autonomy and relatedness. In J. Strauss & G. R. Goethals (Eds.), *The self: Interdisciplinary approaches* (pp. 208–238). New York: Springer-Verlag.

Ryan, R. M. (1993). Agency and organization: Intrinsic motivation, autonomy, and the self in psychological development. In J. E. Jacobs (Ed.), *Nebraska symposium on motivation: Developmental perspectives on motivation* (Vol. 40, pp. 1–56). Lincoln: University of Nebraska Press.

Ryan, R. M., & Connell, J. P. (1989). Perceived locus of causality and internalization: Examining reasons for acting in two domains. *Journal of Personality and Social Psychology, 57,* 749–761.

Ryan, R. M., Connell, J. P., & Deci, E. L. (1985). A motivational analysis of self-determination and self-regulation in education. In C. Ames & R. E. Ames (Eds.), *Research on motivation in education: The classroom milieu* (pp. 13–51). New York: Academic Press.

Ryan, R. M., Connell, J. P., & Grolnick, W. S. (1992). When achievement is not intrinsically motivated: A theory of internalization and self-regulation in school. In A. K. Boggiano & T. S. Pittman (Eds.), *Achievement and motivation: A social-developmental perspective* (pp. 167–188). New York: Cambridge University Press.

Ryan, R. M., & Grolnick, W. S. (1986). Origins and pawns in the classroom: Self-report and projective assessments of individual differences in children's perceptions. *Journal of Personality and Social Psychology, 50,* 550–558.

Ryan, R. M., Mims, V., & Koestner, R. (1983). The relationship of reward contingency and interpersonal context to intrinsic motivation: A review and test using cognitive evaluation theory. *Journal of Personality and Social Psychology, 45,* 736–750.

Ryan, R. M., & Powelson, C. L. (1991). Autonomy and relatedness as fundamental to motivation and education. *Journal of Experimental Education, 60,* 49–66.

Ryan, R. M., Rigby, S., & King, K. (1993). *Two types of religious internalization and their relations to religious orientations and mental health.* Unpublished manuscript, University of Rochester.

Ryan, R. M., & Stiller, J. (1991). The social context of internalization: Parent and teacher influences on autonomy, motivation, and learning. In M. L. Maehr & P. R. Pintrich (Eds.), *Advances in motivation and achievement* (Vol. 7, pp. 115–149). Greenwich, CT: JAI Press.

Sackeim, H. A. (1983). Self-deception, self-esteem, and depression: The adaptive value of lying to oneself. In J. Masling (Ed.), *Empirical studies of psychoanalytic theories* (Vol. 1, pp. 101–157). Hillsdale, NJ: Analytic Press.

Salili, F. (1994). Age, sex, and cultural differences in the meaning and dimensions of achievement. *Personality and Social Psychology Bulletin, 20,* 635–648.

Salomon, G. (1984). Television is "easy" and print is "tough": The differential investment of mental effort in learning as a function of perceptions and attributions. *Journal of Educational Psychology, 76,* 647–658.

Sarason, I. G. (1984). Stress, anxiety, and cognitive interference: Reactions to tests. *Journal of Personality and Social Psychology, 46,* 929–938.

Schank, R. C. (1979). Interestingness: Controlling inferences. *Artificial Intelligence, 12,* 273–297.

Scheier, M. A., & Kraut, R. E. (1979). Increasing educational achievement via self-concept change. *Review of Educational Research, 49,* 131–150.

Schiefele, U. (1991). Interest, learning, and motivation. *Educational Psychologist, 26,* 299–323.

Schiefele, U. (1992). Topic interest and levels of text comprehension. In Renninger, K.

A., Hidi, S., & Krapp, A. (Eds.), *The role of interest in learning and development* (pp. 151–182). Hillsdale, NJ: Lawrence Erlbaum.

Schlenker, B. R., & Leary, M. R. (1982). Social anxiety and self-presentation: A conceptualization and model. *Psychological Bulletin, 92,* 641–669.

Schmidt, G., & Weiner, B. (1988). An attribution-affect-action theory of motivated behavior: Replications examining judgments of help-giving. *Personality and Social Psychology Bulletin, 14,* 610–621.

Schunk, D. H. (1982). Effects of effort attributional feedback on children's perceived self-efficacy and achievement. *Journal of Educational Psychology, 74,* 548–556.

Schunk, D. H. (1983). Goal difficulty and attainment information: Effects on children's achievement behaviors. *Human Learning, 2,* 107–117.

Schunk, D. H. (1985). Participation in goal settings: Effects on self-efficacy and skills of learning disabled students. *Journal of Special Education, 19,* 307–317.

Schunk, D. H. (1987). Peer models and children's behavioral change. *Review of Educational Research, 57,* 149–174.

Schunk, D. H. (1989a). Self-efficacy and achievement behaviors. *Educational Psychology Review, 1,* 173–208.

Schunk, D. H. (1989b). Self-efficacy and cognitive skill learning. In C. Ames & R. Ames (Eds.), *Research on motivation in education: Goals and cognition* (Vol. 3, pp. 13–44). San Diego: Academic Press.

Schunk, D. H. (1991). Self-efficacy and academic motivation. *Educational Psychologist, 26,* 207–231.

Schunk, D. H., & Cox, P. D. (1986). Strategy training and attributional feedback with learning disabled students. *Journal of Educational Psychology, 77,* 313–322.

Schunk, D. H., Hanson, A. R. (1985). Peer models: Influence on children's self-efficacy and achievement. *Journal of Educational Psychology, 77,* 313–322.

Schunk, D. H., & Hanson, A. R. (1989). Self-modeling and children's cognitive skill learning. *Journal of Educational Psychology, 83,* 155–163.

Schunk, D. H., Hanson, A. R., & Cox, P. D. (1987). Peer-model attributes and children's achievement behaviors. *Journal of Educational Psychology, 79,* 54–61.

Schunk, D. H., & Zimmerman, B. J. (1994). *Self-regulation of learning and performance: Issues and educational applications.* Hillsdale, NJ: Lawrence Erlbaum.

Seligman, M. E. P. (1975). *Helplessness: On depression, development, and death.* San Francisco: W. H. Freeman.

Seligman, M. E. P. (1990). *Learned optimism.* New York: Alfred A. Knopf.

Seligman, M. E. P., Abramson, L. Y., Semmerl, A., & von Baeyer, C. (1979). Depressive attributional style. *Journal of Abnormal Psychology, 88,* 242–247.

Shaalvik, E. M., & Hagtvet, K. A. (1990). Academic achievement and self-concept: An analysis of causal predominance in a developmental perspective. *Journal of Personality and Social Psychology, 58,* 292–307.

Shapira, Z. (1976). Expectancy determinants of intrinsically motivated behavior. *Journal of Personality and Social Psychology, 34,* 1235–1244.

Shirey, L. L., & Reynolds, R. E. (1988). Effect of interest on attention and learning. *Journal of Educational Psychology, 80,* 159–166.

Simmons, R. G., & Rosenberg, F. (1975). Sex, sex roles, and self-image. *Journal of Youth and Adolescence, 4,* 229–258.

Simpson, C. (1981). Classroom structure and the organization of ability. *Sociology of Education, 54,* 120–132.

Skinner, E. A. (1991). Development and perceived control: A dynamic model of action in context. In M. R. Gunnar & L. A. Sroufe (Eds.), *Self processes in development: Minnesota symposium on child psychology* (Vol. 23, pp. 167–216). Chicago: University of Chicago Press.

Skinner, E. A., & Belmont, M. J. (1993). Motivation in the classroom: Reciprocal effects of teacher behavior and student engagement across the school year. *Journal of Educational Psychology, 85,* 571–581.

Skinner, E. A., Chapman, M., & Baltes, P. B. (1988). Beliefs about control, means-end, and agency: A new conceptualization and its measurement during childhood. *Journal of Personality and Social Psychology, 54,* 117–133.

Skinner, E. A., Wellborn, J. G., & Connell, J. P. (1990). What it takes to do well in school and whether I've got it: The role of perceived control in children's engagement and school achievement. *Journal of Educational Psychology, 82,* 22–32.

Slavin, R. E. (1984). Students motivating students to excel: Cooperative incentives, cooperative tasks, and student achievement. *Elementary School Journal, 85,* 53–64.

Slavin, R. E. (1995). *Cooperative learning,* 2nd ed. Boston: Allyn and Bacon.

Smith, III, A. C., & Kleinman, S. (1991). Managing emotions in medical school: Students' contacts with the living and the dead. *Social Psychology Quarterly, 52,* 56–69.

Smith, T. W., Snyder, C. R., & Handelsman, M. M. (1982). On the self-serving function of an academic wooden leg: Test anxiety as a self-handicapping strategy. *Journal of Personality and Social Psychology, 42,* 314–321.

Smith, T. W., Snyder, C. R., & Perkins, S. C. (1983). The self-serving function of hypochondriacal complaints: Physical symptoms as self-handicapping strategies. *Journal of Personality and Social Psychology, 44,* 787–797.

Smith-Lovin, L. (1990). Emotion as confirmation and disconfirmation of identity: An affect control model. In T. D. Kemper (Ed.), *Research agendas in the sociology of emotions.* New York: SUNY Press.

Smith-Lovin, L., & Heise, D. R. (Eds.). (1988). *Analyzing social interaction: Advances in affect control theory.* New York: Gordon & Breach.

Snyder, C. R., & Higgins, R. L. (1988). Excuses: Their effective role in the negotiation of reality. *Psychological Bulletin, 104,* 23–35.

Soar, R. S., & Soar, R. M. (1979). Emotional climate and management. In P. Peterson & H. Walberg (Eds.), *Research on teaching: Concepts, findings, and implications.* Berkeley, CA: McCutchan.

Spielberger, C. D., & Starr, L. M. (1994). Curiosity and exploratory behavior. In H. F. O'Neil, Jr., & Drillings, M. (Eds.), *Motivation: Theory and research* (pp. 221–243). Hillsdale, NJ: Lawrence Erlbaum.

Spink, K. S. (1978). Win–lose causal attributions of high school basketball players. *Canadian Journal of Applied Sports Sciences, 3,* 195–201.

Stein, G. L., Kimiecik, J. C., Daniels, J., & Jackson, S. A. (1995). Psychological antecedents of flow in recreational sport. *Personality and Social Psychology Bulletin, 21,* 125–135.

Stipek, D. J. (1981). Children's perceptions of their own and their classmates' ability. *Journal of Educational Psychology, 73,* 404–410.

Stipek, D. J. (1983). A developmental analysis of pride and shame. *Human Development,* 26, 42–56.

Stipek, D. J. (1984). Young children's performance expectations: Logical analysis or wishful thinking? In J. G. Nicholls (Ed.), *The development of achievement motivation* (pp. 33–56). Greenwich, CT: JAI.

Stipek, D. J., & MacIver, D. (1989). Developmental change in children's assessement of intellectual competence. *Child Development, 60,* 521–538.

Strang, H. R., Lawrence, E. C., & Fowler, P. C. (1978). Effects of assigned goal level and knowledge of results on arithmetic computation: A laboratory study. *Journal of Applied Psychology, 63,* 446–450.

Swann, W. B., Jr. (1983). Self-verification: Bringing social reality into harmony with the self. In J. Suls & A. G. Greenwald (Eds.), *Psychological perspectives on the self* (Vol. 2, pp. 33–66). Hillsdale, NJ: Lawrence Erlbaum.

Swann, W. B., Jr. (1985). The self as architect of social reality. In B. Schlenker (Ed.), *The self and social life* (pp. 100–125). New York: McGraw-Hill.

Swann, W. B., Jr. (1987). Identity negotiation: Where two roads meet. *Journal of Personality and Social Psychology, 53,* 1038–1051.

Swann, W. B., Jr. (1990). To be adored or to be known: The interplay of self-enhancement and self-verification. In R. M. Sorrentino & E. T. Higgins (Eds.), *Handbook of motivation and cognition: Foundations of social behavior* (Vol. 2, pp. 408–448). New York: Guilford Press.

Swann, W. B., Jr., Pelham, B. W., & Krull, D. S. (1989). Agreeable fancy or disagreeable truth: Reconciling self-enhancement and self-verification. *Journal of Personality and Social Psychology, 57,* 782–791.

Swann, W. B., Jr., & Predmore, S. C. (1985). Intimates as agents of social support: Sources of consolation or despair? *Journal of Personality and Social Psychology, 49,* 1609–1617.

Taylor, S. E. (1989). *Positive illusions.* New York: Basic Books.

Taylor, S. E., & Brown, J. D. (1988). Illusion and well-being: A social psychological perspective on mental health. *Psychological Bulletin, 103,* 193–210.

Taylor, S. E., & Brown, J. D. (1994). Positive illusions and well-being revisited: Separating fact from fiction. *Psychological Bulletin, 116,* 21–27.

Taylor, S. E., & Lobel, M. (1989). Social comparison activity under threat: Downward evaluation and upward contacts. *Psychological Review, 96,* 569–575.

Teasdale, J. D., & Fogarty, S. J. (1979). Differential effects of induced mood on retrieval of pleasant and unpleasant events from episodic memory. *Journal of Abnormal Psychology, 88,* 248–257.

Tennen, H., & Affleck, G. (1990). Blaming others for threatening events. *Psychological Bulletin, 108,* 209–232.

Tennen, H., & Eller, S. J. (1977). Attributional components of learned helplessness and facilitation. *Journal of Personality and Social Psychology, 35,* 265–271.

Terborg, J. R. (1976). The motivational components of goal setting. *Journal of Applied Psychology, 61,* 613–621.

Thomas, E. L., & Robinson, H. A. (1972). *Improving readings in every class: A sourcebook for teachers.* Boston: Allyn and Bacon.

Thomas, J. W. (1980). Agency and achievement: Self-management and self-regard. *Review of Educational Research, 50,* 213–240.

Thornton, J. W., & Powell, G. D. (1974). Immunization to and alleviation of learned helplessness in man. *American Journal of Psychology, 87,* 351–367.

Tobias, S. (1994). Interest, prior knowledge, and learning. *Review of Educational Research, 64,* 37–54.

Trentham, L., Silvern, S., & Brogdon, R. (1985). Teacher efficacy and teacher competency ratings. *Psychology in the Schools, 22,* 343–352.

Tubbs, M. E. (1986). Goal-setting: A meta-analytic examination of the empirical evidence. *Journal of Applied Psychology, 71,* 474–483.

Vallerand, R. J., & Bissonnette, R. (1992). Intrinsic, extrinsic, and amotivational styles as predictors of behavior: A prospective study. *Journal of Personality, 60,* 599–620.

Vallerand, R. J., Deci, E. L., & Ryan, R. M. (1985). Intrinsic motivation in sport. In K. B. Pandolf (Ed.), *Exercise and sport sciences reviews* (Vol. 15, pp. 389–425). New York: Macmillan.

Vallerand, R. J., Pelletier, L. G., Blais, M. R., Briere, N. M., Senecal, C., & Vallieres, E. F. (1992). The Academic Motivation Scale: A measure of intrinsic, extrinsic, and amotivation in education. *Educational and Psychological Measurement, 52,* 1003–1017.

Vallerand, R. J., & Reid, G. (1984). On the causal effects of perceived competence on intrinsic motivation: A test of cognitive evaluation theory. *Journal of Sport Psychology, 6,* 94–102.

Veitch, R., & Griffitt, W. (1976). Good news—bad news: Affective and interpersonal effects. *Journal of Applied Social Psychology, 6,* 69–75.

Vidler, D. C. (1974). The use of contradiction to stimulate curiosity. *Educational Technology, 14,* 41–43.

Voelkl, J. E. (1993). Academic achievement and expectations among African-American students. *Journal of Research and Development in Education, 27,* 42–55.

Volmer, F. (1986). Why do men have higher expectancy than women? *Sex Roles, 14,* 351–362.

von Glaserfeld, E., & Steffe, L. P. (1991). Conceptual models in educational research and practice. *The Journal of Educational Thought, 25,* 91–103.

Voss, H. G., & Keller, H. (1983). *Curiosity and exploration: Theory and results.* San Diego: Academic Press.

Vygotsky, L. S. (1978). *Mind and society: The development of higher mental processes.* Cambridge, MA: Harvard University Press.

Waterman, A. S. (1988). Identity status theory and Erikson's theory: Commonalities and differences. *Developmental Review, 8,* 185–208.

Weinberg, R., Bruya, L., & Jackson, A. (1985). The effects of goal proximity and goal specificity on endurance performance. *Journal of Sport Psychology, 7,* 296–305.

Weinberg, R., Bruya, L., Jackson, A., & Garland, H. (1987). Goal difficulty and endurance performance: A challenge to the goal attainability assumption. *Journal of Sport Behavior, 10,* 82–92.

Weinberg, R., Bruya, L., Longino, J., & Jackson, A. (1988). Effects of goal proximity and specificity on endurance performance of primary-grade children. *Journal of Sport and Exercise Psychology, 10,* 81–91.

Weinberg, R., Gould, D., & Jackson, A. (1979). Expectations and performance: An empirical test of Bandura's self-efficacy theory. *Journal of Sport Psychology, 1,* 320–331.

Weiner, B. (1979). A theory of motivation for some classroom experiences. *Journal of Educational Psychology, 71,* 3–25.

Weiner, B. (1980). May I borrow your class notes? An attributional analysis of judements of help-giving in an achievement-related context. *Journal of Educational Psychology, 72,* 676–681.

Weiner, B. (1985). An attributional theory of achievement motivation and emotion. *Psychological Review, 92,* 548–573.

Weiner, B. (1986). *An attributional theory of motivation and emotion,* New York: Springer-Verlag.

Weiner, B. (1990). History of motivational research in education. *Journal of Educational Psychology, 82,* 616–622.

Weiner, B., Graham, S., Stern, P., & Lawson, M. (1982). Using affective cues to infer causal thoughts. *Developmental Psychology, 18,* 278–286.

Weiner, B., & Kukla, A. (1970). An attributional analysis of achievement motivation. *Journal of Personality and Social Psychology, 15,* 1–20.

Weiner, B., & Potepan, P. A. (1970). Personality characteristics and affective reactions towards exams of superior and failing college students. *Journal of Educational Psychology, 61,* 144–151.

Wheeler, L., & Miyake, K. (1992). Social comparison in everyday life. *Journal of Personality and Social Psychology, 62,* 760–773.

White, R. W. (1959). Motivation reconsidered: The concept of competence. *Psychological Review, 66,* 297–333.

Wigfield, A., & Karpathian, M. (1991). Who am I and what can I do? Children's self-concepts and motivation in achievement situations. *Educational Psychologist, 26,* 233–261.

Williams, G. C. (1993). *Internalization of biopsychosocial values by medical students.* Unpublished doctoral dissertation, University of Rochester, NY.

Williams, G. C., Wiener, M. W., Markakis, K. M., Reeve, J., & Deci, E. L. (1994). Medical students' motivation for internal medicine. *Journal of General Internal Medicine, 9,* 327–333.

Williams, J. P. (1976). *Individual differences in achievement test presentation and evaluation anxiety.* Unpublished doctoral dissertation, University of Illinois at Urbana-Champaign.

Willig, A. C., Harnisch, D. L., Hill, K. T., & Maehr, M. L. (1983). Sociocultural and educational correlates of success-failure attributions and evaluation anxiety in the school setting for black, Hispanic, and Anglo children. *American Educational Research Journal, 20,* 385–410.

Wills, T. A. (1981). Downward comparison principles in social psychology. *Psychological Bulletin, 90,* 245–271.

Wilson, T. D., & Linville, P. W. (1982). Improving the academic performance of college freshman: Attribution therapy revisited. *Journal of Personality and Social Psychology, 42,* 367–376.

Wilson, T. D., & Linville, P. W. (1985). Improving the performance of college freshman with attributional techniques. *Journal of Personality and Social Psychology, 49,* 287–293.

Winter, D. G., & Healy, J. M., Jr. (1981). *An integrated system for scoring motives in running text: Reliability, validity, and convergence.* Paper presented at the annual meeting of the American Psychological Association, Los Angeles.

Wood, D., Bruner, J. S., & Ross, G. (1976). The role of tutoring in problem solving. *Journal of Child Psychology and Psychiatry, 17,* 89–100.

Wood, J. V. (1989). Theory and research concerning social comparisons of personal attributes. *Psychological Bulletin, 106,* 231–248.

Wood, R. E., & Bandura, A. (1989). Impact of conceptions of ability on self-regulatory mechanisms and complex decision making. *Journal of Personality and Social Psychology, 56,* 407–415.

Wood, R. E., Bandura, A., & Bailey, T. (1990). Mechanisms governing organizational performance in complex decision-making environments. *Organizational Behavior and Human Decision Processes, 46,* 181–201.

Wood, R. E., & Locke, E. A. (1987). The relation of self-efficacy and grade goals to academic performance. *Educational and Psychological Measurement, 47,* 1013–1024.

Wood, R. E., Mento, A. J., & Locke, E. A. (1987). Task complexity as a moderator of goal effects: A meta-analysis. *Journal of Applied Psychology, 72,* 416–425.

Woolfolk, A. E. (1995). *Educational Psychology,* 6th ed. Boston: Allyn and Bacon.

Wortman, C. B., & Brehm, J. W. (1975). Responses to uncontrollable outcomes: An integration of reactance theory and the learned helplessness model. In L. Berkowitz (Ed.), *Advances in experimental social psychology* (Vol. 8, pp. 277–336). New York: Academic Press.

Zanna, M. P., Goethals, G. R., & Hill, J. F. (1975). Evaluating a sex-related ability: Comparison with similar others and standard setters. *Journal of Experimental Social Psychology, 11,* 86–93.

Zillman, D. (1978). Attribution and misattribution of excitatory reactions. In J. H. Harvey, W. Ickes, & R. F. Kidd (Eds.), *New directions in attribution research* (Vol. 2, pp. 335–368). Hillsdale, NJ: Lawrence Erlbaum.

Zillman, D. (1980). Anatomy of suspense. In P. H. Tannenbaum (Ed.), *The entertainment functions of television* (pp. 133–163). Hillsdale, NJ: Lawrence Erlbaum.

Zimmerman, B. J. (1986). Development of self-regulated learning: Which are the key subprocesses? *Contemporary Educational Psychology, 16,* 307–313.

Zimmerman, B. J. (1989). A social cognitive view of self-regulated academic learning. *Journal of Educational Psychology, 81,* 329–339.

Zimmerman, B. J., & Bandura, A. (1994). Impact of self-regulatory influences on writing course attainment. *American Educational Research Journal, 31,* 845–862.

Zimmerman, B. J., Bandura, A., & Martinez-Pons, M. (1992). Self-motivation for academic attainment: The role of self-efficacy beliefs and personal goal-setting. *American Educational Research Journal, 29,* 663–676.

Zimmerman, B. J., & Martinez-Pons, M. (1986). Development of a structured interview for assessing student use of self-regulated learning strategies. *American Educational Research Journal, 23,* 614–628.

Zimmerman, B. J., & Ringle, J. (1981). Effect of model persistence and statements of confidence on children's self-efficacy and problem-solving. *Journal of Educational Psychology, 73,* 485–493.

Zoeller, C. J., Mahoney, G., & Weiner, B. (1983). Effects of attribution training on the assembly task performance of mentally retarded adults. *American Journal of Mental Deficiency, 88,* 109–112.

Name Index

Subject Index